Ruling by Statute

What are the main factors that allow presidents and prime ministers to enact policy through acts of government that carry the force of law? Or, simply put, when does a government actually govern? The theory presented in this book provides a major advance in our understanding of statutory policy making. Using a combination of an original analytical framework and statistical techniques, as well as historical and contemporary case studies, the book demonstrates that, contrary to conventional wisdom, variations in legislative passage rates are the consequences of differences in uncertainty, not partisan support. In particular, it shows that a chief executive's legislative success depends on the predictability of legislators' voting behavior and whether buying votes is a feasible option. From a normative standpoint, the book reveals that governability is best served when the opposition has realistic chances of occasionally defeating the executive in the legislative arena.

Sebastián M. Saiegh is an associate professor in the Department of Political Science at the University of California, San Diego. He received his Ph.D. in Politics from New York University and has previously taught at the University of Pittsburgh. His research interests cut across the fields of comparative politics, positive political theory, and political economy. His work has been published in the *American Journal of Political Science*, the *British Journal of Political Science, Comparative Political Studies, Comparative Politics, Economics and Politics*, the *Journal of Politics*, and *Legislative Studies Quarterly*.

To the memory of my parents, Lidia and Rafael H. Saiegh

Ruling by Statute

How Uncertainty and Vote Buying Shape Lawmaking

SEBASTIÁN M. SAIEGH

University of California, San Diego

CAMBRIDGE
UNIVERSITY PRESS

CAMBRIDGE UNIVERSITY PRESS
Cambridge, New York, Melbourne, Madrid, Cape Town,
Singapore, São Paulo, Delhi, Tokyo, Mexico City

Cambridge University Press
32 Avenue of the Americas, New York, NY 10013-2473, USA

www.cambridge.org
Information on this title: www.cambridge.org/9781107005655

First published 2011

Printed in the United States of America

A catalog record for this publication is available from the British Library.

Library of Congress Cataloging in Publication Data
Saiegh, Sebastián M., 1970–
    Ruling by statute: how uncertainty and vote buying shape
    lawmaking / Sebastián M. Saiegh.
        p.   cm.
    Includes bibliographical references and index.
    ISBN 978-1-107-00565-5 (hardback)
    1. United States. Congress–Voting.   2. Legislative bodies–Voting.
    3. Legislators–United States.   4. Legislation–United States.   I. Title.
    JK1051.S25 2011
    328.73′0775–dc22   2011002456

ISBN 978-1-107-00565-5 Hardback

Contents

List of Figures	*page*	viii
List of Tables		ix
Acknowledgments		xi

PART I INTRODUCTION

1	Introduction	3
	1.1 Ruling by Statute	4
	1.2 Empirical Patterns	8
	1.3 Normative Implications	10
	1.4 Plan of the Book	11

PART II THEORETICAL FOUNDATIONS

2	On Statutory Policy Making	17
	2.1 Lawmaking as a Strategic Game	18
	2.2 Cross-Pressured Legislators and Lawmaking	21
	2.3 Decisiveness, Bribes, and Voting Coalitions	25
	2.4 Concluding Remarks	34
3	A Model of Statutory Policy Making under Uncertainty	36
	3.1 Legislative Stage	37
	3.2 Proposal Stage	50
	3.3 Empirical Implications	51
	3.4 Concluding Remarks	57

PART III EMPIRICAL IMPLICATIONS

4	Measuring Chief Executives' Statutory Performance	61
	4.1 Common Measures of Legislative Achievements	61
	4.2 Chief Executives' Box Scores	66

4.3	*The Appropriateness of Using Box Scores*	70
4.4	*Concluding Remarks*	74
5	**Patterns of Statutory Policy Making Around the World**	**76**
5.1	*Political Regimes and Statutory Policy Making*	77
5.2	*Constitutional Structures and Passage Rates*	84
5.3	*Government Status and Passage Rates*	87
5.4	*Multivariate Analysis*	89
5.5	*Bill Initiation and Passage Rates*	92
5.6	*Concluding Remarks*	94
6	**Political Prowess or "Lady Luck"?**	**95**
6.1	*Legislative Performance: A Sabermetric Approach*	96
6.2	*Lawmaking under Uncertainty*	103
6.3	*Actual and Expected Performance*	106
6.4	*Concluding Remarks*	111
7	**Buying Legislators**	**114**
7.1	*The Wallet of King George*	115
7.2	*Say Cheese!*	125
7.3	*Concluding Remarks*	131
8	**Electoral Rules and Lawmaking**	**133**
8.1	*Ballot Access and Legislative Behavior*	134
8.2	*Ideological Cohesiveness and Legislative Behavior*	142
8.3	*Concluding Remarks*	153

PART IV   NORMATIVE IMPLICATIONS

9	**The Political Gap**	**157**
9.1	*Government Performance and Political Instability*	159
9.2	*Cross-National Analysis*	161
9.3	*Governing without Surviving?*	166
9.4	*Concluding Remarks*	172

PART V   CONCLUSIONS

10	**Conclusions**	**177**
10.1	*Ruling by Statute: A Summary*	180
10.2	*Directions for Future Research*	181
10.3	*Final Remarks*	182

PART VI   APPENDICES

| **A** | **Proofs (Chapter 3)** | **187** |
| **B** | **Data and Sources** | **195** |

C   Statistical Analysis (Chapter 8)   202
D   Statistical Analysis (Chapter 9)   206

Bibliography   209
Index   227

Figures

1.1	Distribution of chief executives' box scores	*page* 10
2.1	The "median" voter and policy outcomes: An illustration	20
3.1	Preferred policies of legislators' principals – An example	49
3.2	Simulated cost of winning coalition	57
5.1	Distribution of democratic chief executives' box scores	78
5.2	Distribution of autocratic chief executives' box scores	83
5.3	Box scores by constitutional structure	85
5.4	Box scores by government status	88
5.5	Bill initiation and statutory achievements	93
8.1	Electoral rules and passage rates	137
8.2	Party control over ballot	139
8.3	Majority status and passage rate	141
8.4	Chilean legislators (2002)	148
8.5	Colombian legislators (2002)	151
9.1	Riots and passage rates (democracies)	163
9.2	Riots and passage rates (autocracies)	165
9.3	Bolivian legislators (2003)	171

Tables

3.1	Voting strategies when no bribes are offered	*page* 42
3.2	Simulated coalitions and total cost	54
4.1	Legislative production in nine countries	64
4.2	Fate of government bills: Portugal, 1976–1997	72
5.1	Committees' activism in Poland (1952–1972)	81
5.2	Passage rates: Multivariate analysis	91
6.1	Performance of individual chief executives	99
6.2	Simulated and actual passage rates	109
7.1	Divisions in Commons (1779–1782)	125
7.2	Factions and bribes under Fujimori	129
C1	Ballot access and passage rates	204
C2	Ballot access and passage rates	205
D1	Riots and passage rates (democracies)	207
D2	Riots and passage rates (autocracies)	208

Acknowledgments

This book, as most, has been a long time in the making. It is the end result of a ten-year journey that started when I was a graduate student in the Department of Politics at New York University. As such, several people have lent invaluable advice and assistance in the process of writing this book. My greatest debt of gratitude, though, goes to Adam Przeworski. As my graduate advisor, he has been central to the project's development from the very beginning. His deep intellectual curiosity, his passion for politics, and his commitment to his students, together with a generous amount of his academic and professional guidance, have profoundly influenced me. The completion of this project, as well as many other achievements in my academic career, are largely due to his guidance. A true *mentor*, coauthor, and friend, Adam has been there every step of the way. I have been truly fortunate to be able to constantly learn from him throughout all these years.

This study would not have been possible without the support of many other colleagues and friends. For exceptionally valuable advice in the early stages of this project, I am grateful to John Ferejohn, John Londregan, and Mariano Tommasi. It was John Londregan who initially challenged me to think about my argument more carefully. Since then he has been a constant source of support and inspiration. As a graduate student, I also received useful input from Youssef Cohen, Stathis Kalyvas, Bernard Manin, Antonio Merlo, Jonathan Nagler, John Roemer, Shanker Satyanath, and Leonard Wantchekon. My colleagues, Suzy Fry, Joseph Gochal, Matt Golder, Sona Nadenichek Golder, Wonik Kim, Jeff Lax, Carmela Lutmar, Covadonga Meseguer, Jillian Schwedler, and Melissa Schwartzberg, also deserve grateful acknowledgment in this regard. Special thanks go to my *goombahs*, Jennifer Gandhi, Patricio Navia, and James Vreeland, as well as my dear friend Naomi Darenblum.

Part of the book was written at the University of Pittsburgh, where I spent three years as an assistant professor. My colleagues offered advice and friendship throughout my time in Pittsburgh. I especially want to thank Barry Ames, David Bearce, Dan Berkowitz, Chris Bonneau, Chris Carman, Michael Goodhart, Mark Hallerberg, Bill Keech, George A. Krause, Scott Morgenstern, Anibal Pérez-Liñan, and Mitch Seligson. Nita Rudra, a marvelous colleague and loyal friend, deserves special recognition.

I would also like to thank my colleagues at the University of California, San Diego (UCSD), where the rest of the book was completed. I learned from conversations with Marisa Abrajano, Amy Bridges, Gary Cox, William Chandler, Scott Desposato, Steve Erie, Peter Galderisi, Peter Gourevitch, Steph Haggard, Thad Kousser, Mat McCubbins, Megumi Naoi, Keith Poole, Christina Schneider, Branislav Slantchev, Peter Smith, Kaare Strom, and Langche Zeng. I would especially like to thank Gary for his suggestions on how to improve the estimation of the chance models, Keith for instructing me in multidimensional scaling, and Mat for his encouragement during the long summer of 2009. I am also particularly grateful to Peter Smith, who read a close-to-final draft of the entire manuscript and whose suggestions greatly improved the substance and style of the book. Marisa painstakingly read the entire manuscript and helped me make it much better. Without her detailed comments, editorial advice, and constant support, this book would have never come to fruition.

Very special thanks go to two individuals who contributed to making this book possible through their insights and their friendship. William Keech, whose guidance literally accompanied me all the way from Pittsburgh to San Diego, was extremely generous with his time. Bill gracefully volunteered to read the entire manuscript and provided valuable feedback and much helpful advice. I do not know if I was able to successfully address all his concerns, but I am sure that the quality of this book is higher for attempting to do so. James Vreeland was also instrumental in the development of this book. I must thank him for insisting that I write a book in the first place, and for providing me with countless pages of detailed comments. Jim was always willing to help in any way he could – and he certainly did. His value as a scholar is surpassed only by his value as a friend.

Two graduate research assistants at UCSD – Daniel Maliniak and
Nicole Bonoff – did a great job helping me revise and expand the data
used in this project, for which I am very grateful. A handful of oth-
ers have played an important role in the writing of this book. For the
assistance I received along the way, I sincerely thank Octavio Amorim
Neto, Lee Alston, Cristobal Aninat, Juliana Bambaci, Bob Barros, Kathy
Bawn, Jenna Bednar, Ernesto Calvo, Royce Carroll, Argelina Cheibub-
Figueiredo, Brian Crisp, Tulia Faletti, Flavia Fiourucci, Jorge Gordín,
Carlos Guevara Mann, John Huber, Matías Iaryczower, Mark P. Jones,
Tasos Kalandrakis, Kris Kanthak, Fabrice Lehoucq, Fernando Limongi,
Germán Lodola, Skip Lupia, Andrés Mejía Acosta, Rebecca Morton,
Gabriel Negretto, Mónica Pachón, Lucio Renno, Nils Ringe, David
Samuels, Carlos Scartascini, Pablo T. Spiller, Ernesto Stein, Michael Thies,
Barry Weingast, Erik Wibbels, and Eduardo Zimmermann. I would also
like to thank Manuel Alcántara and the PELA team for sharing their data
with me. Finally, I must acknowledge the collaboration of several peo-
ple with whom I have coauthored. In particular Eduardo Alemán, Zé
Cheibub, Jennifer Gandhi, and Adam Przeworski will find that parts of
our joint work appear here and there in the book.

Research for this project was presented at Princeton University's Political Economy Workshop; the University of Pennsylvania's Comparative
Politics Workshop; the Political Economy Discussion Society at the University of Washington; Stanford University's Public Policy Program; the
Sixth Annual EITM Institute at the University of California at Los Angeles; the Department of Political Science at the University of Pittsburgh;
the Department of Political Science at Yale University; the Department of
Political Science at the University of California at San Diego; Doshisha
University in Kyoto; the Yale Conference on Political Parties and Legislative Organization; the Conference on Representation and Democratic
Politics in Latin America at the Universidad de San Andrés (Buenos Aires);
the Conference on Institutions, Behavior and Outcomes at CEBRAP (Sao
Paulo); the Conference *Quo Vadis, Argentina?* at CEDLA (Amsterdam);
the Princeton University Conference on Globalization and the Rise of the
Left in Latin America; the Seminário Internacional Legislativo Brasileiro
em Perspectiva Comparada at the Universidade de Brasilia; and meetings
of the American Political Science Association, the Midwest Political Science Association, and the Latin American Studies Association. Numerous
participants in these various forums have offered useful comments and
suggestions for which I am grateful.

Financial support for various parts of the research program that led to this book was provided by the Fundación Antorchas of Argentina; the Bradley Foundation; the Center for Latin American Studies and the School of Arts and Sciences at the University of Pittsburgh; and the Committee on Research and the Faculty Career Development Program at the University of California, San Diego. I thank all these sources as well as the Hellman Family Foundation for awarding me a Fellowship, during the course of which I completed the manuscript.

I would also like to thank the anonymous reviewers of the manuscript for their excellent suggestions, and my editor at Cambridge, Lewis Bateman, for his interest in the project and his help throughout. Some of the materials in Chapter 5 appeared in the *British Journal of Political Science*; part of Chapter 6 draws from an article that appeared in the *Journal of Politics*; and some of the analysis presented in Chapter 8 appeared in *Legislative Studies Quarterly*. I thank the publishers for granting permission to use those materials here.

On a personal note, I also wish to express my appreciation to all my friends (from Buenos Aires, my years in New York City, the University of Pittsburgh, and from Los Angeles and San Diego) who shared with me the ten-year odyssey that culminated in this book. The list is far too long to name each and every single one of you. But you know who you are. And rest assured that I am extremely grateful for your care and support throughout these years.

Finally, I dedicate this book to my family. My parents, Lidia and Rafael Saiegh, encouraged my intellectual interests since childhood. Their teachings have served as an endless source of motivation for me, and my decision to pursue an academic career was due to their influence. Their untimely deaths made this book a much harder undertaking. My immediate family members, Gustavo, Sandra, Tomás, and Dominique Saiegh, provided loving support all along. I must particularly acknowledge Sandra's help. My big sister not only took care of me while I was a graduate student in New York, but also continuously shows me how much she cares. Above all, I owe a great deal to my wife, Marisa Abrajano. She deserves the most credit for the completion of this book. Most importantly, I am thankful for her unconditional support and for bringing balance to my life. I also dedicate this book to her and to our daughter Sofia, with all my love and gratitude.

PART I

INTRODUCTION

1

Introduction

On July 27, 2002, after almost eighteen months of debate and delay, the Republican-controlled Congress granted President George W. Bush "fast-track" authority to negotiate international trade pacts. Most Democrats railed against the bill as a nail in the coffin of the U.S. manufacturing sector. In contrast, most Republicans supported the measure and argued that it would bring economic growth and lower consumer prices. Yet, trade is always a difficult issue in the House, and fearful that free trade would cost jobs in their districts, many Republicans broke ranks and joined the opposition. Meanwhile, Democrats from export-dependent districts were supportive of the measure. Democratic leaders, however, wished to keep most of their party voting against the bill to force Republicans from vulnerable areas to cast a "yes" vote that could be used against them in the November election. With such powerful crosscurrents, GOP leaders were wary of forcing members to take such a controversial vote. Anticipating that only his personal involvement could break the logjam, President Bush went to the Capitol and told Republicans that the economic future of the country was at stake. But even after the president's direct intervention, the outcome of the vote remained uncertain. Senior administration officials worked side by side with majority whip, Tom DeLay, trying to round up votes. When the bill came to the floor, these efforts paid off. A handful of Republicans succumbed to these pleas, including two legislators who changed their votes after securing commitments from Bush to help their districts. DeLay also picked up the votes of five additional pro-business Democrats, who resisted pressure from their party leadership. With victory assured, Republicans in districts with strong anti-fast-track constituencies (like Robin Hayes of textile-rich North Carolina), were let off the hook by their leaders, and voted "no." At 3:30 A.M., the House passed the Trade Act by a razor-thin 215-to-212 vote, with 190 Republicans and 25 Democrats making up the majority.

President Bush was not so fortunate a few months later. On March 1, 2003, U.S. government officials were stunned when Turkey's Parliament narrowly rejected a government bill to let 62,000 American troops on Turkish soil. The defeat also took Turkey's political leaders by surprise. Prime Minister Abdullah Gul and the chief of the governing party, Recep Tayyip Erdogan, supported the resolution, and both men urged their party, which controlled a large majority of the Parliament, to support it. The U.S. military wanted to open a second front against Iraqi forces in Kurdish-controlled northern Iraq, using Turkey as the launchpad. With dozens of American warships anchored off Turkey's eastern Mediterranean shores, Erdogan endorsed the request, arguing that the American relationship was too valuable to spurn. In addition, Erdogan had obtained the promise of billions in American economic aid to cushion the financial effects of the war. But the American request placed Turkey's lawmakers in a difficult position, as polls indicated that as many as nine out of ten Turks opposed involvement in a war against Iraq. Hours before the vote, Erdogan and Gul held a straw ballot of the 300-plus Justice and Development Party members who dominated the 550-seat Parliament. Only about fifty members, made up of the party's core of Islamist-minded politicians, expressed opposition. The alleged support should have given the resolution a comfortable majority. Erdogan, however, underestimated the strength of dissent within his own party. More Turkish lawmakers supported the measure than opposed it (the final vote was 264 votes in favor to 251 against), but the resolution failed because there were 19 abstentions. Under the Turkish Constitution, a resolution can become law only if it is supported by a majority of the lawmakers present. Presuming that the measure had passed, many lawmakers left the Parliament and boarded planes to return home. By the time Gul and Erdogan realized they had miscalculated, it was too late to change the outcome.

1.1 RULING BY STATUTE

This book is about ruling by statute. Chief executives can create policy in different ways: through executive orders, decrees, and even through international agreements.[1] Acting without the explicit consent of the legislative branch, however, has its drawbacks. The main disadvantage is that these policy-making instruments are particularly sensitive to judicial review. The legislative approval of statutes, in contrast, usually allows chief executives to better insulate their policy choices from legal review. Chief executives thus often find it more desirable to enact policy through statutes rather than by circumventing the legislature and acting on their own. This book investigates the factors that allow presidents and prime ministers to enact policy through acts of government that carry the force of law. It examines the role and influence of the executive and the legislative branches in creating law by winning legislative majorities.

The two examples – Bush's trade victory and Erdogan's defeat – illustrate several general features of statutory lawmaking: how political parties, the executive, and cross-pressured legislators interact with each other; how uncertainty affects the possibility of success or failure; and how legislators' vote intentions may change in response to incentives. These examples also focus on executive-sponsored legislation and highlight an intriguing puzzle.

In most contemporary democracies, chief executives play a dominant role in the lawmaking process. They sponsor a significant proportion of bills, and in some countries they even have the monopoly to introduce legislation on important issues. Given their proposal powers, chief executives should seldom be defeated. If a government knows that a bill will not have enough support, it can just refrain from sending it to the legislature and save face. In practice, however, chief executives experience numerous legislative defeats. Even on the floor of the British House of Commons, which may be regarded by many as the least possible scenario for such an occurrence, many divisions exist in which a whip is imposed and the government is defeated. This book thus addresses the following questions: Why does executive-initiated legislation ever get defeated? What explains the variation in the ability of chief executives to pass their legislative agendas?

Patterns of statutory legislation are a product of the interactions among a group of actors who are central to policy making in democratic systems:

---

[1] For example, as Vreeland notes, the executive branch tends to enter unilaterally into International Monetary Fund (IMF) agreements (Vreeland 2003). These arrangements are usually spelled out in a "Letter of Intent", and sent to the IMF Managing Director by a country's finance minister (and/or the central bank governor), whom the IMF recognizes as the *proper* authority over the economy (Vreeland 2007).

political parties, the legislature, and the executive. Hence, it is in the realm of lawmaking that we should examine the various combinations of institutional and partisan considerations that determine whether or not legislators will support a chief executive's legislative agenda. Most scholars are careful to note that the powers the executive derives from partisan support in the legislature can be as important as those derived from authority constitutionally vested in the office. Numerous studies have noted that party systems influence the workability of executive-legislative relations. Conflicting arguments and findings about the effect of inter-branch bargaining on the policy-making process, however, leave open the questions of *why* and *when* chief executives are able to successfully enact policy changes through statutes.

This book addresses these questions. Throughout its chapters, I develop and test a new theory of statutory policy making. Using a combination of an original analytical framework and statistical techniques, as well as historical and contemporary case studies, the analysis demonstrates that variations in legislative passage rates are the consequences of differences in uncertainty, not partisan support. In particular, I identify two major factors that shape lawmaking: the unpredictability of legislators' voting behavior, and the availability of resources to engage in *vote buying*.

The conventional wisdom states that chief executives' legislative passage rates depend on their degree of partisan support. According to this view, if a chief executive's party holds a majority of seats in the legislature, and if all of its members favor her proposal over the existing policy, then she can confidently anticipate a legislative victory. Conversely, if the chief executive's party is in the minority, then the partisan distribution of seats would have an opposite effect on her legislative passage rates. The implicit assumption is that a shared partisan affiliation automatically translates into legislative support. Notice that by this logic, every chief executive could strategically adjust her agenda to her degree of partisan support, and thus should never suffer any costly defeats. Expectations would change radically, however, if one believes that partisan identities do not necessarily reflect legislators' policy positions.

The consequences of uncertainty. Legislative defeats are typically associated with situations where chief executives cannot fully predict legislators' voting behavior. The source of the uncertainty is the existence of cross-pressured legislators. Lawmakers either belong to the governing party/coalition or the opposition, and this is common knowledge. Legislators, however, are also responsive to their respective supporters. Even if chief executives can observe the partisan distribution of the legislature, they may still be unable to identify the policy preferences of legislators' supporters. Given their prior beliefs about the latter distribution, chief executives may send a proposal to the legislature. Yet, as the Turkish example demonstrates, chief executives may lose such legislative gambit by miscalculating their support. A government may, of course, try to handle the effects of cross-voting with "deep pockets" or "big sticks." However, if the total cost of securing these votes exceeds the value of policy change, the government may be better off conceding defeat.

Modeling the legislative process as a game of incomplete information elucidates the empirical puzzle posed by chief executives' legislative defeats. It also leads to some clear empirical implications regarding the relationship between the uncertainty about how legislators may vote and statutory policy making. The existence of a winning voting coalition depends on the distribution of the policy preferences of legislators' constituencies. If a legislator's partisan identity accurately predicts her constituency's ideal policies, then a chief executive may be able to calculate more accurately how she will cast her votes. In contrast, if partisanship is weakly correlated with constituency interests, chief executives are more likely to make mistakes. Thus, a systematic relationship exists between a set of factors that generate more unpredictability and the passage rates of executive-initiated legislation. For example, the extent to which legislators represent a "national" rather than a "local" constituency is an important institutional factor that affects the correlation between partisan's and districts' ideal policies. In this book, I consider the different underlying causes of unpredictability of legislators' behavior.

Buying legislative votes. The Republican party's success at mustering enough votes to secure the passage of the "fast-track" bill illustrates the government's ability to incentivize legislators to adopt the chief executive's preferred policy outcome. These incentives are ubiquitous in legislative policy making, and common terms, such as "horse trading" or "deal making," accurately reflect the phenomenon of vote buying. As mentioned earlier, governments may resort to their "pocketbook" in order to handle the effects of cross-voting. However, chief executives would only offer compensation if the resulting outcome would make them better off than being defeated at a sufficiently low cost. If the chief executive could offer rewards under the condition that legislators be decisive, this cost would be negligible (by promising to reward at least one more voter than he/she needs to win, all legislators become nondecisive, and no payments need to be made). Yet, in deciding how to vote, legislators usually have to balance their own ideal policy, the wishes of the chief executive, and the pressures from specific constituencies. Legislators' responsiveness to their constituencies makes it impossible to use a compensation scheme that is contingent on the collective legislative outcome. On the other hand, considering that enacting legislation implies winning a majority of votes, the chief executive should often be interested only in corralling just enough votes to win, not in maximizing the amount of legislative support. As the "fast-track" example highlights, whenever their votes are nondecisive, some legislators will be free to vote with their constituencies. A chief executive may therefore be able to get her bills approved by rewarding one or few "marginal" legislator(s). In other words, vote buying does not result in supermajority coalitions. In fact, a chief executive may just need to buy a minimum winning coalition or even fewer votes to secure passage of her ideal policy.

I.2 EMPIRICAL PATTERNS

An understanding of the differential abilities of chief executive's to create statute law is hampered by the theoretical limitations described earlier. It is also hindered by the lack of truly cross-national research on this subject matter. Whereas the study of presidential legislative success in the United States has a long and fruitful tradition, these analyses seldom provide systematic comparisons with other countries. Likewise, most comparative research on this topic relies on either case studies of particular acts of government or from country studies.[2]

This book presents a novel approach by bridging together general theories and data over time and space. The studies in Döring (1995a) likely constitute the clearest effort to carry out a comparative study of lawmaking. But, as Gamm and Huber (2003) point out, most of the analyses were motivated by theoretical frameworks developed to examine the U.S.

---

[2] For example, a number of studies examine the statutory achievements of U.S. presidents (Edwards 1980; Spitzer 1983; Shull 1983; Hammond and Fraser 1984b; Rivers and Rose 1985; Bond and Fleisher 1990; Peterson 1990; Covington et al. 1995; Bond et al. 1996; Lockerbie, Borrelli, and Hedger 1998; Rudalevige 2002, Cameron and Park 2007; Barret 2005). Similarly, Coppedge (1994), Crisp (2000), and Amorim Neto and Magar (2000) study presidential policy making in Venezuela. Calvo (2006) and Alemán and Calvo (2007) analyze how institutional and contextual factors explain the approval of presidential initiatives in Argentina. Jones (1995) and Kellam (2006) provide some cross-national evidence from Latin American countries. In the former, however, the focus is more on executive-legislative conflict rather than on the ability of chief executives to pass their legislative agendas, whereas the latter concentrates in the stability of multiparty presidential coalitions in the legislature.

Congress. A few studies examine statutory policy making applying a more general theoretical approach. Yet, they rely almost overwhelmingly on data published by the Inter-Parliamentary Union in 1986 (see Tsebelis 1995). Such data are at most outdated or even inappropriate to study the passage rates of government legislative proposals under different conditions. This books departs from that tradition in that most of the analyses use time-series cross-national data. These data, which where specially collected for this project, document the pattern of chief executives' statutory achievements in more than fifty countries in Western and Eastern Europe, North and Latin America, Asia, and the Middle East for the period between 1946 and 2008.[3]

How can one evaluate a chief executive's statutory performance? Or, to borrow from Huntington (1968: 1), when does a government really *govern*? A substantial impediment to conducting research on statutory policy making at the cross-national level is the lack of a clear definition of legislative success. I measure success with the use of a *box score*. This indicator is calculated as the percentage of executive initiatives that are approved by the legislature over a period of time. Despite some of its limitations (which I discuss in Chapter 4), this is a tangible indicator that makes it possible to compare different chief executives and to assess their relative performance under varying circumstances.

Figure 1.1 presents the distribution of *box scores* in a sample of fifty two countries over the period 1946–2008. Two important trends are worth mentioning. First, the approval rates of executive-initiated bills varies considerably across countries and through time within countries. Second, on average, three-fourths of chief executives' initiatives are approved.[4]

This simple example underscores the importance of a theory of statutory policy making. The empirical patterns indicate that government's legislative defeats, such as the one described in Turkey, are hardly extraordinary events. They also present a direct challenge to the conventional wisdom regarding the relationship between chief executives' statutory performance and partisan support: Legislative passage rates are seldom 100 percent. Hence, any reasonable theory of statutory policy needs to account for the variation in chief executives' passage rates reflected in Figure 1.1.

---

[3] Information about the composition of the sample and the sources from which the data were obtained are listed in Appendix B.

[4] I analyze these patterns in more detail, including the variation in the passage rates of chief executives under authoritarian regimes, in subsequent parts of this book.

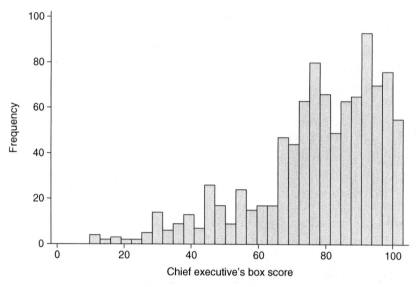

Figure 1.1. Distribution of chief executives' box scores.
Notes: Distribution of chief executives' *box scores*. This measure is calculated as the percentage of executive initiatives approved by the legislature over a period of time. Two important trends are worth mentioning. First, the data indicate that the approval rates of executive-initiated bills varies considerably across countries and through time within countries. Second, on average, three-fourths of chief executives' initiatives are approved. The sample includes observations from fifty two countries over the period 1946–2008 (additional information about the composition of the sample and the sources from which the data were obtained are listed in Appendix B).

1.3 NORMATIVE IMPLICATIONS

The question of how to improve *governability* while simultaneously protecting government *responsiveness* or *accountability* is one of the critical challenges inherent in assessing the quality of democracy. Understanding the conditions under which chief executives will succeed or fail in the legislative arena, where constituency interests are often represented, is of utmost importance. Nonetheless, although the concern with *governability* has been central for both political scientists and policy makers, it is remarkable that much remains unknown regarding the relationship between executive-legislative conflict, stalemate, and political instability.

By linking the notion of governability to chief executives' ability to enact policy changes, this book examines whether chief executives unable to accommodate change are threatened. Specifically, it studies the link between chief executives' box scores and social/political unrest in the developing world. Recent research in comparative politics has demonstrated that executive-legislative confrontation is not a necessary condition for political instability (Pérez-Liñan 2007). Instead, the ability of the opposition to remove a chief executive from office ultimately hinges on the degree of popular mobilization against the government.

It should be noted, though, that social conflict, turmoil, and even violence can be the product of the government's incapacity to solve urgent societal problems. These phenomena, however, can also be the result of unpopular policies. Therefore, governments often have to decide the form and degree to which they accommodate and/or repress popular demands. But, since policies tend to affect all aspects of the governability of a polity, these decisions usually entail a number of dilemmas and trade-offs. I evaluate these dilemmas both from an empirical and a normative standpoint. Empirically, I uncover the relationship between chief executives' legislative passage rates and social upheaval. The evidence indicates that political stability can be undermined when the opposition has no chance to block particular proposals of the executive (i.e., the government is institutionally too powerful). From an normative standpoint, this paradoxical finding suggests that, in terms of *governability*, some degree of control of the executive by the legislature is actually optimal.[5]

1.4 PLAN OF THE BOOK

The remainder of the book develops the arguments presented in this chapter. In Part II, I discuss the two main ideas of this book: (1) the notion that differences in uncertainty, not partisan support, drive the variations in chief executives' ability to enact policy changes through statute law; and (2) the view that in the presence of vote buying, winning coalitions will not be oversized (they will be either strictly minimal or they will include a majority of legislators plus one). I contrast these ideas with existing views on statutory policy making and vote buying in Chapter 2, and I formalize them in Chapter 3. In addition to the main findings previously summarized, the model also yields a number of ancillary empirical implications.

---

[5] This finding does not necessarily contradict the main tenets of the so-called *veto players* approach (cf. Tsebelis 2002). As Franzese notes, this perspective makes no prediction about policy outcomes; such predictions require information about the identity, powers, and preferences of *agenda setters*, and about the location of *status quos* in specific policy-making instances (Franzese 2010: 5).

As such, the model not only provides an explanation of the variation in chief executives' legislative performance, but also expands our understanding of interbranch bargaining, agenda control under uncertainty, and party discipline in legislatures.

Part III of the book turns to the main implications derived from my model. They are tested using my database of chief executives' legislative passage rates. This original dataset draws on and updates the Cheibub, Przeworski, and Saiegh's (2004) governments data set, as well as data on political institutions collected by the World Bank. These sources include data on government's partisan composition, the distribution of seats in the legislature, electoral rules, and the policy-making powers granted by the constitution to chief executives, as well as their statutory performance. In addition, because the model focuses on lawmakers' voting decisions, I also use data gathered from interviews with political elites to estimate legislators' preferences at the individual level.

In Chapter 4, I present a clear and simple indicator to measure how much a government *governs*. The chapter addresses some conceptual and measurement questions regarding executive-legislative relations. I compare and contrast different measures used in the literature, and focus on the merits and limitations of the *box score*. I demonstrate that, by summarizing a chief executive's legislative performance, the box score is an ideal measure to conduct cross-national research on statutory policy making.

Chapter 5 documents the pattern of chief executives' statutory achievements around the world. The empirical evidence clearly shows that chief executives do not get their proposals approved by the legislature all the time. The analyses also reveal that: (1) autocratic rulers have higher legislative passage rates than democratic chief executives, but they occasionally suffer legislative defeats, too; (2) the percentage of government bills approved in the legislature is higher under parliamentarism than under presidentialism, regardless of government coalition or majority status; (3) single-party minority presidents can often avoid "legislative impasse," "deadlock," or "stalemate"; (4) the notion that chief executives can manipulate their box scores by withholding legislation is not supported by the evidence; (5) chief executives display higher legislative passage rates when legislators' represent a national rather than a local constituency.

In Chapter 6, I introduce a metric for measuring chief executives' legislative performance. The approach enables me to compare individual rulers against each other. In addition, I present a standard to evaluate chief executives' lawmaking abilities when legislators' voting behavior is unpredictable. I examine the issue statistically, representing an uncertain world as one in which legislative outcomes are decided by chance. Specifically, I use data that are generated by simulated agents in a simulated system, performing simulated actions (i.e., Monte Carlo experiments). The analysis reveals that, on average, chief executives' performances are not much different from what would be expected if legislators flip coins to decide how to respond to their proposals. Furthermore, the findings highlight the need to assess the relative performance of chief executives in conjunction with the particular informational environment under which they operate.

Next, I consider the different strategies that chief executives employ to induce cross-pressured legislators to adopt their preferred policy outcomes. Chapter 7 presents evidence on legislative vote buying involving favors, *partisan rewards*, and outright bribery. I focus on England during the period before the accession of George III and the aftermath of the American Revolutionary War (1754–1783), and Peru under Alberto Fujimori (1990–2000). In these two historical cases, detailed records of the monetary payments made to members of the legislature in exchange for their support exist. The findings in this chapter support two important implications drawn from the formal model. First, the amount paid in bribes by the British and Peruvian governments were not excessively large. Second, the pattern of bribes in England and Peru validate the notion that, when governments engage in vote buying, winning coalitions are not oversized.

In Chapter 8, I demonstrate that governments effectively use a variety of partisan resources to incentivize legislators to support their policies. In particular, I analyze the impact of candidate selection and ideological cohesion on legislative behavior using multiple levels of analyses. At the cross-national level, my findings suggest that majority governments in parliamentary democracies use their control of candidate nominations to get their bills approved. The results also indicate that presidents have a particularly difficult time obtaining support for their legislative initiatives when they are in the minority and face individual legislators who have little control over party labels. I also investigate how candidate recruitment in Chile and Colombia affects legislators' preferences at the individual level. The findings suggest that party leaders can effectively use candidate selection rules to recruit individuals with similar preferences. Chief executives who receive the support of ideologically cohesive parties also enjoy higher legislative passage rates than those who have to deal with unwieldily legislative coalitions.

In Part V, I examine some of the normative implications derived from the theory of statutory policy making presented in this book. Specifically, Chapter 9 addresses how governmental *performance* (i.e., a chief executive's ability to enact policy changes through statutes) influences governability in developing countries. The analysis suggests that chief executives' legislative passage rates and social unrest have a *U-shaped* relationship. Governability, at least in the developing world, is best served when the chief executive can pass some of its agenda through the legislature but not when the opposition has little chances of blocking some of the government's proposals. Note that this conclusion is reminiscent of the argument, common in the new growth literature, that placing some limitations on a government's scope of action may be conducive to economic development.

PART II

THEORETICAL FOUNDATIONS

2

On Statutory Policy Making

Scholars of comparative politics have traditionally argued that chief executives, both under presidentialism and parliamentarism, require adequate partisan support in the legislature to govern as well as to survive in office. Consider the case of Argentina's Fernando de la Rúa. The fate of his presidency was sealed on the night of October 14, 2001. After almost two years in power, his administration lost control of the two Houses of Congress to the Peronist party. Two months later, on December 19, 2001, thousands of people marched on the Casa Rosada calling for his resignation. After de la Rua stepped down, Adolfo Rodríguez Saá became interim president. But he also had to resign a week later when he lost the support of fellow Peronist governors. A Peronist-controlled Congress eventually chose Eduardo Duhalde to complete De la Rúa's term. These events show the degree to which a chief executive with little legislative support can unleash a dangerous spiral that renders a country increasingly ungovernable.

Chief executives whose parties do not control the legislature are common in all countries. Still, it is not always the case that these chief executives are doomed to failure. Moreover, even chief executives with considerable partisan support in the legislature and significant agenda-setting powers may find it difficult to muster sufficient votes in the legislature and obtain passage of each and every one of their proposals. Peru's Alberto Fujimori is a case in point. Despite having very strong legislative powers, thanks to a 1993 tailor-made constitutional reform and a considerable legislative contingent, he needed to bribe or intimidate both his opponents and legislators of his own party, *Perú 2000*, to obtain their support. Curiously enough, many bribery situations were recorded on video tape, and the revelation of these tapes led to Fujimori's resignation in November 2000.

In this chapter, I outline two of the main ideas of this book. First, I discuss the role of uncertainty regarding legislators' voting behavior as the key factor that shapes a chief executive's capacity to successfully enact policy changes through acts of government by winning legislative majorities. Second, I examine how vote buying shapes legislative voting. In particular, I assume that legislators are concerned with both policy outcomes and the position-taking aspect of their voting decisions. This conceptualization of legislative behavior gives rise to the other main conclusion of this book; the idea that in the presence of vote buying, winning coalitions will not be oversized.

My theory of statutory policy making can be understood in varying degrees of mathematical precision and generality. In this chapter, I present a descriptive framework which is relatively intuitive and example-based. A formal exposition is introduced in Chapter 3.

2.1 LAWMAKING AS A STRATEGIC GAME

Chief executives can create policy in a variety of ways. For example, they can act without the explicit consent of the legislative branch and "legislate" on their own through executive orders, decrees, or regulatory ordinances. Yet, the use of executive prerogatives as a source of law has important limitations. Decrees, for example, are usually seen as an exceptional policy-making instrument, and thus are particularly sensitive to judicial review. And, in some countries, they can be overturned by legislature. In contrast, the legislative approval of statutes often allows chief executives to better insulate their policy choices from legal review (Remington et al. 1998; Amorim Neto 2006). Chief executives may thus find it preferable to enact policy by winning legislative majorities for statutes rather than by circumventing the legislature and acting on their own.

Statutory implementation of policy, though, is often more complex because it depends on the interactions between the executive and the legislature. Legislators are purposive agents, and their aims may be in conflict with those of the executive's. When a chief executive attempts to gain legislative approval for her bills, she must anticipate and overcome resistance to her plans. In other words, she must have a *strategy*, a plan of action appropriate to such interactive decisions.

Given these considerations, a useful way to analyze the lawmaking process is to represent it as a game of strategy. Players in the game include the chief executive and the members of the legislature. Assume for now that there is just one issue; it could be a general liberal-conservative split, a continuum on which liberal policies are located on the left, moderate policies are located in the center, and conservative policies are located on the right. We represent this issue and all possible positions on it by a line. Each player has an *ideal point* in this line, that is, a policy that yields greater benefits to the player than all other policies. Each player's preferences are *single-peaked*, meaning that any outcome farther from his or her ideal point is less desired by that player than policies closer to his or her most preferred policy. Finally, an exogenous *status quo point* represents existing policy.

As Dixit and Nalebuff (1991) note, the essence of a game of strategy is the interdependence of players' decisions. These reciprocal actions emerge in two ways. First they can be *sequential*: The players make alternating moves; second, they can be *simultaneous*: The players act at the same time, without knowing the current actions of others. The lawmaking process examined here contains elements of both types of interactions.

Consider first the move of the chief executive. For any given issue, she can either send a bill to the legislature with a new policy or she can keep the existing one (i.e., the status quo). If she decides to initiate legislation, then it will be the turn of the legislature to make its move. By definition, a legislature is a collective body, hence, its choice depends on the aggregation of its members' individual choices. To keep things as simple as possible, we take the legislature to be a set of n individuals, where n is an odd number and where everyone casts a vote. It makes decisions by majority rule, and no amendments can be proposed.

To make this more precise, imagine that we can place the executive's proposal on the liberal-conservative scale discussed earlier. Legislators express their preference by choosing between the executive proposal or the status quo. Since the issue is one-dimensional, legislators' preferences are single-peaked, and a majority is needed to win, we can calculate how each and every legislator will vote. Moreover, if the proposed policy yields greater benefits to the legislator with the *median* position than the status quo, then it will be approved. To see this, consider what would happen if the status quo is the ideal point of the legislator with the median position. This type of situation is illustrated in Panel A of Figure 2.1. The legislator with the median position divides the legislature in two equal halves: There are exactly as many legislators who want the policy to move left of the

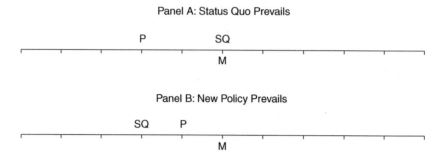

Figure 2.1. The "median" voter and policy outcomes: An illustration.
Notes: An illustration of how the location of the "median voter" vis-á-vis alternative policy proposals affects legislative outcomes when the issue under consideration is one-dimensional, legislators' preferences are single-peaked, and a majority is needed to win. Relative locations of the ideal policy of the legislator with the *median* position (M), the status quo (SQ), and the new policy proposal (P) are shown on a unidimensional space. The legislator with the median position divides the legislature in two equal halves. The top panel shows that no alternative proposal that can beat the status quo under majority rule exists. The bottom panel shows that a coalition in support of the new policy will include the legislator with the *median* position. The new policy will thus be the majority choice in this case.

status quo as to move right. Hence, no alternative proposal that can beat the status quo under majority rule exists.

Suppose now that the status quo is anywhere other than at the ideal point of the legislator with the *median* position, and that the proposed policy is closer to him or her than the status quo. This alternative scenario is depicted in Panel B of Figure 2.1. In this case, the coalition in support of the new policy will include the legislator with the *median* position. By definition of *median*, no more than one-half of all legislators minus one can be to his or her left (or his or her right). Therefore, the proposed policy will be the majority choice. In fact, any bill that is closer to the location of the legislator with the median position that the status quo will be approved by the legislature in this environment.

Turning our attention back to the chief executive, it is safe to assume that a prudent politician will anticipate the legislative outcome and exercise foresight. In this case, the chief executive will try to count "noses" and assess how much support exists for the bill in the legislature. In particular, she will likely only send a bill to the legislature if the legislator with the median position prefers this new policy to the status quo. Otherwise, assuming that suffering a legislative defeat will entail a political cost for the chief executive, she may be better off by not sending any legislation to the legislature at all.[1]

2.2 CROSS-PRESSURED LEGISLATORS AND LAWMAKING

Notice that by predicting the legislature's actions, any chief executive could strategically take advantage of the sequential structure to the decision making, and avoid costly defeats. Following this logic, many scholars have developed models of statutory policy making where proposers are never defeated (Shepsle and Weingast 1987; Alesina and Rosenthal 1995; Groseclose and Snyder 1996; Heller 2001). For example, Shepsle and Bonchek (1997) offer no explanation as to why a proposer would send a bill that will be defeated, other than a proposer's own sheer stupidity.[2]

Acting strategically, however, it is not always so easy. In particular, consider the role of information. The way the argument was presented suggests that chief executives can successfully identify the location of legislators' ideal policies (including the preferred policy of the legislator with the median position). But where would this information come from? It could be argued that legislators' partisan affiliations contain enough information to allow any observer to predict their preferences. Hence, in a world where partisan identities accurately reflect policy positions, a chief executive could use her knowledge of the partisan distribution of the legislature to act strategically. For example, if she knows that her party holds a majority of seats in the legislature, and that all of its members favor her proposal over the status quo, then she can confidently anticipate a legislative victory. Notice that if this were the case, then for every possible bill, any chief executive would be able to strategically tailor her legislative agenda to her degree of partisan support. And, again, per the

---

[1] Some scholars argue that chief executives may sometimes actually choose to be defeated in order to send a particular signal to the general public (Matthews 1989; Ingberman and Yao 1991; Groseclose and McCarty 2001). According to this view, a chief executive may occasionally adopt a strategy of "triangulation" – positioning herself between her own party and the opposition forces in the legislature to build popularity. If there are opposition forces in the legislature that need to be exposed in front of the general public, then this strategy may be palatable for a chief executive. Yet, if the public views the legislature as a natural extension of the chief executive's authority, it may not be a good idea for her to force defeats too frequently.

[2] As these authors note, if a committee and a legislature's floor want to move policy in opposite directions, the committee will refuse to open the gates. But, "... if they did stupidly open the gates, then any proposal they made to improve their lot would be voted down ..." (Shepsle and Bonchek 1997: 332).

law of anticipated reactions, legislative passage rates should always be 100 percent.[3]

Expectations would change radically if one believes that legislators' preferred policies cannot be fully predicted in advance. For example, suppose that a chief executive has to propose to a legislature composed of legislators who belong to political parties, but who must respond to various pressures. In particular, assume that in deciding how to vote, legislators consider a variety of influences, including their personal values, announced positions, the views of their constituents, and the preferences of their party leadership. If these pressures are not aligned, then legislators are cross-pressured (Fiorina 1974; Fenno 1978; King and Zeckhauser 2003).

The existence of *cross-pressured* legislators as a source of incomplete information is well illustrated by the recent experience of Henry Paulson. A former Goldman Sachs's CEO, Paulson served as the seventy fourth United States Treasury Secretary and had a leadership role in the Bush administration's efforts to cope with the 2008 financial crisis. As *Vanity Fair* reporter Todd Purdum notes, at Goldman, Paulson had played his share of high-stakes office politics; yet, when it came to Washington, he found he had much to learn. Paulson's candid revelation to Purdum, while he was still in office, tells us why:

... I found that at Goldman Sachs, to be effective as a leader, you had to build consensus when you're managing smart people who've got other alternatives. I'm in that situation today to a much greater extent than I ever was at Goldman Sachs, because the people I'm trying to bring together are *truly* independent. Oftentimes, they may even agree [with me] in private, but because of their constituencies or because of their parties or because of their committee chairmen or because of what the American people think, you know, won't agree in public. So I have to get used to people saying, Boy, that's reasonable – I really think a trade agreement

---

[3] The main problem with the traditional accounts is the "Hicks paradox," which holds that bargaining failures like strikes, wars, vetoes, or legislative defeats are irrational in a setting of complete and perfect information (Kennan 1986; Gartzke 1999; Cameron 2000). Other scholars have also stressed the role of incomplete information. Cameron (2000) relies on incomplete information to explain the existence of bargaining failures across the branches of government in the United States. Diermeier and Vlaicu (2007) model the legislative process as a multiperiod bargaining game under uncertainty to rationalize the fact that legislative success rates of chief executives are lower in presidential than in parliamentary democracies. They argue that bills proposed to the legislature are more likely to be accepted when legislators expect that failing to do so would lead to the collapse of the government. However, unlike Cameron (2000) and Diermeier and Vlaicu (2007), who do not identify the source of the uncertainty about legislators' preferences, I explicitly assert that incomplete information originates in the existence of *cross-pressured* legislators.

with Colombia is great, but I can't be for it. ... If you need my vote to get it done, I'll vote with you, but, fortunately, you don't, and I can take a pass ... (cited in Purdum 2009: 5)

Paulson's perplexity is illustrative of Washington's way of doing business. In fact, it reflects more broadly an essential feature of statutory policy making stressed in this book: how the unpredictability of legislators' voting behavior affects chief executives' ability to pass their legislative agenda.

In addition to anecdotal evidence, the fact that legislators account for different sets of interests when deciding how to cast their votes is well documented in the literature (Covington 1988; Kalt and Zupan 1990; Levitt 1996; Londregan 2000). Most of the theoretical models previously mentioned, however, do not incorporate these constraints in legislators' voting decisions.[4] A notable exception is Denzau et al. (1985); they examine the idea that principals (supporters) not only induce preferences in agents (legislators) but also constrain their mode of behavior. As Denzau et al. (1985) note, lawmakers vote in the legislature, but they secure support, campaign resources, and electoral rewards outside the legislative arena. Thus, legislators are judged not only by the collective choices made by themselves and their colleagues, but also by their own individual actions (Fiorina and Noll 1978; Denzau et al. 1985; Rasmusen and Ramseyer 1994; Groseclose and Milyo 2009).

For expositional purposes, throughout the book I will refer to a legislator's principal as her *constituency*. Still, legislators may wish to remain in the good graces of a group (or person) distinct from her electorate or constituency. These different principals may include a set of influential voters in the legislator's district, as exemplified in the U.S. case described in Chapter 1, but also the leadership of a specific interest group (such as a labor union or a business association), a local party boss, or even a higher authority (which may be embodied in a legislator's allegiance to a given set of religious or moral principles).

The identity of the principal, and the nature of the agency relationship with his or her representative, is likely to be shaped by legislators' electoral

---

[4] For example, in Groseclose and Snyder's (1996) model, legislators are primarily concerned with the position-taking aspect of their voting decisions, not with policy outcomes (i.e., they derive utility simply from taking part in decision making, even if they are indifferent to the collective outcome). This seems to be a particularly unrealistic assumption. As Barry cleverly points out, "a committee made up entirely of people who had no interest in pursuing some particular outcome but were fascinated by the process as such would be as frustrating as a brothel all of whose customers were voyeurs" (1980: 184).

incentives. Legislators who are elected by plurality rule in single-member districts are often responsive to influential voters in their district. In contrast, when legislators are elected via closed regional party lists and votes are pooled, they may give deference to the preferences of the regional party leadership.[5] Yet, regardless of the principal's identity, the agency relationship between legislators and their supporters implies that the former will not always be party loyalists. Conflicting pressures can induce them time and again to challenge the party line.[6]

From the chief executive's perspective, the fact that a group of legislators may face conflicting influences implies that in order to behave strategically, she needs to assess how these legislators would cast their votes. As previously mentioned, legislators are usually elected as members of organized parties, and their partisan affiliations are public information. In addition, a legislator's membership in a given political party or legislative bloc is often stable over time.[7] In other words, a legislator's partisan affiliation does not vary across issues, and certainly not in conjunction with a bill's content. In contrast, whether a legislator's principal likes a given piece of legislation will depend on the specific content of the bill. Therefore, although the partisan composition of the legislature is *a priori* observable, the policy preferences of legislators' principals are not.

Here, then, lies the main difficulty that even the most strategic chief executives must confront: When they send a proposal to the legislature, chief executives usually know with certainty what the legislators' partisan affiliations are, but they only have incomplete information about the policy preferences of the legislators' principals. Otherwise, as previously discussed, a strategic chief executive could always tailor the content of the legislation to accommodate the policy preferences of a majority of legislators and avoid being defeated (i.e., calculate *ex-ante* an optimal policy proposal).

---

[5] In Argentina, for example, the process by which provincial party lists are formed affects which candidates run on each party list, their ranking, and consequently their chances of winning a seat in Congress. In almost every province, local party bosses dominate the construction of party lists. Legislators' ability to adopt their own independent positions is thus substantially curtailed: To pursue a successful legislative career, they must maintain a good relationship with their local party bosses (De Luca et al. 2002; Jones et al. 2002).

[6] In the Argentine case, legislators tend to respond to their provincial party bosses. As a result, a president's ability to influence each of his or her co-partisans will depend in part on whether the legislator's provincial party boss supports the administration or not.

[7] Even in those countries where *party switching* is frequent, legislators publicly announce their decisions to defect/join a party and they often do not make these decisions in between terms (Desposato 2006).

2.3 DECISIVENESS, BRIBES, AND VOTING COALITIONS

We are now ready to examine the second type of interaction that characterizes the lawmaking process: The interdependence of legislators' voting decisions. Suppose that even without having an accurate representation of the policy preferences of legislators' constituencies, a chief executive decides to send a bill to the legislature with a new policy. Recall that such proposal can be represented by a point in a line (i.e., a general liberal-conservative continuum). Assume also that once a bill is filed, its content becomes public and that all lawmakers receive a mandate from their constituents. When this information is revealed, it becomes possible to identify the location of legislators' ideal policies. To make this situation interesting, it should be assumed that the chief executive cannot change the bill's content at this point (otherwise, she would tailor it to accommodate the preference of a majority of legislators and avoid a costly defeat).

It is now the legislature's turn to move. It has two choices: pass the bill or keep the status quo. By virtue of the requirement that majority vote is needed to pass legislation, the actions of individual legislators are linked. And, just as in any collective situation, strategic issues arise in voting. In particular, each vote can have two effects. It can be instrumental in determining the collective outcome, or it can be a "voice" that reflects the preferences of a legislator's constituency without altering the outcome. To determine whether the former is more important to a legislator than the latter, we need to consider the interdependence of legislators' decisions.

Consider a three-person legislature (composed of legislators A, B, and C) operating under majority rule. Suppose that legislators A and B, who favor the proposal over the status quo, realize that their constituents also support the policy change. The remaining legislator also likes the proposal, but he knows that his constituents will not be pleased with the new policy. How should legislator C vote? Note that there are only two circumstances for C to consider. If he votes yea, the bill will pass with three votes, and he will displease his constituents. But, given that A and B support the bill, C knows that if he votes nay the bill will also pass. So, legislator C is in the best of all possible worlds: By voting nay, he can please his constituents and have his preferred policy enacted as well.

Suppose the situation is the same as before, but now legislator B opposes the proposal, an opinion that she shares with her constituents. In this case, there is a split vote (one yea and one nay); as such, legislator C's vote is decisive. Legislator C knows that if he votes yea, the bill will pass, but if he votes nay, it will fail. Unlike the previous situation, his vote now has the power to unilaterally change the outcome. His choice will depend on whether he cares about the policy consequences or the position-taking aspect of his voting decision. If he cares about the former, then he will vote yea even at the expense of displeasing his constituents. In contrast, if he cares most about reflecting his constituency's preferences, he will vote nay, even though he is personally in favor of the policy change.

This simple three-member legislature example leads to an important conclusion of wider applicability: Only if a vote is tied or is within one vote of a tie can a single legislator be decisive and affect the outcome by unilaterally changing his own actions. When the final tally does not involve a one-vote margin, a legislator's vote will have no effect on the outcome, and the only relevant factor in his calculation is the benefit associated with position taking.[8]

Consider now the implications of this characterization of legislative behavior for vote buying.[9] Suppose that, based on the legislators' announced positions, a vote is expected to result in a tie. Undoubtedly, this state of affairs would indicate that the chief executive miscalculated the support for her bill at the proposal stage. Nonetheless, she may still be capable of influencing the legislative outcome. In particular, if the chief executive wishes to get her proposal approved, she needs to procure exactly one more vote. As stated before, the chief executive cannot change the content of her proposal. She may still be able to incentivize the decisive legislator to adopt her preferred policy outcome. In other words, suppose that before voting takes place, the chief executive can offer a *bribe* to the relevant legislator. These bribes may include favors, sinecures, or political rewards, and votes can also be traded in exchange for monetary payments.

An important question, of course, is whether under such circumstances bribes are actually needed. It turns out that because legislators care about both policy and position taking, it might be possible for the chief executive to get her proposal approved without having to offer any bribes. For this to happen, the only requirement is that a single legislator who likes the proposal, and whose vote is decisive, takes the "bitter pill" (i.e., sides

---

[8] In light of this possibility, some authors have raised doubts as to the relevance of interpreting legislative "prowess" as decisiveness, suggesting as more relevant the notion of "satisfaction," which is defined as the likelihood of having the result one favors irrespective of whether one's vote was crucial for it or not (Barry 1980; Laruelle and Valenciano 2005; Laruelle, Martinez and Valenciano 2006).

[9] I develop a formal treatment of vote buying in situations where legislators care non-negligibly about how they vote in the next chapter.

against his constituency). So, going back to the second example of the three-member legislature, if we assume that the legislation was proposed by the chief executive, and that legislator *C* cared most about changing the status quo, then the bill would have been approved without any bribes being dispensed. Representative Marjorie Margolies-Mezvinsky's vote on President Clinton's budget-reconciliation bill suggests that a situation like this is not just a theoretical possibility.

The first Democrat in seventy-six years to be elected from a heavily Republican district, Margolies-Mezvinsky pledged to her constituents in her campaign that she would vote against higher taxes. Early in the 103rd Congress, she was the only Democratic freshman to vote against both Clinton's budget proposal and his economic stimulus package. But on August 5, 1993, the administration needed her vote to pass the budget-reconciliation bill. With nine hours left before the vote, the Democratic leadership was still 10 votes short of the 218 it needed to win. Indeed, when the vote began at 9:55 in the evening, it looked like the proposal was set for defeat. But, when time expired, the count stood at 216-215 in favor of the bill. With three more Democrats (Pat Williams, Ray Thornton, and Margolies-Mezvinsky) waiting to cast their votes, two of them had to vote "yes" or the bill would fail. As Hager and Pianin (1997) note, to the whips and the Democratic leaders, what had to happen was clear: Williams and Thornton would have to support the bill so that Margolies-Mezvinsky could vote no. Williams initially planned to vote against the bill, but he told the party leadership that he was willing to change his vote if needed. Tension mounted when Thornton signaled his intention to oppose the bill. Democratic Representative Bill Richardson intercepted him and stated: "Ray, you told the president that you were with us," but Thornton replied that he promised his constituents that he would vote against the bill (Hager and Pianin 1997). Now the vote was 216-216. If the tie held, the bill would die. Hager and Pianin (1997) recount the remainder of the story in the following way:

Margolies-Mezvinsky was waiting 30 feet away next to the vote computer on the Democratic side of chamber .... [The Speaker of the House] Foley walked up and told her they needed her vote. Barely glancing at him, she hesitated and then began to walk slowly down the aisle toward the well ... A Democrat handed her the green card she would need to vote yes. She joined Williams at the desk at the foot of the Speaker's dais. Williams signed his card and handed it in and, finally, agonizingly slowly, Margolies-Mezvinsky did the same. After a few seconds' delay, the orange lights displaying the vote total blinked out the changes: from 216-216 to 217-216 and finally to 218-216. It was over.

Margolies-Mezvinsky's service to the president did not go unnoticed. Bill Clinton subsequently recognized her action by speaking at a seminar on deficit reduction that she sponsored in her district. Clinton's gesture, however, was hardly an equitable compensation for her vote change. In her 1994 reelection bid, John D. Fox, the man that Margolies-Mezvinsky had defeated two years before, defeated her by more than 8,000 votes. As *Congressional Quarterly* puts it, he had a powerful weapon to use against her in the form of what came to be called "The Vote".[10]

This historical example highlights those situations in which votes are "close enough" (i.e., there is a tie) to make it worthwhile for a cross-pressured legislator to favor her party rather than her constituency when casting a vote. On most votes, though, there are usually multiple legislators whose vote can potentially change the collective outcome. In these cases, "narrow victory" coalitions may unravel unless rewards are appropriately dispensed.

Consider the following example. Suppose that the chief executive introduces a bill to a five-person legislature (composed of legislators A, B, C, D, and E). As before, assume that every legislator casts a vote, the body makes decisions by majority rule, and no amendments can be proposed. Legislator A likes the proposal, and she knows that her constituents will also be pleased with the new policy. Legislator E opposes the proposal, an opinion that is shared with his constituents. The remaining legislators like the proposal, but they know that their constituents will not be pleased with it. How should legislators B, C, and D vote? Let's focus first on legislator B. He knows that A will vote yea, and that E will vote nay. With respect to C and D, there are three circumstances for B to consider (2 nay votes, 2 yea votes, or a split in their vote). If C and D support the bill, B knows that if he votes nay the bill will pass (with three votes against two). So, by voting nay, he can please his constituents and have his preferred policy enacted anyhow. If there is a split vote between C and D, then legislator B's vote is decisive. So, if he cares most about changing the status quo, he will have to take the "bitter pill" and vote yea (the bill will pass with three votes against two). Notice that this case is analogous to Margolies-Mezvinsky's situation described earlier. Finally, if both C and D vote nay, then legislator B would definitively vote nay. By voting yea under such circumstances, he cannot please his constituents, and he

---

[10] Incidentally, on July 31, 2010, almost seventeen years after Marjorie Margolies-Mezvinsky cast her famous vote, her son, Marc Mezvinsky, married Bill Clinton's daughter, Chelsea Clinton.

would not have his preferred policy enacted anyhow. How about legislators C and D? Both of them face the same incentives as legislator B, so the same logic holds for them. Therefore, it is possible that, under the impression that the other two legislators will vote nay, each one of these legislators (B, C, and D) will vote nay. Namely, all potentially decisive legislators would end up voting against their preferred policy outcome. In consequence, the chief executive would suffer a legislative defeat (the proposal would lose by four votes against one).

As this example demonstrates, the strategic behavior on the part of individual legislators may sometimes lead to a collective dilemma, a situation in which an undesirable outcome prevails. The problem is the interdependence and simultaneity of decisions: The jointly preferred outcome arises when each chooses a somewhat *selfless* strategy. Each legislator is tempted to behave as a "free rider" (if there are already two yeas, and I am the remaining legislator, then by voting nay I can "have the cake and eat it too").

It should be noted that all three legislators could be better off if they could make a binding agreement to cooperate with one another (i.e., correlate strategies) when casting a vote. For example, if they all belong to the same political party, they could exchange promises to take turns when decisive votes are needed. Yet, as the example of Representative Ray Thornton highlights, the promises of cross-pressured legislators are seldom credible. Hence, it is probably safer to assume that in any given vote, each legislator will choose her own optimal action, holding the choices of all other legislators fixed.[11]

Turning back to the last example, it is clear that the chief executive may not be able to pass the new policy without offering bribes (for example, when legislators B, C, and D vote nay). So, how many legislators should be bribed? And who should be the recipient(s) of such compensations? In principle, the chief executive needs to "buy" two additional votes (only legislator A will clearly cast a vote in favor of the proposal). Yet, consider what happens when only one additional vote is bought. Suppose that the chief executive extends an offer to legislator B to make sure than he votes yea. Now, only one additional vote will be needed to pass the bill. Suppose

---

[11] In addition to the issue of credibility, another reason to assume noncooperative behavior is that the simplest way of bringing concerted action, a Strong Nash Equilibrium (which occurs when players cannot do better even if they are allowed to communicate and collaborate before the game), adds no new equilibria to those analyzed as ordinary Nash (Denzau et al. 1985).

that you are legislator *C*. If you expect *D* to vote yea, then you should vote nay (you can please your constituents and have your preferred policy enacted anyhow). But, if you think that legislator *D* will vote nay, and you care most about changing the status quo, then you should vote yea. Legislator *D* faces the same incentives as legislator *C*, so the same logic holds for him. Hence, only two possible outcomes can occur: (1) *A*, *B*, and *C* vote yea and *D* and *E* vote nay; or (2) *A*, *B*, and *D* vote yea and *C* and *E* vote nay. In both cases, though, the chief executive's bill wins for sure.

Suppose now that instead of bribing legislator *B*, the chief executive decides to reward legislator *E* in exchange for his vote in favor of the proposal. Again, only one additional vote will be needed to pass the bill. But, now, there are still three available voters (*B*, *C*, and *D*). How should these legislators vote? Consider first legislator *B*. If both *C* and *D* vote nay, then if he cares most about changing the status quo, he should vote yea (otherwise, the bill would not be approved). As before, the other two legislators face the same incentives as *B*. Therefore, three possible outcomes can occur: (1) *A*, *B*, and *E* vote yea and *D* and *C* vote nay; (2) *A*, *C*, and *E* vote yea and *B* and *D* vote nay; or (3) *A*, *D*, and *E* vote yea and *B* and *C* vote nay. In all three cases, the chief executive's bill wins for sure.

But, regardless of who receives the bribe (legislator *B* or legislator *E*), in both cases, the chief executive only needs to buy one more additional vote instead of two to secure her bill's passage. Thus, this last example illustrates how a strategic chief executive interested in obtaining a majority of votes may be able to do so by spending as little as possible. In this case, the chief executive's strategy consists of buying enough votes so that one of the cross-pressured legislators who like the proposal would find herself in the position of being able to unilaterally change the collective outcome with her vote.

More generally, the number of legislators the chief executive will need to buy, and the total cost of a winning coalition in support of her proposal, will depend on the policy preferences of legislators and their supporters. For example, suppose that a chief executive needs to buy additional votes from legislators who dislike her proposal but whose constituents support it. In particular, suppose that legislator *A* likes the proposal and knows that her constituents will also be pleased with the new policy. Legislator *E* opposes the proposal, an opinion that is shared with his constituents. The remaining legislators dislike the proposal, but they know that their constituents will be pleased with it. To win for sure, the chief executive needs to "buy" two additional votes.

Consider what happens if the chief executive buys legislator E's vote. Now, only one additional vote will be needed to pass the proposal, and there would still be three votes up for grabs (those of legislators B, C, and D). How should these legislators vote? Consider first legislator B. If both C and D vote nay, then if he cares most about keeping the status quo, he should vote nay (otherwise, the bill would be approved). But, if both C and D vote yea, then he should also vote yea (since he cannot unilaterally prevent the proposal's passage, at least he can please his constituents). Legislators C and D face the same incentives as B. Therefore, two possible outcomes can occur: (1) A and E vote yea and B, C, and D vote nay; (2) everybody votes yea. Note that if only one additional vote is bought, there is no guarantee that the bill will pass.

Suppose now that the chief executive extends an offer to legislator B rather than E to vote yea. Once again, only one additional vote will be needed to pass the bill. Suppose that you are legislator C. If you expect D to vote yea, then you should also vote yea (since you cannot unilaterally prevent the proposal's passage, at least you can please your constituents). But, if you think that legislator D will vote nay, and you care most about keeping the status quo, then you should vote nay. Legislator D faces the same incentives as legislator C, so the same logic holds for him. In consequence, only two possible outcomes can occur: (1) A, B, C, and D vote yea, and E votes nay; or (2) A and B vote yea and C, D, and E vote nay. So, to make sure that the bill will pass, the chief executive needs to buy one more vote.

Unlike the example previously discussed, in this case, the chief executive's strategy consists of buying enough votes so that none of the cross-pressured legislators who dislike the proposal would find themselves in the position of being able to unilaterally change the collective outcome with their votes. What the two examples have in common, though, is that in both cases, it would be be possible for the chief executive to buy a minimum winning coalition (i.e., two votes out of three) or even fewer votes (i.e., one out of three) to get her proposal passed. In fact, whenever a chief executive engages in vote buying, winning coalitions will never be oversized.

I provide formal proof of my last statement in the following chapter; for now, the following examples provide the intuition of these results. In particular, I focus on some recent events that took place in Argentina. These real-world cases illustrate some of the main lessons from the abstract theory discussed in this chapter.

After a marathon session that started the previous day, Argentina's lower house narrowly approved a government tax program for agricultural exports on Saturday July 5, 2008. The bill's passage was just another chapter of a bitter battle between farmers and President Cristina Fernández de Kirchner. The conflict originated when Kirchner issued a decree in March raising taxes on agricultural exports. The measure set off a rebellion in Argentina's countryside. Enraged farmers blocked roads nationwide, paralyzing grain and meat sales that caused food shortages across the country. The government responded to the protests by staging its own progovernment demonstrations. The president also attacked the leaders of the four major farmer associations and cast the farmers as greedy oligarchs or unpatriotic plotters intent on overthrowing the government. This discursive strategy backfired, as most opinion polls showed that her uncompromising line on the farm revolt damaged her popularity. On June 16, with a new round of protests under way, Kirchner sought to legitimize the tax program by allowing Congress to vote on the measure. This was an unexpected move, because her government, as well as the government of her predecessor and husband, Néstor Kirchner, had not asked Congress to approve any major government action.

The president's Peronist party held comfortable majorities in both houses of Congress. Yet, a significant number of legislators came from agricultural districts. When the bill reached the lower house's floor late on July 4, the government still did not have the votes needed for its passage. The majority Peronist leader Agustín Rossi had to exert enormous pressure on recalcitrant deputies to ensure the bill's approval. Despite these efforts, Felipe Solá, a former Peronist governor of Buenos Aires, and seventeen other *Kirchneristas* openly defied the government and announced that they would vote against the bill. At that point, the count stood at 124-122 against the bill, with six legislators still unsure of how to cast their votes (the remaining legislator, a Peronist from a heavily agricultural district, had already announced that she was going to abstain). In the wee hours of Saturday morning, after the government promised to eliminate the export tax on apples and pears exported by their respective provinces, the deputies Julio Arriaga and Fabiana Rossi switched away from the Solá camp. By securing the defection of these two deputies from the opposition, the government ensured that none of the remaining legislators could affect the outcome by unilaterally changing their votes. Released from the burden of being individually decisive, five of the legislators voted "yes" and the remaining one cast an abstention. At 12:13 P.M., the bill passed with a majority of 129 votes, just one more than the minimum the government needed for approval.

In the aftermath of the House vote, public attention shifted to the Senate. The government needed thirty seven out of seventy two votes in a Peronist-dominated Senate to get the bill approved. Yet, pressure against the tax program kept mounting. Massive demonstrations, designed to influence various undecided senators, were organized by each side. After a number of tumultuous days, at about 4:20 A.M. on July 17, 2008, the Senate rejected the bill.

The events that led to the government's defeat had began to take shape during the previous day. Peronist Senator Teresita Quintela from La Rioja publicly announced that she would vote against the bill. After her defection, the count in favor of the bill stood at thirty four votes plus three undecided Senators. This state of affairs still gave the government a chance to pull off a favorable outcome. In contrast to the situation in the lower house, however, the Senate turned into a complicated game. By 6:00 P.M., and with three undecided votes still left, the priority of the leadership of the Peronist party was to avoid a tie. Three hours later, two undecided Peronist Senators announced their support for the bill. However, with the addition of these two legislators to the government coalition, Senator Julio Rached became the decisive voter. Rached was under intense pressure from the governor of his province to support the bill, but he personally opposed the measure. Forced to cast the decisive vote, Rached revealed that he would vote against the bill. At this point, the count stood at thirty-six to thirty-six, and every Senator had already publicly announced his or her vote intention.

With millions of Argentines following the debate live on television broadcast, the Peronist leadership knew that it would be impossible to convince anyone to change their votes. At this point, only one person, the unpredictable Vice President Julio Cobos, was in play. Cobos had challenged the President's authority a few weeks earlier by making a call to reach a compromise with the farmers. A turncoat member of the Unión Cívica Radical (UCR), a party that traditionally opposed the Peronists, he was selected by President Kirchner as her running mate to win voters outside her party's electoral base. When Cobos took the floor, the Senate hushed. In a weary, cracking voice Cobos said that although he understood that President Kirchner expected him to support the bill, he would vote against it because passing the measure would not offer a solution to the conflict. When the Senate finally voted, thirteen Peronists and twenty three members of different opposition parties voted no, tying the roll call at thirty-six to thirty-six. Vice president Julio Cobos broke the tie, squeaking out a loss, thirty-six to thirty-seven.

This real-world example clearly illustrates how despite having a solid majority in both houses of Congress, the Peronist party could not take the vote of some of its members for granted. In fact, the events that occurred in the Chamber of Deputies lend additional support to the view that chief executives may need to compensate a few vote switchers; yet, they will not necessarily need to buy too many votes or pay for votes in a losing effort. In the case of the Argentine Senate, the events that took place there vividly demonstrate how the collective decision of a legislature ultimately depends on the interdependent decisions of several individual legislators.

2.4 CONCLUDING REMARKS

The aim of this chapter was to introduce the reader to the theory of statutory policy making advanced in this book. In particular, the analysis sought to highlight the role of uncertainty regarding legislators' voting behavior as the key factor that shapes the capacity of chief executives to successfully enact statutes. Both the analytical as well as the historical examples illustrate some of the general features of statutory policy making: (1) how chief executives and legislators strategically interact with each other to produce policy changes; (2) how the existence of cross-pressured legislators affects the likelihood of a bill's passage; and (3) how legislators' vote intentions change in response to incentives.

This chapter also examined the consequences of legislative behavior for chief executives' vote-buying strategies. As the examples demonstrate, vote-buying opportunities depend on the properties of statutes and the manner in which they are produced. To reiterate, legislation possesses the characteristics of what economists call *public goods*. If a new tax rate is introduced, it will please those legislators who favor it and will displease those who do not. But, as Barry (1980) notes, the gains are not confined to those who voted on the winning side, nor are the losses confined to those who were on the losing side. The bill creates its own winners and losers by its content: If one is advantaged or disadvantaged by it, that will be so whether one voted in favor or against or did not vote at all (Barry 1980). The exception, of course, are those legislators who can unilaterally change the outcome (i.e., when a vote is tied or is within one vote of a tie). The analytical examples discussed in this chapter indicate that whenever additional votes are needed, a strategic chief executive should buy enough votes to ensure that all (none) of the cross-pressured legislators who like (dislike) her proposal find themselves in a position to unilaterally change the outcome.

The discussion of Argentina's failed tax program provide additional support for the arguments presented in this chapter. Specifically, the dilemma faced by the Peronist leaders when only three undecided legislators where left shows how, when cross-pressured legislators act strategically, even the most clever of vote buyers may end up with an undesirable policy outcome. The model presented in the next chapter explicitly identifies those situations in which strategic behavior on the part of individual legislators can lead to unanimously disliked outcomes.[12]

---

[12] I encourage those readers who are interested in this particular implication of the model to examine Lemmas 3–6 in Appendix A, as the events that took place in the Argentine Senate are represented almost to the detail in some of the examples that I use there to prove Propositions 1 and 2.

3

A Model of Statutory Policy Making under Uncertainty

In the previous chapter, I presented an intuitive and example-based framework for understanding how uncertainty and vote buying shape statutory policy making. This theme is developed further in this chapter with the introduction of a relatively simple mathematical model. Its main goal is to shed light on how party loyalty, conflicting influences, and vote buying affect chief executives' legislative performance.

There is obviously no such thing as the right degree of abstraction for all analytic purposes. In the mathematical representation of the lawmaking process that I present in this chapter, I ignore many details and make a series of simplifications. The model is thus tractable, yet rich enough to generate interesting testable propositions.[1]

Throughout the chapter, I attempt to keep the exposition of the main ideas as simple as possible, without losing mathematical precision and generality. In some passages, I rely on figures and numerical examples to convey intuition about the results. Technical details are left to the footnotes, and formal proofs can be found in Appendix A. For expositional purposes, I adopt the following convention: Legislators are identified as female and chief executives as male.

---

[1] The importance of generalization and abstraction in thought and science is cleverly illustrated in *Funes the Memorious*, a short story by the Argentine writer Jorge Luis Borges: "Without effort [Funes] had learned English, French, Portuguese, Latin. I suspect, nevertheless, that he was not very capable of thought. To think is to forget a difference, to generalize, to abstract. In the overly replete world of Funes there was nothing but details, almost contiguous details." (Borges 1962: 115). In a similar vein, Paul Krugman (1994) argues that the utility of modeling stems from useful simplification.

3.1 LEGISLATIVE STAGE

I assume the legislative process starts when the chief executive chooses between two alternatives. He can either send a proposal x^* to the legislature or keep the status quo policy x^{sq}, both elements of the set of real numbers, **R**. If the chief executive decides to do the former, then the legislature chooses between adopting the bill and making x^* the new policy, or killing it and keeping the status quo policy x^{sq}.

I analyze first the second stage of the game, namely legislative behavior once the chief executive has sent a proposal to the legislature. In the next section, I turn to the proposal stage.

Environment and Players. Two kinds of players exist: the chief executive and the legislators. The legislature is composed of an odd number of legislators, $i = 1, 2, \ldots, n$ $(n \geq 3)$. Each legislator casts a vote v_i for or against the proposal. Thus, the action space for every legislator is the set $V = \{yes, no\}$. Let v be the vector of cast votes $[v_1, v_2, \ldots, v_n] \in V^n$. This voting profile determines the legislature's decision through a decision rule $r(v)$. I assume that this decision rule is simple majority.

I make the assumption that if the bill is adopted, the chief executive derives utility $u_E(x^*) > u_E(x^{sq})$; however, if the bill is rejected, he pays a political cost $c > 0$, and gets $u_E(x^{sq}) - c$. Therefore, the chief executive strictly prefers the new policy x^* to the status quo.

If the proposal does not command a majority, the chief executive may be able and willing to bribe some legislators to affect the outcome. Let $\tau_i(v) \geq 0$ denote the bribe offer by the chief executive to legislator i under the realized voting profile v. The chief executive's payoff can be then written as:

$$u_E(x, c) + \left[\Pi(v) - \sum_{i=1}^{n} \tau_i(v) \right] \tag{3.1}$$

where $\Pi(v)$ is his fixed budget to buy off individual legislators.

Let $\theta_E = u_E(x^*) - u_E(x^{sq})$ denote the value of policy change for the chief executive. It follows that if $\theta_E > \sum_{i=1}^{n} \tau_i(v) - c$, then the chief executive would rather pass the new policy and make bribes than tolerate the status quo policy, as well as pay a cost c and keep his vote-buying budget.[2]

---

[2] But, if the total cost of securing these votes exceeds the value of policy change, the chief executive may be better off by conceding defeat.

For a legislator i, let $\theta_i = u_i(x^*) - u_i(x^{sq})$ denote the value of policy change. I assume that legislators belong to legislative parties, and that, absent any further pressures, they would follow the party line when deciding how to vote. I do not take a position regarding the particular sources of legislators' partisan alignment. Whether legislators vote with their parties because of ideological affinity (Krehbiel 1993) or for other reasons, such as protecting the party's brand name or to enjoy privileged access to legislative posts (Cox and McCubbins 1993, 2005) is not germane to the argument. Regardless of their motivation, I assume that legislators' ideal policy, $\hat{x}_i$, corresponds to their party's preferred alternative:

$$\hat{x}_i = \delta_i x^* + (1 - \delta_i)x^{sq} \tag{3.2}$$

where the parameter δ indicates legislator i's party, and takes the value of $\delta = 1$ if legislator i belongs to a government party, and $\delta = 0$ otherwise. Therefore, θ_i is identical for all legislators who belong to the same party.

As I argued in Chapter 2, legislators vote in the legislature, but they secure support, campaign resources, and electoral rewards outside the legislative arena. Therefore, I assume that legislators act as agents of particular constituencies (their principals), and that these principals may not only induce preferences in the legislators but also constrain their mode of behavior. For simplicity, I make the assumption that each legislator has a single principal $j \in J$; each principal j is characterized by the intensity of his/her preference of x^* over x^{sq}:

$$\omega_j = u_j(x^*) - u_j(x^{sq}) \tag{3.3}$$

I further assume that both principal and legislator have the same information throughout the relationship. That is, a legislator and her principal share common information as to all relevant characteristics of the chief executive's proposal, and legislator i's behavior is verifiable, so every principal can check if she has voted in accordance to its views. Since the legislator's behavior and the final result of the relationship are observable, the principal can introduce these variables explicitly into the terms of the contract. I assume that the payoff that legislator i receives from her principal j is contingent on how she casts a vote. These payoffs may take either negative or positive values (i.e., legislators can either receive a punishment or a reward), and they materialize in different forms. One can think of them as the reaction of the principal in the next election, campaign contributions, media exposure, and so on.

In terms of her utility from choosing x, I assume that it is additively separable between: (i) the utility the legislator derives from the policy that is collectively chosen by the legislature, denoted by x; (ii) the bribes (τ_i) offered to her by the chief executive; and (iii) the utility she derives from her principal's reaction to how she votes, denoted by s_i.

Therefore, the payoff of legislator i can be written as:

$$u_i(x, \tau_i, s_i | v_i) = u_i(x) + \tau_i + u_i(s_i | v_i) \tag{3.4}$$

where v_i stands for legislator i's vote; and s_i, the principal's punishment or reward is given by:

$$s_i = \begin{cases} |\omega_j| & \text{if } \omega_j > 0 \text{ and } v_i = yes \text{ or } \omega_j < 0 \text{ and } v_i = no \\ -|\omega_j| & \text{if } \omega_j < 0 \text{ and } v_i = yes \text{ or } \omega_j > 0 \text{ and } v_i = no \end{cases} \tag{3.5}$$

For example, the utility of legislator i when the collective outcome would be x^* regardless of how she votes, and she casts a vote in favor of x^* is represented by $u_i(x^*, \tau_i, s_i | yes)$. The utility of legislator i when the collective outcome would be x^{sq} regardless of how she votes, and she votes for x^*, is $u_i(x^{sq}, \tau_i, s_i | yes)$.[3]

One final assumption is that within each party, legislators are only distinguishable by the intensity of their principals' preferences. Let m denote the size of the government's legislative contingent. Legislators can then be ordered separately according to the intensity of their principals' preference of x^* over x^{sq}. Government legislators can be ordered in the following form: $\omega_1^{\delta=1} \leq \omega_2^{\delta=1} \leq \ldots \leq \omega_m^{\delta=1}$. Opposition legislators can be ordered as $\omega_1^{\delta=0} \leq \omega_2^{\delta=0} \leq \ldots \leq \omega_{n-m}^{\delta=0}$. Note that for each legislator i, ω_j defines her ω_i, so herein I use the latter notation.

Sequence. The sequence of play is as follows.

1. *Bill Introduction.* The chief executive sends a bill to the legislature without knowing the ideal policy of legislators' principals but has some prior on $\omega_i^{\delta=1} \sim N(\mu_1, \sigma_1^2)$ and $\omega_i^{\delta=0} \sim N(\mu_0, \sigma_0^2)$.
2. *Vote Buying.* Once the bill is sent to the legislature, lawmakers receive a mandate from their principals that defines ω_i for each one of them. At this point, everyone knows everything (i.e., the ω_is become common knowledge). Once this information is revealed, a voting profile v is realized. The chief executive can now "count noses" and decide whether to offer each legislator a schedule $\tau_i(v)$ of payments for voting for x^*.

---

[3] The analysis in Rasmusen and Ramseyer (1994) characterizes legislative voting behavior in a similar way.

3. *Legislative Voting.* Each legislator simultaneously casts a vote $v_i \in$ {*yes, no*}. The chief executive observes a voting profile v and delivers payments according to $\tau_i(v)$. The collective outcome x is determined by majority rule.

Strategies. I assume that once the chief executive sends a bill x^* to the legislature, he cannot change its content.[4] Therefore, his strategy at this stage consists of an n-dimensional bribe vector **p** with components $\tau_i \in \wp \equiv \{V : \{yes, no\}^n \rightarrow 0 \cup \mathbf{R}_+\}$ mapping a voting profile v into payments for voting for x^*. Legislator i's strategy $v_i : x \times \wp^n \rightarrow \{yes, no\}$ maps the chief executive proposal x^* and the payment schedules into a vote.

Given the sequentiality of the decisions by the chief executive and by the legislature, I use *subgame perfection* as my solution concept. A subgame perfect equilibrium requires each player's strategy to be optimal, given the other players' strategies, not only at the start of the game but after every possible sequence of events (Osborne 2004). First, I analyze equilibrium outcomes where the chief executive does not offer any bribes; then, I examine vote-buying situations.

3.1.1 Equilibrium Outcomes without Bribes

As I discussed in Chapter 2, I rule out the possibility that legislators can make binding agreements to cooperate with one another (i.e., correlate strategies) when casting a vote. Instead, I consider that in any given vote, each legislator chooses her own optimal action while holding the choices of all other legislators fixed.

I also assume that legislators do not use mixed strategies. I believe that this is an appropriate assumption for any voting body that allows legislators to change their votes after seeing all other votes, and does not allow the presiding officer to end the voting period when there are still legislators who want to record or change their vote (i.e., to invoke a "quick gavel"). Voting models that allow mixed strategies are consistent with the quick-gavel norm. Most legislatures around the world, however, specify a minimum amount of time for voting, and legislators can continue to vote even after the official time has expired (Groseclose and Milyo 2009). Hence, in this model, votes are the legislators' pure strategies, which I

---

[4] As I discussed in Chapter 2, if the chief executive can change the content of the legislation, then he would be able to tailor it to accommodate the policy preferences of a majority of legislators and avoid being defeated.

take to be history-independent (i.e., voting strategies only depend on the existing proposal).

Recall that legislators have preferences over which alternative wins. Therefore, legislator i's vote will only have an effect on the utility she derives from the collective outcome if she is decisive. Otherwise, legislator i will only be concerned with her principal's reaction to how she votes. Taking this into account, legislators can be arranged according to how much their principals like the proposal relative to their own taste.

For each proposal x^*, six legislative *factions* or voting blocks can be defined. The composition for each is a function of: (i) whether a legislator shares the same party as the chief executive; (ii) how much a legislator's principal values policy change; and (iii) the possible collective outcomes whenever legislator i's vote is decisive.

Formally, each legislator can be characterized as being of the type t_i: $\{\omega_i, \delta_i\}$. Let n_t be the measure of a faction composed by type-t legislators, where n_t is positive and integer-valued, so $\sum_{t=1}^{6} n_t = n$. If C is any voting coalition, let $N_t(C)$ be the set of type-t legislators in C. Let $n_t(C)$ be the total number of type-t legislators in C, and let $n(C) = \sum_{t=1}^{6} n_t(C)$ be the total number of legislators in C. I assume that all legislators in the same faction act the same. Specifically, unless they receive any bribes from the chief executive, all legislators who belong to the same faction have the same dominant voting strategy.[5]

Consider now the situation that legislator i faces when the chief executive proposes $\tau_i(v) = 0$ for all legislators. In this case, her utility depends on the policy that is collectively chosen and the individual payoff that she would get from her principal, which is contingent on how she votes. Her vote, as discussed in Chapter 2, can have two effects. It can be instrumental in determining the collective outcome, or it can be a "voice" that reflects her principal's preferences without altering the outcome. To determine whether the former is more important to legislator i than the latter, we need to consider the interdependence of legislators' decisions. Table 3.1 summarizes legislators' voting strategies. The first column identifies each faction. The fourth column shows legislator i's utility from casting her vote in a particular way. Finally the last two columns list the equilibrium strategies of legislator i when her individual vote does not change the collective outcome, and when her vote is decisive.

---

[5] For a somewhat similar approach, see Rasmusen and Ramseyer (1994) and Snyder, Ting, and Ansolabehere (2005).

Table 3.1. *Voting strategies when no bribes are offered*

Faction	Party	Ideal policy of principal	Utility from casting a particular vote	Strategy if she is not decisive	Strategy if she is decisive
N_1(C)	Government	$\omega_i > 0$	$u_i(x, s_i\|yes) > u_i(x, s_i\|no)$	Vote Yes	Vote Yes
N_2(C)	Government	$\omega_i < 0$	$u_i(x^*, s_i\|yes) > u_i(x^{sq}, s_i\|no)$	Vote No	Vote Yes
N_3(C)	Government	$\omega_i < 0$	$u_i(x, s_i\|yes) < u_i(x, s_i\|no)$	Vote No	Vote No
N_4(C)	Opposition	$\omega_i < 0$	$u_i(x, s_i\|yes) < u_i(x, s_i\|no)$	Vote No	Vote No
N_5(C)	Opposition	$\omega_i > 0$	$u_i(x, s_i\|yes) < u_i(x, s_i\|no)$	Vote Yes	Vote No
N_6(C)	Opposition	$\omega_i > 0$	$u_i(x^*, s_i\|yes) > u_i(x^{sq}, s_i\|no)$	Vote Yes	Vote Yes

Notes: This table shows how the interdependence of legislators' decisions affects their individual voting strategies when no bribes are offered. Given proposal x^*, six factions can be defined. The composition of each faction depends on: (i) a legislator's party; (ii) the ideal policy of her principal $j \in J$, denoted by $\omega_i \equiv u_j(x^*) - u_j(x^{sq})$; and (iii) the collective outcome if her vote is decisive. Without bribes, a legislator's utility from choosing x is additively separable between the utility she derives from: (i) the policy that is chosen by the legislature (x); and (ii) her principal's reaction to how she votes (s_i). For example, her utility when the outcome is x^* and she casts a vote in favor of x^* (i.e., she votes *yes*) is represented by $u_i(x^*, s_i\|yes)$. Legislators in factions N_1(C) and N_6(C) will always vote in favor of x^*. Conversely, legislators in factions N_3(C) and N_4(C) will never vote in favor of x^*. In the case of legislators in factions N_2(C) and N_5(C), their vote will depend on whether they are decisive. The former constitute the set of *potentially decisive* government legislators, whereas the latter are *potentially decisive* opposition legislators.

Legislators in faction $N_1(C)$ are government legislators whose principals like the proposal. To gain some intuition, consider Republican president George W. Bush's free-trade legislation discussed in Chapter 1. Most Republicans supported the president's measure, whereas most Democrats opposed it. Still, some Democrats from export-dependent districts were in favor of the bill, whereas Republicans from protectionist districts railed against it. In this particular example, free-trade Republicans from export-dependent districts should thus be considered members of this faction.

Faction $N_6(C)$ is composed of the opposition legislators whose principals like the government proposal so much that they are more than compensated for the disutility they incur by voting in favor of x^*. One can think of these legislators as the Democrats from export-dependent districts in the free-trade legislation example.

Faction $N_3(C)$ is composed of government legislators whose principals strongly oppose the proposal. In keeping with the same example, one can think of these legislators as Republicans from protectionist districts. Republican representative Chris Smith of New Jersey's 4th congressional district is a case in point. He voted against Bush's proposal, as well as other free-trade agreements such as NAFTA, CAFTA, and PNTR for China and Vietnam.

Legislators in faction $N_4(C)$ are opposition legislators whose principals also oppose the proposal. In the case of Bush's free-trade legislation, most Democrats opposed the bill arguing that it would bleed American jobs. These legislators should thus be considered members of this faction.

Faction $N_2(C)$ is composed of legislators who favor x^* but whose principals mildly oppose the proposal. The strategy of these legislators depends on whether their vote changes the collective outcome. If their vote is not decisive, they will always vote in favor of x^{sq}. This will make them better off because they will be able to reap the benefits from the policy that is collectively chosen and at the same time act on behalf of their principals. Robin Hayes of textile-rich North Carolina, who voted against Bush's free-trade legislation after its victory was assured, embodies the legislator who belongs to this faction.

Finally, the $N_5(C)$ faction comprises those legislators who are opposed to x^* but have principals who mildly support the measure. This support, however, is not sufficient to compensate for the disutility these legislators may incur by voting in favor of x^*, should such vote change the collective outcome. If their vote is not decisive, they will vote in favor of x^*, otherwise they will vote for x^{sq}. Turning back to the example, one can think of these legislators as the twenty five Democrats who supported Bush's free-trade proposal.

In the absence of bribes, given a proposal x^*, the outcome depends entirely on the distribution of types in the legislature. Legislators in factions $N_1(C)$ and $N_6(C)$ will always vote in favor of x^*. Conversely, legislators in factions $N_3(C)$ and $N_4(C)$ will never vote in favor of x^*. In the case of legislators in factions $N_2(C)$ and $N_5(C)$, their vote will depend on whether they are decisive. The former constitute the set of *potentially decisive* government legislators, whereas the latter are *potentially decisive* opposition legislators.

Obviously, a proposal x^* will be adopted without any bribes if a majority of *unconditional supporters* in the legislature exists; namely, if:

$$n_1(C) + n_6(C) \geq \frac{n+1}{2} \tag{3.6}$$

In this case, legislators in factions $N_1(C)$ and $N_6(C)$ will vote in favor of x^* and the remaining legislators would cast their votes according to their principals' preferences. Legislators in factions $N_2(C)$, $N_3(C)$, and $N_4(C)$ will vote against x^*. Legislators in $N_5(C)$ will cast a vote in support of the bill.

Conversely, a proposal x^* will be not adopted without any bribes if there is a majority of *unconditional opponents* in the legislature; namely, if:

$$n_3(C) + n_4(C) \geq \frac{n+1}{2} \tag{3.7}$$

In this case, legislators in factions $N_3(C)$ and $N_4(C)$ will vote against x^* and the remaining legislators will cast their votes according to their principals' preferences. Legislators in factions $N_1(C)$, $N_5(C)$, and $N_6(C)$ will vote for x^*. Legislators in $N_2(C)$ will cast a vote against the bill.

Suppose now that neither unconditional supporters nor unconditional opponents constitute a majority. Let k be the number of additional votes needed to pass x^*, once the votes from the unconditional supporters are accounted for. Formally, let:

$$k = \frac{n+1}{2} - n_1(C) + n_6(C) \tag{3.8}$$

The outcome depends on how the potentially decisive legislators cast their votes. This reasoning leads to the following proposition.

Proposition 1 *A pure-strategy equilibrium outcome, where the chief executive offers no bribes and* x^* *wins, exists. In every equilibrium, legislator* i *will never vote against her principal unless her vote is decisive.*

Proof. All proofs are in Appendix A.

An important feature of these equilibrium outcomes is that each legislator's vote will affect the collective decision and hence her own payoff. This is the case because legislators have preferences over which policy alternative wins. A government legislator, however, would only take the "bitter pill" and vote contrary to her principal's wishes if her vote is the decisive one.[6]

Another characteristic of these equilibria is their symmetry. This is another significant feature because it implies that strategic behavior on the part of individual legislators may lead to Pareto-inefficient outcomes. Specifically, whenever the set of potentially decisive government legislators or the set of potentially decisive opposition legislators is empty, the existence of "surplus" votes generates a kind of multilateral prisoners' dilemma. By playing dominant strategies, all potentially decisive legislators end up voting in favor of a policy outcome that is undesirable for them. In consequence, when more than one additional vote is needed to change the outcome, the chief executive may not be able to pass the new policy x^* without offering bribes.[7]

When there are both government and opposition potentially decisive legislators, two situations arise. Either the legislative stage of the game has no pure strategy equilibrium outcomes, or in equilibrium every legislator votes with her principal. As such, the size and partisan make-up

---

[6] As Denzau et al. (1985) note, when legislators are monitored and evaluated by constituents who care both about legislative outcomes and about legislative behavior, "... result-oriented strategic calculation and sophisticated behavior in the legislative arena may require actions that run contrary to the nominal preferences of important constituents ..." (Denzau et al. 1985: 1118). The authors examine these situations and find that when voting behavior is consistent with a pure strategy Nash equilibrium, legislators should only act sophisticatedly in the knife-edge case of a tie. Similarly, Groseclose and Milyo (2009) demonstrate that legislators with preferences over policy and the positions that they take (i.e., the way in which they vote when they are not pivotal), will rarely engage in sophisticated voting.

[7] When the chief executive does not offer any bribes, there are several pure strategy equilibrium outcomes where this is not the case. However, in all of these situations, the "strongest" voting profile is the one where all potentially decisive legislators vote as if they were not casting the decisive vote, as it involves (weakly) dominant strategies. See Dal Bo (2007) for a similar treatment.

of unbribed winning coalitions can be characterized in the following way:

Comment 1 *In the absence of bribes, minimum-winning voting coalitions where the chief executive wins for sure only occur if:*

1. $n_1(\mathbf{C}) + n_6(\mathbf{C}) = \frac{n+1}{2}$, *and* $n_5(\mathbf{C}) = 0$;
2. $n_1(\mathbf{C}) + n_6(\mathbf{C}) < \frac{n+1}{2}$, $k > 1$, $n_2(\mathbf{C}) > 0$, *and* $n_5(\mathbf{C}) = k + 1$;
3. $n_1(\mathbf{C}) + n_6(\mathbf{C}) < \frac{n+1}{2}$, $k = 1$, $n_2(\mathbf{C}) > 0$, *and* $n_5(\mathbf{C}) = 0$.

If unconditional supporters constitute a majority of the legislature, or if unconditional supporters plus one potentially decisive opposition legislator constitute a majority (given $k = 1$), then x^* wins for sure. In both cases, however, all members of faction $\mathbf{N}_5(\mathbf{C})$ will vote for x^*. And as these legislators join the winning coalition, its size becomes larger than minimum.

We know that an equilibrium outcome where all legislators vote with their principals always exist in pure strategies when $n_5(\mathbf{C}) > k$. In this case, a minimum-winning coalition will only exist if $n_5(\mathbf{C}) = k + 1$. Without bribes, a cross-partisan minimum-winning coalition will be an equilibrium outcome only if unconditional supporters are exactly a majority of the legislature and there are no potentially decisive opposition legislators, or if: (1) neither unconditional supporters nor unconditional opponents constitute a majority; (2) there are some potentially decisive opposition legislators; (3) more than one additional vote is needed to change the outcome; and (4) the set of potentially decisive opposition legislators is equal to the number of additional votes needed to pass x^* plus one.

An all-government – or *nonflooded*, in Groseclose and Snyder (1996) terms – minimum-winning coalition will only happen if: (1) neither unconditional supporters nor unconditional opponents constitute a majority; (2) there are some potentially decisive government legislators; (3) exactly one additional vote is needed to change the outcome; and (4) there are no potentially decisive nor unconditional supporters in the opposition. The prediction that nonflooded minimum winning coalitions would only rarely occur (i.e., under a very restrictive set of circumstances) is consistent with the literature (Groseclose and Snyder 1996; King and Zeckhauser 1999) and evidence from roll-call votes in the U.S. Congress.

3.1.2 Equilibrium Outcomes with Bribes

I now turn my attention to the analysis of the chief executive's strategy. The chief executive would only offer bribes if he can achieve a better outcome than being defeated at a sufficiently low cost. In principle, every chief executive would like to make an offer such that each legislator would actually receive the reward if and only if her vote happens to be decisive. As Dal Bo (2007) shows, by promising to reward at least one more voter than she needs to win, all legislators become nondecisive, and therefore the chief executive would not need to make any payments at all. Nonetheless, when legislators are cross-pressured, chief executives cannot use these so-called *pivotal offers* to manipulate the collective decision at virtually no cost (Rasmusen and Ramseyer 1994; Dekel et al. 2005; Dal Bo 2007).

It should now be clear why this is the case. A legislator who votes in favor of a policy that damages her principal would suffer a loss equal to her principal's punishment, no matter what the other legislators do. In other words, the agency relationship with her principal shields every legislator from the externalities caused by other legislators' votes. The chief executive will therefore be unable to accomplish much by offering pivotal contracts.

To reiterate, unless a legislator is actually decisive, she will never cast a vote that contradicts her principal's preferences. By the same logic, whenever she is not decisive, the policy component of her utility is irrelevant to her voting decision. As a result, a chief executive could exploit this aspect of legislative behavior and buy legislators' votes at a cost of $\tau_i(v) = 2s_i$ each. This "price" reflects the fact that in order to cast a vote against her principal, a legislator would have to be compensated for contradicting her (which entails forgoing her reward and suffering her punishment).

If this stage of the legislative game has been reached, it means that every legislator's ω_i has become common knowledge. In consequence, the chief executive can use this information to compute the optimal n-dimensional bribe vector using the following algorithm. Denote by $\mathbf{B}$ the set of bribed legislators. Let $\mathbf{N}_t(\mathbf{B})$ be the set of type-t legislators in $\mathbf{B}$. Let $n_t(\mathbf{B})$ be the total number of type-t legislators in $\mathbf{B}$, and let $n(\mathbf{B}) = \sum_{t=2}^{5} n_t(\mathbf{B})$ be the total number of legislators in $\mathbf{B}$. The cost of a winning coalition increases in $n(\mathbf{B})$, thus, the optimal bribing strategy consists in picking the "cheapest" legislators such that $n(\mathbf{B}) \leq \frac{n+1}{2} - n_1(\mathbf{C}) - n_6(\mathbf{C})$.

The following proposition identifies this strategy, which I call the Least Expensive Bribed Majority strategy (LEBM) for the chief executive:

Proposition 2 *The LEBM strategy, whereby the chief executive buys* k *or fewer votes, guarantees a victory to* x*.*

This proposition presents one of the main findings in this book. A chief executive may be able to buy a minimum winning coalition, or even fewer votes than those needed to pass x^* (once the votes from the unconditional supporters are accounted for) and get his initiative approved. Proposition 2 also leads to the following observation about the size of "bribed" majorities:

Comment 2 *In the presence of vote buying, winning coalitions are either strictly minimal or include* $(\frac{n+3}{2})$ *legislators.*

This conclusion follows directly from the fact that legislators are cross-pressured. Given legislators' policy preferences and responsiveness to their principals, these types of coalitions are the least expensive ones available. Whether the coalition is minimum-winning or includes one additional legislator depends on the distribution of types in the legislature. Occasionally, it will be cheaper for a chief executive to buy some votes and add enough legislators to the winning coalition so that no opposition legislator is actually decisive.

Example 1 *Let* $n = 101$, *the decision rule* $r(v)$ *be simple majority,* $\omega_i^{\delta=1} \sim N(\mu_1, \sigma_1^2)$, *and* $\omega_i^{\delta=0} \sim N(\mu_0, \sigma_0^2)$.

A possible distribution of the ω_is in this legislature is represented in Figure 3.1. Suppose that the government and opposition legislative contingents are almost of equal size (i.e., the government has fifty one seats and the opposition has fifty). As shown in Figure 3.1, legislators can be ordered according to their ω_is. All legislators in $N_1(C)$, $N_5(C)$, and $N_6(C)$ are located to the right of $\omega_i = 0$. All legislators in $N_2(C)$, $N_3(C)$, and $N_4(C)$ are located to the left of $\omega_i = 0$. With regard to legislators' utilities, assume that for government legislators, $u(x^*) = 1$ and $u(x^{sq}) = -1$. Likewise, for opposition legislators, $u(x^*) = -1$ and $u(x^{sq}) = 1$. Hence, everything is measured in the metric of $u(x^*) - u(x^{sq})$.

Given these parameter values, a legislator in $N_2(C)$ could have a $\omega_i = -.8$, and if the outcome is already decided in favor of x^*, she will vote against x^*, receive no bribes, and still have a positive utility of 1.8. Suppose, however, that she would only vote in support of x^* if she receives a bribe. The chief executive would have to compensate her for casting a vote in favor of x^* and being punished by her principal. Therefore, the cost of buying this legislator's vote becomes $2s_i = 1.6$. In the case of a

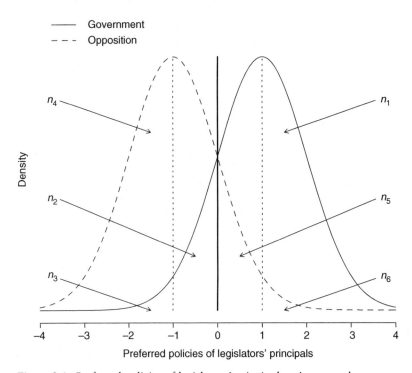

Figure 3.1. Preferred policies of legislators' principals – An example.
Notes: This figure illustrates how principals' policy preferences shape the size and composition of legislative factions. The example is based on a 101-member legislature operating under majority rule, where the government has 51 seats and the opposition has the remaining 50. The ideal policies of legislators' principals (ω_is) are given by $\omega_i^{\delta=1} \sim N(1, 1)$ for government legislators and by $\omega_i^{\delta=0} \sim N(-1, 1)$ for those in the opposition. Legislators are ordered according to their ω_is. To the right of $\omega_i = 0$ are $n_1(C)$, $n_6(C)$, and $n_5(C)$ legislators. To the left of $\omega_i = 0$ are $n_2(C)$, $n_3(C)$, and $n_4(C)$ legislators. Regarding legislators' utilities, everything is measured in the metric of $u(x^*) - u(x^{sq})$, where $u(x^*) = 1$ and $u(x^{sq}) = -1$ for government legislators and $u(x^*) = -1$ and $u(x^{sq}) = 1$ for opposition legislators. In this example, a $\omega_i = -.8$ may correspond to a *potentially decisive* government legislator. Whenever her vote is not decisive and the new policy is supported by a legislative majority, this legislator would vote against the proposal, receive no bribes, and still have a positive utility of 1.8.

legislator in $N_5(C)$, she could have a $\omega_i = .5$. If the outcome is already decided, she will vote for x^* and get a utility of 1.5 if x^{sq} is the winning policy and -.5 otherwise. If her vote is needed to change the outcome, then she can sell it and her vote will be worth $2s_i = 1$.

Because voting coalitions in support of x^* can be conformed by buying different types of legislators, a chief executive will always buy the least expensive votes to achieve x^*; but their individual cost is given by $2s_i$, and these "prices" depend on the realization of the ω_is. Therefore, to complete the analysis, the total cost of a bribed winning coalition needs to be calculated.

Let the "approval" cost function be $Y: g(\tilde{\omega}) \to \mathbf{R}$ where $g(\tilde{\omega}) = g(\omega^{\delta=1}, \omega^{\delta=0})$ denotes the realization of $\omega_i^{\delta=1}$ and $\omega_i^{\delta=0}$. Then, the expected total cost of bribes can be expressed as:

$$\hat{Y} = \int \int g(\tilde{\omega}) f_{\omega^{\delta=1}} f_{\omega^{\delta=0}} \, d\omega^{\delta=1} \, d\omega^{\delta=0} \tag{3.9}$$

The optimal bribe vector $\mathbf{p}$ depends on the total cost of a winning coalition and on $\Pi(v)$, the chief executive's budget to buy those individual votes. If the total cost of bribes is larger than his budget ($Y > \Pi(v)$), then the status quo will prevail. Likewise, if the total cost of securing these votes exceeds the value of policy change plus the political costs ($Y > \theta_E + c$), then the chief executive would actually be better off by conceding defeat.

3.2 PROPOSAL STAGE

Turning to the proposal stage, the chief executive's decision entails sending a proposal x^* to the legislature or keeping the status quo policy x^{sq}. Because each legislator's reservation value depends on a proposal's content, the chief executive would like to send a bill x^* that maximizes his policy objectives and minimize his payments (i.e., by compromising on policy). Nonetheless, as I argued in Chapter 2, because the chief executive sends his bills to the legislature without knowing the ideal policy of legislators' principals, he cannot calculate *ex-ante* such optimal proposal.

Given some prior on $\omega_i^{\delta=1}$ and $\omega_i^{\delta=0}$, the chief executive adopts a *sending* strategy of the form: $\rho : [\underline{Y}, \overline{Y}] \to \{1, 0\}$, where $\rho(\hat{Y}) = 1(0)$ means that the chief executive sends (does not send) a bill to the legislature if the expected cost of securing majoritarian support for the bill is $\hat{Y}$. Therefore, the sending strategy ρ depends on the probability that the total cost of bribes would not exceed either the chief executive's vote-buying budget or the sum of the value of policy change and the political costs of defeat to him.

These considerations lead to the following proposition:

Proposition 3 *The game has an equilibrium in pure strategies where the chief executive sends a bill to the legislature and is defeated.*

The chief executive would only send a bill to the legislature when he estimates that his vote-buying budget is large enough to secure majoritarian support. Depending on the particular realization of Y, the chief executive may be able, if needed, to gather sufficient support for such bill or not. Even with well-defined priors, the draws of Y may be quite different. If the chief executive sends a bill to the legislature, and the realization of Y is larger than $Y = \theta_E + c$, then he may have to concede the issue. In addition, even if it is worthwhile for the chief executive to buy some additional votes and make x^* the new policy, if $\Pi(v) < Y < \theta_E + c$, the chief executive is unable to secure the bill's passage.

Defeat, of course, is not the only possible equilibrium outcome. As the total cost of a bribed winning coalition decreases, the chief executive would be able to pay the necessary compensations to achieve his preferred policy. He also would not need to resort to his "pocketbook" in order to handle the effects of cross-voting if the total cost of bribes drops to zero. If that is the case, a bill would pass with majority support and no payments would be necessary.

3.3 EMPIRICAL IMPLICATIONS

As discussed in Chapter 2, the model stresses the role of uncertainty regarding legislative voting behavior as the key factor shaping the capacity of chief executives to successfully enact policy changes through government acts that carry the force of law by winning legislative majorities. The importance of this distinction can be seen by explicitly examining how agenda setting and the number of legislators who belong to the chief executive's party/coalition affect the passage of legislation in this model.

Numerical Examples. To get a sense of the model's predictions, it is helpful to first work through several numerical examples. Let the chief executive be the proposer of legislation (i.e., the agenda-setter), $n = 101$, and the decision rule $r(v)$ be simple majority. Let $\omega_i^{\delta=1} \sim N(\mu_1, \sigma_1^2)$, and $\omega_i^{\delta=0} \sim N(\mu_0, \sigma_0^2)$. Also $u(x^*) = 1$ and $u(x^{sq}) = -1$ for government legislators; and $u(x^*) = -1$ and $u(x^{sq}) = 1$ for opposition legislators. Let $c = .5$.

Example 2 *Suppose the chief executive's party has 45 seats in the legislature. Let* $\Pi(v) = 2.5$, *and* $\hat{Y} = 2.5$.

In this case, the chief executive would adopt a sending strategy $s(\hat{Y}) = 0$. Therefore, the final outcome is that no bill is sent to the legislature, the status quo policy x^{sq} remains unchanged, and the chief executive does not pay any political costs of defeat.

Example 3 *Suppose the chief executive's party has 53 seats in the legislature. Let* $\Pi(v) = 3$, $\hat{Y} = .5$, *and* $Y = 2.6$.

Suppose the chief executive adopts a sending strategy $s(\hat{Y}) = 1$. Once the bill is sent to the legislature, he has enough resources to buy additional votes. However, buying the additional votes to make x^* the new policy is not a dominant strategy for the chief executive. Therefore, the bill x^* is defeated, the status quo policy x^{sq} remains unchanged, and the chief executive pays the political costs of defeat.

Example 4 *Suppose the chief executive's party has 55 seats in the legislature. Let* $\Pi(v) = .5$, $\hat{Y} = 0$, *and* $Y = .45$.

Suppose the chief executive adopts a sending strategy $s(\hat{Y}) = 1$. In this case, despite the miscalculation, the chief executive can buy the additional votes to make x^* the new policy. As a result, the bill x^* becomes the new policy after some payments are made.

Example 5 *Suppose the chief executive's party has 55 seats in the legislature. Let* $\Pi(v) = .5$, $\hat{Y} = 0$, *and* $Y = 1$.

Suppose the chief executive adopts a sending strategy $s(\hat{Y}) = 1$. In this case, buying the additional votes to make x^* the new policy is worthwhile for him (e.g., $\theta_E + c > Y$). Yet, as the chief executive miscalculated the total cost of bribes, his vote-buying budget is not large enough to make such payments. Therefore, the bill x^* is defeated, the status quo policy x^{sq} remains unchanged, and the chief executive pays the political costs of defeat.

Simulation Results. I now examine the model's predictions using simulated data. As before, let the chief executive be the proposer of legislation (i.e., the agenda-setter), $n = 101$, and the decision rule $r(v)$ be simple majority. Legislators' ω_is were randomly generated assuming that $\omega_i^{\delta=1} \sim N(1,1)$, and $\omega_i^{\delta=0} \sim N(-1,1)$.

Table 3.2 presents how majority sizes, composition, and the total cost of winning coalitions vary as a function of ω_i for these simulated values. I restrict attention to situations where the party of the chief executive controls between 45 and 61 seats in the 101-member legislature. The first six columns indicate the number of legislators in each faction. The following two columns indicate the average ω_i for that draw, for both the government and opposition legislators. The ninth column indicates the composition of the voting coalition in support of x^*. The following column indicates the size of the coalition. The eleventh column indicates how many legislators have to be bribed. The final column indicates the total cost. These estimates are also examined according to the total number of government and opposition seats. The first three panels correspond to situations where the party of the chief executive fails to have a majority of seats in the legislature. The reminder of the table presents situations where government legislators have a majority of seats.

Take, for example, the first entry in Table 3.2. Government legislators hold 45 seats in the legislature, $n_1(C) = 36$, $n_2(C) = 6$ and $n_3(C) = 1$. The opposition is composed of 56 legislators; 42 legislators in $N_4(C)$, 11 in $N_5(C)$ and 3 legislators in $N_6(C)$. The average ideal policy for government legislators' principals, $\overline{\omega}^{\delta=1}$ is 0.73, and the average ideal policy for opposition legislators' principals, $\overline{\omega}^{\delta=0}$ is -0.69. The least expensive coalition includes 52 legislators from factions $N_1(C)$, $N_2(C)$, $N_4(C)$, $N_5(C)$, $N_6(C)$. The logic goes as follows: the chief executive can buy just two legislators to make all legislators in $N_5(C)$ nondecisive. Given the reservation value of the two least costly legislators (in this case, one legislator in $N_2(C)$, and one legislator in $N_4(C)$), the total cost of putting together a voting coalition in support of x^* is 0.34.

Consider now what happens in the scenario represented in the fourth entry of Table 3.2. There are also forty five government legislators and fifty six opposition legislators. But in this case, the government has to bribe eight legislators (excluding one potentially decisive government legislator) to make all legislators in $N_5(C)$ nondecisive. In this case the total cost of a winning coalition in support of x^* (including three legislators in $N_2(C)$, and five in $N_4(C)$) is 3.78. Alternatively, it can buy all five legislators in $N_5(C)$ plus six more legislators and make a legislator in $N_2(C)$ decisive. In this case, the cost would be 5.5. To have a sense of what this means in substantive terms, the cost of a winning coalition that accounts for the value of policy change for the chief executive is $\theta_E = 2$. In this last case, the cost of the least expensive coalition is almost twice as large than the utility loss for the chief executive from keeping the status quo.

Table 3.2. *Simulated coalitions and total cost*

n_1	n_2	n_3	n_4	n_5	n_6	$\bar{\omega}^{\delta=1}$	$\bar{\omega}^{\delta=0}$	Types included	Size	Bribed Legs.	Total Cost ($\sum_{i=1}^{n} \tau_i(v)$)
36	6	3	42	11	3	0.73	−0.69	1, 2, 4, 5, 6	52	2	0.34
39	6	0	50	5	1	0.98	−1.06	1, 2, 4, 5, 6	52	7	1.97
37	7	1	50	6	0	1.13	−1.19	1, 2, 4, 5	52	9	1.88
39	6	0	51	5	0	1.08	−1.09	1, 2, 4, 5	52	8	3.78
34	11	0	46	8	2	1.11	−0.99	1, 2, 4, 5, 6	52	8	2.26
41	4	2	41	13	0	1.19	−1.07	1, 5	54	0	0
34	12	1	42	11	1	0.72	−1.05	1, 2, 4, 5, 6	52	6	1.93
38	7	2	46	7	1	1.02	−1.12	1, 2, 4, 5, 6	52	6	2.25
38	8	1	43	9	2	1.06	−0.75	1, 2, 4, 5, 6	52	3	0.77
39	8	0	47	7	0	1.11	−1.04	1, 2, 4, 5	52	6	1.11
43	4	2	42	8	2	1.07	−1.16	1, 5, 6	53	0	0
41	8	0	46	5	1	1.09	−1.11	1, 2, 4, 5, 6	52	5	0.59
39	10	0	45	7	0	0.94	−0.96	1, 2, 4, 5	52	6	3.01
42	6	1	44	7	1	1.05	−1.17	1, 2, 4, 5, 6	52	2	0.28
40	7	2	46	5	1	0.91	−1.12	1, 2, 4, 5, 6	52	6	1.31
42	8	1	42	8	0	0.83	−0.99	1, 2, 5	52	2	0.55
42	9	0	40	9	1	0.82	−0.88	1, 5, 6	52	0	0
41	9	1	43	6	1	0.66	−1.02	1, 2, 4, 5, 6	52	4	0.73
43	8	0	45	3	2	0.88	−1.11	1, 2, 4, 5, 6	52	4	0.65
43	8	0	43	7	0	0.91	−0.98	1, 2, 4, 5	52	2	0.16
40	12	1	42	5	1	0.97	−0.98	1, 2, 4, 5, 6	52	6	0.51
47	5	1	39	8	1	1.17	−0.94	1, 5, 6	56	0	0
42	10	1	41	5	2	0.96	−0.79	1, 2, 4, 5, 6	52	3	0.11
41	11	1	42	6	0	0.87	−0.97	1, 2, 4, 5	52	5	1.62
45	7	1	37	10	1	0.92	−0.98	1, 5, 6	56	0	0

49	4	2	43	2	1	0.99	−0.98	1,5,6	52	0	0
45	8	2	39	5	2	0.83	−0.92	1,5,6	52	0	0
49	6	0	39	7	0	1.01	−1.01	1,5	56	0	0
47	6	2	39	5	2	0.87	−0.93	1,5,6	54	0	0
45	10	0	36	9	1	1.11	−0.74	1,5,6	55	0	0
53	4	0	39	4	1	1.07	−1.19	1,5,6	58	0	0
44	10	3	38	6	0	0.64	−0.95	1,2,4,5	52	2	0.45
51	5	1	34	10	0	1.02	−0.99	1,5	61	0	0
46	11	0	38	5	1	0.95	−1.35	1,5,6	52	0	0
46	10	1	36	7	1	0.93	−1.07	1,5,6	54	0	0
45	13	1	41	1	0	0.88	−1.42	1,2,5	51	5	1.55
52	6	1	33	9	0	1.02	−0.88	1,5	61	0	0
50	8	1	35	6	1	1.05	−1.12	1,5,6	57	0	0
47	10	2	37	5	0	0.89	−1.24	1,5	52	0	0
49	8	2	34	6	2	0.88	−0.93	1,5,6	57	0	0
51	7	3	29	8	3	0.89	−0.70	1,5	62	0	0
54	7	0	34	5	1	0.96	−1.05	1,5,6	60	0	0
50	9	2	36	4	0	1.06	−1.22	1,5	54	0	0
53	6	2	37	3	0	1.05	−1.11	1,5	56	0	0
48	13	0	32	6	2	1.13	−1.07	1,5,6	56	0	0

Notes: This table shows how majority sizes, composition, and the total cost of winning coalitions vary as a function of the ideal policies of legislators' principals. The outcomes are based on simulated data for a 101-member legislature operating under majority rule. Legislators' mandates from their principals (ω_js) were randomly generated assuming that $\omega_i^{\delta=1} \sim N(1,1)$ for government legislators and $\omega_i^{\delta=0} \sim N(-1,1)$ for those in the opposition. The first six columns indicate the number of legislators in each faction. Columns 7 and 8 indicate the average ω_i for that draw, for the government and opposition legislators, respectively. Column 9 indicates the composition of the voting coalition in support of x^*. Column 10 indicates the size of the coalition. Column 11 indicates how many legislators have to be bribed. Column 12 indicates the total cost. The first three panels correspond to situations where the party of the chief executive fails to have a majority of seats in the legislature. The remainder of the table presents situations where government legislators have a majority of seats.

Moving down in Table 3.2, one can see more generally how the composition of the legislature and the distribution of the ω_is affect the cost of a winning coalition. For instance, when the chief executive's party is in the minority (i.e., it has fewer than fifty one seats) the average cost of a winning coalition is 1.43, including a maximum of 3.78 and a minimum of 0 (i.e., no bribes are needed). In all these cases, the chief executive receives all the votes from the potentially decisive opposition legislators for free without giving out any bribes or buying legislators from other factions.

Notice what occurs when the chief executive's party controls a majority of seats in the legislature. Take the cases where it has fifty one or fifty three seats. The average coalition cost is 0.43, with a maximum of 1.62 and a minimum of 0. In some cases, despite having a majority of seats, the chief executive may need to buy some of his own legislators to win with certainty. In some other cases, bribes will not be necessary given a "surplus" of potentially decisive opposition legislators. The variance in $\omega^{\delta=1}$ and $\omega^{\delta=0}$, which reflects the principal's influence, plays an important role both in favor and against the government. Finally, when the party of the chief executive has an ample majority of seats, the effects of the principals' influence are mitigated. When it has more than 55 seats, voting coalitions in support of x^* are costless or very cheap. Still, in some cases where legislators' principals really dislike a bill, some payments will have to be made to get x^* approved. For example, in one of the cases, government legislators hold 59 seats in the legislature, but unconditional supporters constitute a minority: $n_1(C) = 45$, $n_2(C) = 13$, and $n_3(C) = 1$. In the opposition, there are 41 legislators in faction $N_4(C)$, 1 in $N_5(C)$, and no legislators in $N_6(C)$. In this case, the legislator in $N_5(C)$ is always decisive. The chief executive, can thus buy 6 legislators (4 in $N_2(C)$, and 2 in $N_4(C)$) at a cost of 1.82. Alternatively, it can bribe the potentially decisive opposition legislator and buy 4 more legislators (all in $N_2(C)$) at a cost of 1.55, and make a legislator in $N_2(C)$ decisive. The latter option is the least expensive one, but still considerably high when considering that the government controls an ample majority of seats.

Figure 3.2 presents a graphical representation of the distribution of Y, the costs of securing majoritarian support for a bill, based on the simulated values. As Figure 3.2 indicates, most of the time, the total cost of bribes is smaller than the value of policy change for the chief executive. However, there are some draws for which the value of $Y > \theta_E$. Therefore,

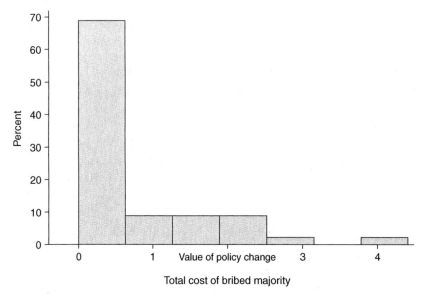

Figure 3.2. Simulated cost of winning coalition.
Notes: This figure presents a graphical representation of the simulated cost of a winning coalition. These values correspond to those in column 12 of Table 3.2. In most cases, the total cost of bribes is smaller than 2, the value of policy change for the chief executive. However, there are some draws for which the total cost of securing additional votes exceeds the value of policy change.

as the model predicts, when chief executives cannot identify the policy preferences of legislators' principals, they may suffer defeats.

3.4 CONCLUDING REMARKS

As discussed in the previous chapter, the existing literature does not provide us with a good explanation of why chief executives suffer legislative defeats. Most models are inadequate on two counts. First, they are unrealistic in their predictions that executive-initiated bills are never defeated. Second, they often neglect the role of cross-pressured legislators.

The model introduced in this chapter explains the main puzzle posed in this book: Even if a proposer has no intention to be defeated, his initiatives can fail at the legislative stage. The results suggest that it takes very little uncertainty for a chief executive to miscalculate his legislative support. The analysis also reveals that when a bill commands too much opposition (and thus the total cost of a bribed winning coalition is too high), chief executives will be unwilling or unable to pay the necessary compensations to achieve their preferred policies.

Beyond explaining why executive-initiated bills sometimes fail, the model also provides new insights into statutory policy making. My findings indicate that: (1) cross-partisan minimum-winning coalitions would occur only under a very restrictive set of circumstances when no bribes are paid; (2) without bribes, minimum-winning coalitions composed exclusively of government legislators would occur only under an even more restrictive set of circumstances; (3) equilibrium vote-buying behavior does not result in supermajority coalitions.

The model's predictions are borne out by the outcomes generated using simulated data. Moving beyond the simulations, the model also yields several important implications with regard to the variation in chief executives' legislative passage rates that are observed in the real world. I examine this variation using data from fifty two countries in the period between 1946 and 2008 in Part II of the book.

PART III

EMPIRICAL IMPLICATIONS

4

Measuring Chief Executives' Statutory Performance

When does a government actually *govern*? Or, simply put, how can one gauge a chief executive's effectiveness? I argue for the use of the *box score*. This indicator is calculated as the percentage of executive initiatives approved by the legislature. It is analogous to a batting average (i.e., number of hits as a proportion of times at bat). As such, the box score summarizes a chief executive's record of wins and losses (Bond et al. 1996).[1]

In this chapter, I compare and contrast the box score with several other commonly used measures in the literature. After addressing some common criticisms against the use of box scores, I explain why this indicator is the most appropriate measure to analyze chief executives' statutory achievements in the context of this work.

4.1 COMMON MEASURES OF LEGISLATIVE ACHIEVEMENTS

In addition to the box score, students of executive-legislative relations use several measures of legislative success and various units of analysis. In fact, passage, success, productivity, support, concurrence, dominance, control, and influence all appear in the scholarly literature (Edwards 1980, 1989; Shull 1983; Bond and Fleisher 1990; Peterson 1990) and sometimes are used interchangeably.

One commonly used indicator is the "supply" of legislation, or total legislative productivity. For instance, most of the literature focusing on the effect of divided government on lawmaking examines the number of

---

[1] This measure is a commonly used indicator in the literature on presidential legislative success in the United States. For those readers familiar with this literature, this measure is similar to Congressional Quarterly's box score.

laws enacted by the U.S. Congress (Coleman 1999; Howell et al. 2000; Krutz 2000). But, legislative output is not necessarily the inverse of grid-lock. Thus, this measure is not a good indicator of a chief executive's capacity to pass its agenda.[2]

Another measure that is frequently used calculates the percentage of all bills approved by the legislature that are of executive origin. This indicator speaks to the question of *who* initiates laws. Therefore, it is typically used to evaluate arguments about how "monopolistic" governments are in the law production process (Crain, Holcombe, and Tollison 1979; Cox and McCubbins 1993). Some scholars argue that if agenda control is divided into a number of agenda-setting centers with different procedural prerog-atives (as it occurs in many democratic countries) and party discipline is not taken for granted, monopolistic production may be an ill-conceived model of the legislative process.[3] As a result, this indicator can be used to adjudicate the usefulness of conceiving law production in monopolistic terms. Or, more broadly, it can be used to analyze the balance between the executive and legislature.[4] This indicator, however, does not reveal anything regarding the ability of a chief executive to win approval for her legislative initiatives. It may be the case that the executive sends 900 bills to the legislature and only 10 percent are approved, and private mem-bers introduce 10 initiatives with an approval rate of 100 percent. It may also be the case that the executive sends 100 initiatives with 90 percent being approved and private members introduce 900 initiatives and only 10 percent are approved.[5]

---

[2] As Binder notes, "... a low level of law production may indicate a high level of political gridlock. Alternatively, it may reflect the response of a Congress and a president facing a limited political agenda, in which case it may indicate a low level of gridlock ..." (Binder 1999: 520).

[3] Even in Britain, where party discipline is reported to be extremely high, party leadership cannot take their backbenchers' support for granted (Saalfeld 1995).

[4] For example, say that in a particular year in country *j*, a total of 100 laws were enacted. Of these laws, 90 resulted from bills introduced by the executive and 10 from legislative initiatives of private members. We can say, then, that out of the laws that were produced in that particular year in country *j*, 90 percent of them were of executive origin. In that sense we can talk of executive "dominance" over the legislature.

[5] This seems to have been the case in Belgium between 1968 and 1996: About nine out of ten of all legislative proposals originate from parliamentary initiative, but of those only one out of ten becomes law (de Winter 1998: 108). In fact, in most countries this seems to be the pattern: A large majority of bills approved by legislatures around the world are introduced to a large extent by the government. And, although individual legislators have everywhere the right to introduce bills, the legislation most likely to be enacted is initiated by governments.

To compare these different measures, Table 4.1 presents cross-national data on legislative production in nine countries. Suppose that one is interested in the issue of executive dominance. Then, the relevant measure is the ratio of government-initiated laws to total laws. In Canada and Spain, a clear dominance of the executive over the legislature exists. The cabinet was responsible for almost 97 and 90 percent of the laws that were passed by the Canadian and Spanish Parliaments, respectively. To a lesser degree in Honduras, Mexico, Turkey, and Italy, a dominance of the executive over the legislature is also apparent: The executive was responsible for more than 75 percent of the approved bills in Honduras, whereas almost 70 percent of the laws enacted by the Turkish Parliament were of government origin. In contrast, in Portugal, Paraguay, and Argentina, the majority of the laws enacted by the legislature were of parliamentary origin. In Paraguay, the president was only responsible for 40 percent of the total number of bills approved by the legislature between 1992 and 2003. Likewise, in the case of Portugal, legislators were responsible for roughly 60 percent of the approved bills. An examination of these data suggests that the executive is most "dominant" in Canada and Spain, somewhat dominant in Mexico, Turkey, Honduras, and Italy, and even less dominant in Argentina, Paraguay, and Portugal.

An alternative way to interpret these data is through box scores. The data indicate that in Canada, the Parliament passed 89 percent of executive-initiated bills and only 2 percent of private member bills. The Mexican Congress approved 97 percent of the bills submitted by the executive and 16 percent of the bills initiated by the legislature. In the case of Turkey, governments had 54 percent of their bills approved by Parliament, whereas only 12 percent of the bills initiated by private members were passed. The executive and private members of Portugal were able to pass 64 and 30 percent of their bills, respectively. In Paraguay, the ratio of bills passed to bills introduced amounted to almost 75 percent in the case of the executive and 47 percent for members of the legislature. Whereas presidents obtained passage for roughly 60 percent of their initiatives, less than 5 percent of legislators' proposals became laws in Argentina. Now, a different picture emerges: In all nine countries the ability of legislators to turn their bills into laws is lower than that of the executive. This is most notable in Canada, Spain, Turkey, and Argentina.

Finally, the data could also be examined as total legislative output. Based on this definition, the Canadian Parliament passed 56 laws per year on average. Of these laws, more than 54 were of government origin and less than 2 were initiated by private members. In the case of Italy, the average number of laws enacted by year amounted to 383, of which

Table 4.1. *Legislative production in nine countries*

	Government Bills	Government Laws	Private Member Bills	Private Member Laws	Total Laws	Share of Gov. Laws (%)	Executive's Box Score
Canada (1945–1976)	1947	1736	2601	57	1793	96.82	89.16
Italy (1948–1994)	14742	11444	37893	6574	18018	63.51	77.62
Portugal(1976–1997)	1092	696	3553	1070	1766	39.41	63.73
Spain (1977–2000)	1296	1024	1031	112	1136	90.14	79.01
Turkey (1983–1999)	2556	1382	4905	596	1978	69.86	54.06
Mexico (1982–2000)	605	588	1465	239	827	71.10	97.19
Honduras(1990–1995)	1150	935	708	305	1240	75.40	81.30
Argentina(1983–1997)	1485	887	21196	1015	1902	46.63	59.73
Paraguay (1992–2003)	1348	1009	3177	1486	2495	40.44	74.85

Notes: This table presents cross-national data on legislative production in nine countries. These figures can be used to construct different measures of legislative achievements. For example, the data in columns 3 and 6 can be used to calculate the percentage of laws enacted by the legislature that are of executive origin (column 7). This indicator speaks to the question of *who* initiates laws. The data suggests that the executive is most "dominant" in Canada and Spain, somewhat dominant in Mexico, Turkey, Honduras, and Italy, and even less dominant in Argentina, Paraguay, and Portugal. An alternative way to interpret these data is to look at chief executives' box scores (column 8). The data reveal that in all nine countries the ability of chief executives to turn their bills into laws is higher than that of the legislature. Data reported in Campbell (1977), Kreppel (1997), Molinas et al. (2004), Taylor-Robinson and Diaz (1999), Leston-Bandeira (2001), Casar (2002), Capo Giol (2003), Turan (2003), Molinelli et al. (1999).

243 were executive-initiated and the remaining 140 were of parliamentary origin. Spain had an average 47 laws per year, of which 42 were initiated by the cabinet and the remaining 5 were of parliamentary origin. In Mexico, the total legislative output amounted to 43 per year, with the president passing 31 laws per year and legislators an average of 12. And in Paraguay, the yearly average legislative output was 208 laws, of which 84 were initiated by the executive and the remaining 124 by the legislature. Thus, depending on the measured used, one can reach very different conclusions regarding the nature of executive-legislative relations in each of these countries.

Other measures are also frequently used in the literature but are not constructed using the number of legislative proposals. Instead, they are calculated from legislative roll-call votes. Several of these measures emphasize the degree of legislative support a chief executive receives on a particular vote, or the frequencies with which she wins on a series of votes. Such measures are known as support scores and *congruence* (or success) scores. The former are based on the percentage of time during a specified period that each legislator votes in agreement with the chief executive's position (when she expresses one); or, alternatively, the percentage of legislators who vote in agreement with the chief executive's position (when she expresses one) in a given time period. The unit of analysis is the member of the legislature rather than a specific vote. The latter are based on the percentage of votes where the chief executive's publicly stated position prevails on the floor of the legislature. Here the unit of analysis is the vote, as opposed to the member of the legislature. In the United States, the best-developed and most-utilized measure is the support score, as evidenced by the fact that *Congressional Quarterly* (CQ) has recorded it since 1953. According to *CQ*'s calculations, in 2005, president George W. Bush's average support score among House Republicans was 81 percent. House Democrats, meanwhile, supported his position 24 percent of the time.[6] In terms of Bush's *success scores*, CQ reports that he prevailed on 78 percent of the roll calls on which his administration took a clear position (Poole 2006). Outside of the United States, measures based on roll-call votes are less developed. Some data exist for a selection of roll calls in several countries. Kellam (2006) uses roll-call votes from Argentina (1985–1997), Brazil (1988–2004), Chile

---

[6] John B. Shadegg (R-Arizona) was the representative who voted most often for President Bush's position (95.6 percent) and representative Sherrod Brown (D-Ohio) was his fiercest opponent (i.e., voted against the president's position 93.5 percent of the time).

(1997–2000), and Ecuador (1999–2002). She finds that the average level of support for chief executives' initiatives amounted to 72.44 percent of all legislators who were present and casted a vote (Kellam 2006: 15).

Another measure calculated from roll-call votes is the party roll rate. This indicator typically seeks to reflect the government's control of the agenda (Cox and McCubbins 2005). This measure is calculated as the number or proportion of times that the government is unable to prevent the passage of a bill that is opposed by its members. If the government controls the agenda, then it should be able to "veto" bills it dislikes and should never (or rarely) suffer rolls (passage of bills that a majority of its members oppose). This measure contrasts with the box score in that it does not count the failure to pass a bill that the government likes as a roll. As Cox and McCubbins (2005) note, such defeats do not suggest that the government cannot control the agenda, because what is being voted on the floor is favorable to the government; rather, they reflect their inability to muster sufficient votes on the floor.[7]

4.2 CHIEF EXECUTIVES' BOX SCORES

As with any measure, the reliability and validity of box scores have been questioned by several scholars. The main empirical problem that led scholars in the United States to criticize this indicator pertains to the ambiguity in identifying actual legislative proposals by the president. This is often referred to as the "denominator" problem (Binder 1999). Put simply, since there are several ways to define how many times the president went to bat, one may end up calculating several different presidential box scores. As a result, the validity of the measure may be compromised.

Note that this criticism is germane to the United States's separation-of-powers system. The president's legislative program has no constitutional or statutory basis in the United States. However, chief executives in other countries formally introduce a significant proportion of bills, and may even have the monopoly of legislative initiative on important issues (Payne et al. 2002; Alemán and Tsebelis 2005).

For instance, among nineteen Latin American presidential systems, the role of the legislature with regard to budgetary legislation is highly limited

---

[7] Cox and McCubbins (2005) calculate roll rates for the 45–105 Congresses in the United States; Amorim Neto, Cox, and McCubbins (2003) provide roll rates for Brazil (1990–1998).

except for Bolivia, Costa Rica, Guatemala, Honduras, and Paraguay. Legislatures in the remaining countries can propose only those amendments that do not increase the deficit or spending, and in several cases they can do so only with the approval of the president. Parliamentary governments play an even more dominant role in the lawmaking process; in Britain, for example, the government can determine what is to be debated and voted on, with the exception of a few Opposition and Private Member Days.

Another concern with the box score is the difficulty in establishing when exactly a proposal is actually passed, that is, the calendar-year constraint (Shull 1997). This is more of an empirical rather than a conceptual problem of the measure. As Döring (1995b) notes, the lifetime of bills before lapsing, should they fail to be adopted, varies considerably between countries. In some countries, legislative proposals can carry over into the following year. In other legislatures, bills that are not considered during a legislative year expire and have to be introduced again to the legislature in the following period. Thus, if a bill does not reach the floor, its "death" can be automatic after some period of time or can "languish" in the legislature. For example, in the British House of Commons, a bill must be passed within the parliamentary session in which it is introduced. Otherwise, the bill must be reintroduced in the next session. The same is true for Denmark and Iceland. In other countries, such as Austria, Finland, Germany, Greece, Ireland, Italy, Norway, and Spain, the lifetime of a bill is equal to that of a legislative term. Therefore, bills do not lapse unless the government falls or the legislative term expires. In the case of Belgium, France, and Portugal, bills usually lapse at the end of a legislative term, although carrying some of them over the next term is possible. Finally, in some other countries, bills never lapse except when they are explicitly rejected by a vote. This is the case, for example, in Argentina, Luxembourg, Netherlands, Sweden, and Switzerland.[8] Therefore, how to account for time constraints ultimately depends on each country's rules and procedure and coding practices.

A second issue associated with using box scores is that the equal weighting of all executive-initiated bills in this measure may not distinguish the important from the trivial (Shull 1997). This is an important shortcoming, but one that is common to most measures discussed earlier, as each ignores the content of the legislation being considered by

---

[8] For a description of legislative rules in different countries see Inter-Parliamentary Union (1986) and Döring (1995b).

the legislature. In all likelihood, the primary reason for this oversight is the difficulty of measuring the content of legislation quantitatively and the subjective nature of it. The best way to address this issue is to examine a subset of bills that are classified by country experts as "relevant" in contrast to "irrelevant" legislation. For example, Molinelli et al. (1999) classify laws enacted by the Argentine Congress between 1983 and 1997 into three different groups according to their degree of importance. They find that chief executives initiated 65 percent of the laws in the "most important" group, 53 percent of the laws in the "intermediate importance" group, and 23 percent of the laws in the "less relevant" group (Molinelli et al. 1999: 444–446). Thus, the executive dominance varies according to the issues at stake. In terms of the Argentine chief executive's box score, Bavastro investigates the fate of executive bills in Argentina during the 1983–1989 period. He shows that for a "selection" of important laws (although his criteria is somewhat different than that of Molinelli et al.), the passage rate of important initiatives amounts to 55 percent, compared to a rate of 66 percent when all government bills are considered (Bavastro 2001: 23). Alemán and Calvo (2006) examine nearly 124,000 public and private bills formally proposed to the Argentine Congress between 1983 and 2001 and uncover a somewhat similar pattern. The authors identify 1,739 executive-initiated proposals, and note that 54 percent were approved by the legislature. However, they claim that, among these initiatives, a large number of formal requests with no substantive importance exists.[9] The reduced sample includes 1,004 proposals, 51 percent of which were approved by Congress between 1983 and 2001 (Alemán and Calvo: 28).

As Tsebelis (2002) notes, the criteria for selection of "significant" or "substantive" initiatives is subjective and can undermine the results of any analysis when one does not share the same criteria for selection. This becomes a particularly important problem for cross-national comparisons of legislative output. A research team at the Mannheim Centre for European Social Research led by Döring identified the number of significant laws for all Western European countries in the area of labor legislation for the period 1981–1991. The analysis produced an "expert rating" of important legislative instruments between 1981 and 1991 (Scholz

---

[9] These requests include: (i) authorization for the president to leave the country; (ii) the confirmation of presidential appointees; (iii) the ratification of goodwill international treaties (Calvo 2007: 15).

and Trantas 1995).[10] Legislative output for all laws regarding working time/conditions and for selected laws are correlated at .33. This correlation suggests that no "trade-off" is evident between passing relevant and irrelevant legislation. No further intuition, however, can be gained from this analysis, because the number of bills proposed in each country (both for relevant and irrelevant legislation) is unknown.

In terms of the content of legislation that is effectively approved by the legislature, many of the same problems persist. The key question here is whether bills that are enacted reflect a chief executive's preferences; or rather, as a result of successive amendments, those bills become substantively different from what was originally proposed. Few cross-country evidence on this respect exists, but some case studies can help shed light on this matter. Barrett (2005), for example, examines the content of 233 significant bills to measure presidential success in the United States (1977–1996). He finds that in approximately 69 percent of the bills that become law, presidents receive most of what they want. Therefore, he concludes that most presidential successes can be characterized as presidential *victories* in terms of the content of legislation (Barret 2005: 149).

The final main criticism directed at the box score measure is that it may fail to account for the strategic behavior of chief executives. The argument is that chief executives may try to fatten their "batting average" by proposing popular but trivial legislation or by withholding unpopular legislation (Ames 2001). In its most extreme formulation, the claim is that some chief executives may not send bills to the legislature at all. This charge is not wholly accurate, as most chief executives need to govern (Cheibub 2007). In particular, outside the United Sates where chief executives are required to take the legislative initiative on important issues, very few can get away with being strategically passive. Hence, most chief executives, albeit reluctantly, have to frequently "step up to bat." In fact, as shown in Chapter 5, chief executives' passage rates do not depend on the number of bills that they send to the legislature. Specifically, chief executives who send few bills to the legislature do not enjoy higher passage rates than those who initiate copious legislation. In addition, there is no evidence that chief executives vary in their use of posturing in systematic

---

[10] The authors used the computerized database NATLEX, compiled by the International Labor Organization (ILO). Döring's team concentrated on a subset of bills that were worth mentioning by the legal experts in Roger Blainpain's *Encyclopedia of Labor Law* to be significant legislative changes in the field of the regulation of labor relations.

and predictable ways. Therefore, absent such knowledge, it would be difficult to predict how their strategic behavior affects box scores measures (i.e., the "direction" of the bias).

By addressing the box score's main criticisms, I have hopefully demonstrated that the claims of its lack of validity and/or reliability are largely unfounded. Of course, this particular indicator has merits and limitations, as it is the case of every other measure discussed.[11]

4.3 THE APPROPRIATENESS OF USING BOX SCORES

As many scholars suggest, the decision to use a particular indicator to measure the outcomes of executive-legislative interactions ultimately depends on the type of question one is trying to answer. (Bond et al. 1996; Shull 1997). If the question is how frequently legislators support chief executive's positions, some variant of the "chief executive support score" should be used.[12] If the goal is to uncover a chief executive's success in preventing unwanted legislation from passing, her roll rates should be the focus. But, considering that my primary aim is to investigate how successful chief executives are in promoting their policy agendas in the legislature, then it is most appropriate to use the box score measure (Lockerbie, Borrelli, and Hedger 1998).

---

[11] For example, take the case of the *congruence* scores discussed earlier. This indicator has some of the same drawbacks as the box score, and in fact some of its problems are even more severe. First, this measure is equally likely to be subject to the calendar year constraint. Second, like the box scores, measures of success based on roll-call votes do not include any weighting that reflects the importance of each proposal. The most serious problem with this measure, though, is selection bias. A large number of important legislation may be killed before it reaches the floor for a roll-call vote. Therefore, this measure of legislative success does not include legislation that fails to reach the floor (defeats in committee, for instance), voice votes, or unrecorded votes (Ames 2001). In addition to these empirical problems, congruence scores are also conceptually inappropriate if the focus is on chief executives' statutory achievements. As Shull notes, this measure is not an indicator of successful chief executive's initiatives to the legislature (the chief executive's agenda) but rather his or her response (position taking) to issues before the legislature that it upholds or rejects (Shull 1997: 83).

[12] For example, support scores are good indicators of a chief executive's influence. This is certainly an important topic, and one profusely studied in the United States since the appearance of Richard Neudstadt's seminal work on the subject, *Presidential Power*. However, as Bond et al. (1996) note, influence may not necessarily translate into policy outputs (i.e., statutes), or a president's preferences may prevail for reasons other than influence. Therefore, presidential influence provides an incomplete understanding of executive-legislative relations (Bond et al. 1996: 104–105).

I focus on chief executives' statutory achievements for several reasons. First, it is safe to assume that in most, if not all, cases, chief executives are not only concerned with whether their initiatives are considered by the legislature, voted on, or almost pass, but also if the proposed legislation is enacted into law. Second, statutes are the definite measure of legislative output, whereas votes and positions on issues are merely means to an end of an uncertain consequence.

Moreover, a box score is a tangible measure that allows one to compare different chief executives and to assess their relative success in the legislature. Indeed, as Rivers and Rose (1985) and King and Ragsdale (1988) note, this is an ideal measure from a conceptual standpoint. The box score also considers the multiple decision points in the legislative process (Bond et al. 1996: 107). To count as a victory, a chief executive's proposal must receive favorable action at every stage of the process. Instances where chief executives' initiatives make it to the legislature's floor but are voted down are exceptional, but do occur. Even on the floor of the British House of Commons, which may be regarded by many as the least possible scenario for a chief executive to lose a vote, divisions in which a whip was imposed and the government was defeated have occurred.[13] However, bills can "die" in the legislature through other means. A negative committee report can kill a bill; no committee report is drafted, so the bill never leaves the committee; a positive committee report is drafted, which makes it possible for the floor to debate the bill, but does not guarantee that the bill will come up for debate; and outright defeat of the bill by the floor. Of course, these factors vary as a function of legislative procedures in each country. Peterson (1990), for example, reports that between 1953 and 1984, the U.S. Congress ignored 24 percent of a random sample of 229 presidential proposals via inaction (Peterson 1990: 96). A proposal thus may fail either because the legislature purposively kills it or because

---

[13] According to Boothroyd (2001), between 1918 and 2001, there were 118 divisions in which the government was defeated. Most of these government defeats were concentrated in the period 1974–1979 and had to do with economic issues (amendments to Finance Bills) and with the Scotish and Welsh referendums. Even a very strong Prime Minister, Margaret Thatcher, experienced parliamentary defeats. The belief that a government that was defeated should either reverse the decision, seek a vote of confidence, or resign was common during the period 1945–1970 (when governments were only very rarely defeated). As Boothroyd notes, only when Heath's government was repeatedly defeated was there a realization that the government need only resign if it loses a vote of confidence (Boothroyd 2001).

Table 4.2. *Fate of government bills: Portugal, 1976–1997*

Legislature	Bills presented total	Bills not discussed at first reading	Bills rejected at first reading	Bills approved at final vote	Bills approved (percent)
1976–1980	382	173	11	198	51.83
1980–1983	141	73	0	68	48.22
1983–1985	103	26	0	70	67.96
1985–1987	44	7	4	15	34.09
1987–1991	176	4	0	167	94.88
1991–1995	118	8	0	105	88.98
1995–1997	128	38	6	73	57.03
Total	1092	329	21	696	63.73

Notes: This table presents data on the fate of government-initiated bills in Portugal between 1976 and 1997. The data reveal that prior to 1987, government bills attained a level of approval of roughly 50 percent, mainly due to the high proportion of bills not discussed at first reading. Between 1987 and 1995, when the government had a clear majority, the situation changed considerably. Government bills attained a high level of approval and nearly all were discussed at first reading. Data reported in Leston-Bandeira (2001).

the legislature takes no action. In both cases, the failure to get approval must count as a defeat (Bond et al. 1996: 107).

Collecting systematic cross-national data on executive-initiated bills that account for the fate of those bills constitutes a very difficult task. Nonetheless, some data of this type exist. In Table 4.2, I present data from Portugal.

As Table 4.2 documents, prior to 1987, government bills attained a level of approval of roughly 50 percent, mainly due to the high proportion of bills not discussed at first reading. In particular, the IVth legislature (1985–1987), which was characterized by a government with minority support in Parliament, exhibits low levels of government legislative success. Between 1987 and 1995, when the government had a clear majority, the situation changed considerably. Government bills attained roughly a 92 percent level of approval and nearly all were discussed at first reading. In the subsequent minority legislature (1995–1997), some government bills were rejected at first reading (although in a smaller proportion than in the 1976–1985 period), and more than half of the bills were approved at final vote (Leston-Bandeira 2001). In the case of Argentina, Bavastro (2001) examines the fate of government bills not enacted into law during the 1983–1995 period. He finds that 57 percent of the bills that were "killed" in the Argentine Congress did not receive legislative study or consideration either from a committee or from the floor.

In sum, although box scores exhibit some limitations, my primary question as well as previous works support the view that they provide a conceptually valid measure of a chief executive's statutory achievements (Shull 1983; Spitzer 1983; Hammond and Fraser 1984b; Rivers and Rose 1985; Covington et al. 1995; Lockerbie, Borrelli, and Hedger 1998; Rudalevige 2002, Barrett 2005; Cameron and Park 2007).[14] Thus, keeping in mind the inevitable drawbacks associated with any measure, the box score makes it possible to compare the performance of chief executives under different circumstances that are unconstrained by geography or time.

A final comment regarding my calculation of box scores is in order. One characteristic that may affect the role played by the legislature in policy-making process is its structure (either unicameral or bicameral). Approximately one-third of the world's countries are bicameral legislatures, so two distinct chambers are involved in their deliberations (Tsebelis and Money 1997). In principle, this organizational difference should be correlated with the political or geographical characteristics of the countries. However, bicameral cases include large countries (such as the United States and Brazil) and small ones (such as Belgium and Uruguay). Thus, the existence of a second chamber has more to do with historical legacies than a conscious decision on the part of the political leadership to adopt a particular institutional design. As Tsebelis and Money (1997) note, depending on the balance of legislative powers between the two chambers, a bicameral legislature can provide a separate veto point in the policy-making process. For instance, a senate elected from a single national district concurrently with the chief executive on a single ballot is less likely to act as an additional veto point; it also fails to dramatically change how territorial interests are represented. However, when senators are elected separately from the president on the basis of provincial districts, and representation is not tied to population size, then a greater possibility exists where the upper house can become a separate veto point and accentuate the extent to which regional interests are represented in policy making. On the other hand, the authors also note that the existence of a second chamber appears to have little effect on the relationship

---

[14] In fact, the prime factor in CQ's decision to drop the box score after 1975 was the threat to the validity of *analyses* using the indicator, rather than the validity of the measure itself (Peterson 1990: 306).

between the legislature and the executive (Tsebelis and Money 1997). Therefore, my analysis focuses mainly on the lower house, or in the case of unicameral congresses, the national assembly. In some cases, the upper chamber may constitute an effective *hurdle* for the passage of legislation. As such, using this criterion may lead to overestimating rather than underestimating the ability of chief executives to enact policy changes through statutes.

4.4 CONCLUDING REMARKS

The ability of chief executives to pass their agendas is an extensively researched phenomenon. Most studies examine how the party system influences the workability of executive-legislative relations. For example, it is often assumed chief executives are more successful if their party controls a majority of seats in the legislature. Nonetheless, the literature offers conflicting arguments on how the partisan makeup of the legislature affects statutory policy making. In the United States, a heated debate exists on whether divided party control of the executive and legislative branches affects the productivity of Congress. The main point of contention concerns the relationship between divided government and legislative gridlock. Studies inspired by David Mayhew's *Divided We Govern* (1990), state that divided government does not necessarily have a negative impact on the enactment of public policy (cf. Krehbiel 1998). Many prominent scholars, however, challenge this argument and contend that divided government results in less policy innovation and more gridlock than does unified control of the institutions by one party (Kernell 1991; Sundquist 1992; Edwards, Barrett, and Peake 1997; Binder 1999; Coleman 1999; Howell et al. 2000; Krutz 2000).

Clearly, this example demonstrates how the divided-versus-unified debate fails to provide a clear blueprint on how to evaluate the effect of the partisan composition of the legislature on a chief executive's legislative performance. This is the case, not only because the research record is mixed, but also because divided government, defined as a situation in which a single majority party in the legislature is not the one of the chief executive, is almost exclusively a U.S. peculiarity. In most presidential systems around the world, a two-party system does not exist; hence, the largest party in the legislature seldom controls a majority of seats (Cheibub et al. 2004).

My theory of statutory policy making contends that the unpredictability of legislators' voting behavior rather than the chief executive's partisan support in the legislature is the key factor explaining the variation in chief executive's statutory performance. The model discussed in the previous chapter indicates how well a chief executive should be expected to fare when legislators are cross-pressured. The simulations suggest that when the party of the chief executive has an ample majority of seats, the effects of the principals' influence on their legislators should be mitigated; however, they also show that sometimes even *majoritarian* chief executives may lack legislative support to pass their bills. Of course, validation for those simulated outcomes is key. So, do such patterns take place in the real world? Unfortunately, despite the centrality of statutory policy making in modern democratic countries, the comparative ability of chief executives to obtain legislative approval of their initiatives has remained understudied in the empirical literature.

In this chapter, I presented a clear and simple indicator to measure how much a government *governs*. Moreover, I demonstrated that by summarizing a chief executive's legislative performance, the box score is an ideal measure to conduct cross-national research on statutory policy making. In the rest of the book, I examine the main implications derived from my theory of statutory policy making using the box score as my main indicator of interest.

5

Patterns of Statutory Policy Making Around the World

What are the main factors that allow chief executives to rule by statute? More specifically, what combination of institutional and partisan considerations determines whether or not legislators will support a chief executive's agenda? Most research on this area relies on either case studies of particular acts of government or country studies. In order to systematically test the theory of statutory policy making presented in this book, however, a truly comparative evaluation is needed. The importance of adopting a cross-national approach is also underscored by the topic's broader theoretical implications. Indeed, the inability of presidents to pass their agendas has been at the heart of a raging debate on the merits of presidentialism itself.[1]

In this chapter, I present new evidence for comparative research into democratic governance. In particular, I document the pattern of chief executives' statutory achievements in more than fifty countries in Western and Eastern Europe, North and Latin America, Asia, and the Middle East for the period between 1946 and 2008. I use the box score to gauge chief executives' statutory performance. As discussed in the previous chapter, this measure is the number of chief executive's proposals approved in the lower house of the national legislature, divided by the total number of proposals introduced by the chief executive.[2]

---

[1] Whereas some authors argue that legislative paralysis invariably leads to regime breakdown (Linz 1978; Mainwaring 1993; Valenzuela 1994) others claim that it is neither pervasive nor is it associated with such outcome (Cheibub 2007). I address some of this issues in more detail in Chapter 9.

[2] Given the controversy surrounding the "correct" box score for the United States' president discussed in Chapter 4, I decided to leave this country out of the sample. None of the

The sample is quite comprehensive, including countries with long democratic traditions, such as the United Kingdom and Denmark, but also a number of countries with less democratic experience, such as Paraguay, Bangladesh, and Pakistan. Finally, some of the countries are simply authoritarian regimes: for example, Ivory Coast between 1965 and 1970, or Jordan between 1974 and 1979. Detailed information about the composition of the sample and the sources from which the data were obtained are listed in Appendix B.[3]

The primary purpose of this chapter is to reinforce the idea that a theory of statutory policy making that accounts for chief executive's legislative defeats is needed. The chapter is more descriptive than theoretical, and the findings only provide a template for evaluating the legislative performance of chief executives. An explanation of these patterns, using the framework developed in Part I of the book, is left for Chapters 6 through 8.

5.1 POLITICAL REGIMES AND STATUTORY POLICY MAKING

I begin my analysis of chief executives' box scores focusing on democratic regimes. Following Przeworski et al. (2000), I classify a country as a democracy if during a particular year it satisfies all four criteria: (1) the chief executive is elected; (2) the legislature is elected; (3) more than one party competes in elections; (4) incumbent parties have in the past or will have in the future lost an election and yielded office. All countries that fail to satisfy at least one of these four criteria are classified as dictatorships (Przeworski et al. 2000: 18–29).[4]

Figure 5.1 presents the distribution of box scores in the sample of democratic countries. The data indicate that, on average, 76.12 percent of chief

patterns that I find in the data are sensitive to the exclusion of this case. In addition, most of the findings regarding the U.S. are extensively discussed in the rest of this book.

[3] In several instances, the data were reported in legislative terms, so to create annual observations, I apportioned longer periods to years, taking as the criterion the state of affairs as of December 31 of each year. While this manipulation of the data places restrictions on the interpretation of annual changes, it addresses the problem of the calendar-year constraint examined in the previous chapter. Some other data of interest (i.e., separation-of-powers system, or partisan composition of the legislature) are sometimes reported annually. To ensure that a potential mismatch in observational units does not lead to wrong inferences, I use averages of those other variables for the same time periods for which I have box score data.

[4] See Gandhi (2008) and Cheibub et al. (2010) for an updated version of Przeworski et al. (2000) index of democracy.

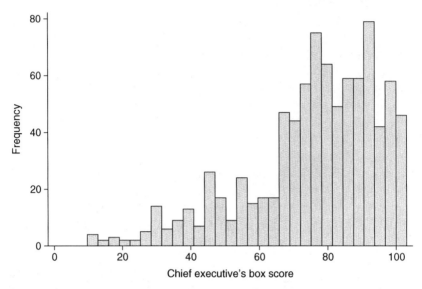

Figure 5.1. Distribution of democratic chief executives' box scores.
Notes: This measure is calculated as the percentage of executive initiatives that
are approved by the legislature over a period of time. The data indicate that,
under democracy, an average of 76.12 percent of chief executives' proposals are
approved by the lower house of their respective national legislatures. Information
about the composition of the sample and the sources from which the data were
obtained are listed in Appendix B. I classify a country as a democracy if during a
particular year it satisfies all four criteria: (1) the chief executive is elected, (2) the
legislature is elected, (3) more than one party competes in elections, (4) incumbent
parties have in the past or will have in the future lost an election and yielded office
(cf. Przeworski et al. 2000). Data on regime type reported in Przeworski et al.
(2000), Gandhi (2008), and Cheibub et al. (2010).

executives' proposals are approved by the lower house of their respective
national legislatures. Based on this sample, one can be 99 percent confident that the population mean lies somewhere in the interval of 74.45
and 77.79 percent.

Chief executives with the lowest box scores represent countries with
fragile democratic institutions, such as Brazil in 1954–1955 and Ecuador
in 1986, but also include some countries with longer democratic traditions, such as Costa Rica in 1989 and Colombia in 1982. Likewise, chief
executives possessing the highest box scores hail from established democracies, such as Canada, Denmark, and the Netherlands, as well as those
with less democratic experience, such as Brazil in the 1980s, Bangladesh
in the 1990s, and Mexico after 2000.

In light of these findings, it is worthwhile to explore whether a systematic relationship exists between differences in institutional arrangements and the variation in chief executives' legislative passage rates. Thus, the next section examines the box scores of authoritarian rulers, followed by a discussion of legislative passage rates of democratically elected chief executives under different constitutional structures.

5.1.1 Statutory Policy Making under Dictatorship

At first blush, it may seem odd to include nondemocratic regimes in a study of legislative policy making. But, as a number of recent studies reveal, authoritarian leaders usually rely on more than just force and tradition to rule (Bueno de Mesquita et al. 2003; Geddes 2004; Gandhi and Przeworski 2006; Magaloni 2006; Gandhi 2008; Svolik 2008; Wright 2008). Nondemocratic rulers often permit various types of party systems, with some dictators establishing a single-party regime from scratch, whereas others allow the remnants of pre-dictatorial parties to exist (Lust-Okar 2005; Gandhi 2008).

Many authoritarian regimes also operate with nominally democratic institutions such as legislatures (Gandhi 2008). These legislative bodies range from ad hoc institutions that only meet sporadically to more permanent institutions that regularly convene and implement systematic internal rules and substructures.[5] This fact is surprising in and of itself, but even more surprising is that government-sponsored bills in such regimes are sometimes defeated.

Take the case of authoritarian Brazil. In 1967, the Brazilian Congress rejected an important tax bill submitted by the military government. In 1968, it blocked an international trade bill. Yet the most stunning blow came later that year when the legislature rejected an urgent presidential demand to lift the immunity of a parliamentarian, Márcio Moreira Alves, whom the military wished to prosecute for insulting the armed forces during a speech. The president, General Costa e Silva, expected the regime's party, Aliança Renovadora Nacional (ARENA), to deliver the necessary majority. But many ARENA deputies decided to vote against the government to protect one of their colleagues who actually belonged to the official opposition party, the Movimiento Democrático Brasileiro (MDB).

---

[5] In addition, members of dictatorial assemblies are often elected. Gandhi (2008) reports that during the 1946–1996 period, only 8.7 percent of all country-years with dictatorial legislatures had appointed members. These legislators, though, often achieve election in very controlled circumstances; voters are offered either just one candidate or a slate of government-approved ones.

Additional anecdotal evidence suggests that similar things occurred in authoritarian regimes around the globe. A study published in 1966 noted that the government of Jomo Kenyatta's Kenyan African National Union (KANU) could afford to pay little attention to the members of the Kenya African Democratic Union (KADU), the government's opposition in the House of Representatives. The government, however, could not ignore parliamentary resistance from members of the backbench of its own party. The backbench did not restrict itself to criticism of the small details of legislation; it challenged the government on major issues of policy such as land reform, nationalization, and education (Gertzel 1966: 497).[6]

Similarly, when Thailand's government led by Prime Minister Thanom Kittikachorn proposed raising taxes on more than 200 commodities in 1970, many legislators, even from the pro-government United Thai People's Party (UTPP), reacted negatively. Legislators believed that a more equitably enforced income tax and new taxes on land, property, and inheritance would be more acceptable to the public. In the end, the government's tax bill passed by only one vote, 102 to 101. In order to pass the bill, Kittikachorn agreed to lower gasoline and cement taxes and permitted voting on the bill by secret ballot (Mezey 1979). As Neher (1971) notes, the latter concession allowed UTPP members to vote for the government without alienating constituencies.

Poland represents another interesting case; civil society presented serious political challenges for the Communist Party leadership during the early years of the Cold War. The Sejm deputies viewed themselves "as separate from the ministries and also as separate from external organs of their respective parties" (Olson and Simon 1982: 50). In fact, as Olson and Simon (1982) report, during the period between 1952 and 1972, legislative committees were quite active in Poland. Such activism can be seen on the voluminous changes made to government proposals by Sejm committees documented by Olson and Simon (1982).[7] The extent of change ranges from none at all to quite substantive modifications. For illustrative purposes, Olson and Simon's data are presented in Table 5.1.

As Table 5.1 indicates, the percentage of substantive changes made to bills decreased over time, but the use of amendments dominated in four out of the six legislative terms. It thus seems that the Polish Sejm provided

---

[6] A study of Kenyan legislators in 1974 indicated that 82 percent of them were concerned with constituency problems (Barkan and Okumo 1974)

[7] See also Chrypinski (1966) on the activity of Polish committees during this period.

Table 5.1. *Committees' activism in Poland (1952–1972)*

	1952–1956 (N=39)	1957–1961 (N=161)	1961–1965 (N=90)	1965–1969 (N=56)	1969–1972 (N=32)	1972 (N=46)
Accepted (%)	41	52.8	34.5	42.9	37.5	73.9
Amended (%)	46.2	37.9	64.4	57.1	56.3	23.9
Substantively Changed (%)	12.8	8.7	1.1		6.3	2.2
Abandoned (%)		0.6				

Notes: This table shows how legislative committees affected government proposals in Poland between 1952 and 1972 (by Sejm term). The data reveal that legislative committees were quite active: The extent of changes made to government proposals range from none at all to quite substantive modifications. The percentage of substantive changes made to bills decreased over time, but the use of amendments dominated in four out of the six legislative terms. Data reported in Olson and Simon (1982).

a forum where groups from civil society could voice their opinions and, to some extent, challenge the regime even if they could not always defeat government-initiated legislation on the floor.

In cases typified by the Brazilian example, however, legislators may muster enough opposition not only to amend an authoritarian regime's legislation, but even to defeat it altogether. Take the case of Jordan. Between 1964 and 1974, the Parliament not only amended 35 percent of the bills it considered, but also rejected 13 percent of them (Mezey 1979: 121). Likewise, Loewenberg and Patterson (1979) report that in the early 1970s, all legislation introduced in the Kenyan Parliament originated in the Cabinet. However, only 70 percent of these executive-sponsored bills were ultimately approved by the legislature (Loewenberg and Patterson 1979: 62).

To gain a systematic understanding of statutory policy making under nondemocratic regimes, I examine the box scores of authoritarian rulers. The data comprise fourteen authoritarian regimes in Africa, Latin America, Asia, and Eastern Europe between 1965 and 1999 (92 country-year observations). Authoritarian regimes are identified using the rules described earlier. Following Gandhi (2008), I consider a legislature to exist under dictatorship only if it has formal lawmaking powers. Therefore, consultative councils, common in monarchies of the Persian Gulf, are not included because their explicitly stated purpose is the provision of advice. Similarly, constitutive assemblies are excluded from the analysis because they typically play no role in determining the content of ordinary legislation. Finally, dictatorial legislatures must have at least twenty members in order to prevent the inclusion of juntas as legislative bodies (Gandhi 2008). In this sample, all legislators were elected (rather than appointed) to their posts.

The distribution of the box scores for these nondemocratic countries is presented in Figure 5.2. On average, 92 percent of the bills introduced by dictatorial governments are approved by their respective national legislatures. The lowest passage rate, 73.23 percent, corresponds to Kuwait in the 1970s. At the other end of the distribution, nine observations exist where the government attained a 100 percent passage rate. They correspond to Czechoslovakia (1969–1973) and Brazil in the 1970s.

These box scores can be compared with those presented in Figure 5.1. As it should be expected, authoritarian chief executives enjoy higher legislative passage rates than their democratic counterparts. Of course, the data should be interpreted with some caution. Authoritarian rulers who routinely receive 100 percent approval of their proposals from

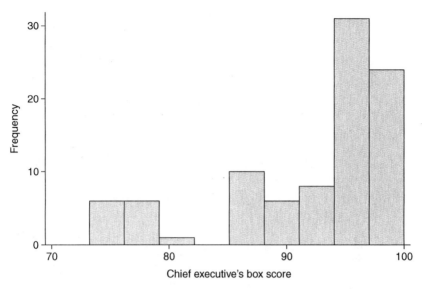

Figure 5.2. Distribution of autocratic chief executives' box scores.
Notes: This measure is calculated as the percentage of executive initiatives that are approved by the legislature over a period of time. Authoritarian chief executives enjoy higher legislative passage rates than their democratic counterparts. On average, 92 percent of the bills introduced by dictatorial governments are approved by their respective national legislatures. Information about the composition of the sample and the sources from which the data were obtained are listed in Appendix B. I classify a country as an autocracy if during a particular year it fails to satisfy at least one of these four criteria: (1) the chief executive is elected, (2) the legislature is elected, (3) more than one party competes in elections, (4) incumbent parties have in the past or will have in the future lost an election and yielded office (cf. Przeworski et al. 2000). Data on regime type reported in Przeworski et al. (2000), Gandhi (2008), and Cheibub et al. (2010).

their assemblies may not even bother to report their legislative output. Therefore it is possible that cases of "lower" legislative success may be overrepresented in the sample.

On the other hand, as the data on the work of the Polish Sejm committees suggest, legislative passage rates may underestimate the influence that opposition groups have within dictatorial legislatures. Legislators under dictatorship may not deign to vote against government bills once they have reached the floor, but they may shape legislation prior to its arrival. Anecdotal evidence abounds of legislative committees amending bills and governments tabling proposals once opposition within committees seemed insurmountable; this suggests that once dictators govern with nominally democratic legislatures, they face pressures and incentives that often force them to act as democrats would. Authoritarian rulers, of course, can override the assemblies' verdicts, and even close them down. Occasionally, however, as the data on Figure 5.2 indicate, authoritarian rulers lose and accept these failures.

5.2 CONSTITUTIONAL STRUCTURES AND PASSAGE RATES

Moving back to the world of democratically elected leaders, I now examine whether the variation in chief executives' box scores is conditional on their country's constitutional structures. I follow Przeworski et al. (2000) to classify countries' constitutional structures. Presidentialism is understood here as a form of government in which: (1) the president is both the head of state and the chief executive and is elected by voters (or an electoral college chosen by them for that sole purpose); and (2) the terms of office for the president and the assembly are fixed and are not contingent on mutual confidence. By contrast, parliamentarism is defined as a form of government in which: (1) there is a head of state and a head of government. Whereas the former plays merely a protocolary role, the latter is the country's chief executive and is elected by, and responsible to, the legislature. (2) The terms of office for the executive and the assembly are not fixed and are contingent on mutual confidence. Other forms of government cannot be classified as parliamentary or presidential based on these criteria. These are countries where the president is elected for a fixed term, but the government serves at the discretion of the parliament. These constitutional structures are often referred to as "premier-presidential," "semi-presidential," or "mixed" (Przeworski et al. 2000).

In Figure 5.3, I use a boxplot to display the distribution of chief executives' box scores by constitutional structure. Each box extends from approximately the first to third quartiles. Observations more than the 1.5 interquartile range beyond the first or third quartile are plotted individually. Three-quarters of the observations in the group of parliamentary countries are on or above the average box score in the whole sample.

As Figure 5.3 demonstrates, chief executives' passage rates vary considerably across as well as within constitutional structures. Consider first parliamentary regimes. For example, in the United Kingdom, the number of government bills approved as a percentage of all government-sponsored bills introduced in the House of Commons amounts to an average of 96.8 and 99.2 percent for the periods between 1946–1979 and 1997–2005,

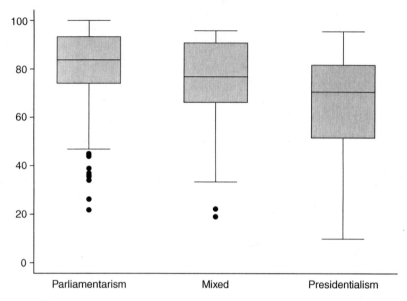

Figure 5.3. Box scores by constitutional structure.

Notes: The box score measure is calculated as the percentage of executive initiatives that are approved by the legislature over a period of time. The data are displayed using a boxplot. Each box extends from approximately the first to third quartiles. Observations more than the 1.5 interquartile range beyond the first or third quartile are plotted individually. Three-quarters of the observations in the group of parliamentary countries are on or above the average box score in the whole sample. The data reveal that democratic chief executives' passage rates vary considerably across as well as within constitutional structures. Information about the composition of the sample and the sources from which the data were obtained are listed in Appendix B. I follow Przeworski et al. (2000) to classify countries' constitutional structures (see main text). Data on constitutional structures reported in Przeworski et al. (2000) and Cheibub et al. (2010).

respectively. In contrast, the percentage of government-sponsored bills passed by the German Bundestag from 1949 to 1990 amounts, on average, to 77.1 percent. The latter figure comprises a maximum of 82.8 percent for the 1973–1976 period and a minimum of 71.9 percent in the 1949–1952 period. The Italian Parliament approved an average of 86.1 percent of government-sponsored bills in the first six legislative periods after World War II (1948–1976); however, only 65.3 percent of those bills passed in the successive six legislative periods (1977–1996). Several outliers with very low box scores are also present. These observations correspond to Italy in 1972, 1979, 1987, and 1995–1996, Turkey in

1996–1999, Lebanon in 1971–1972, Canada in 1974, and South Korea's brief experience with parliamentarism in 1960.[8]

Similar patterns characterize presidential systems. In Uruguay during the 1985–2002 period, on average, 66.3 percent of the executive's legislative agenda was approved by the legislature, including a maximum of 79 percent in 1991 and a minimum of 43 percent in 1994 (both under Luis Lacalle's presidency). In Ecuador during the 1979–2001 period, the legislature only approved an average of 41 percent of government-initiated bills, with a maximum of 65.2 percent in 1992 and a minimum of 10.7 percent during León Febres Cordero's presidency in 1986. The Venezuelan congress approved 67.8 percent of executive-initiated bills between 1959 and 1988, but only passed half these bills in the 1979–1983 legislative period.

In the case of presidential regimes, the overall distribution is negatively skewed by some of the cases mentioned above (Brazil in 1954–1955, Ecuador in 1986, and Costa Rica in 1989). Still, only 40 percent of presidential country observations possess box scores above the average for all democratic regimes (76 percent). Interestingly, one of the highest box scores, 94.5 percent, corresponds to Costa Rica in 1994, the first year of President Figueres' term (1994–1998). In spite of this successful start, Figueres' overall legislative performance was far from spectacular. Of the 224 bills he initiated during his presidency, only 46.9 percent were passed into law during his entire term.

It is also clear from Figure 5.3 that the passage rates of chief executives under parliamentarism are higher than presidential ones. The box scores from these two forms of government are also statistically distinct; a simple two-sample t-test indicates that one can safely reject the null hypothesis that no difference between the two systems exist at the 99 percent confidence level.

One can also reject the hypothesis that box scores are higher under presidential regimes. There are several reasons that explain the underperformance of presidential regimes. They are examined in detail in Chapter 8. For now, it is sufficient to note that the variation in chief

---

[8] Known as the *Second Republic*, parliamentary government only lasted in South Korea for eight months in 1960 and 1961. The Second Republic succeeded the First Republic, which was overthrown by widespread protests known as the "April Revolution" in April 1960. Under the Second Republic, for the first and the only instance, South Korea adopted a parliamentary cabinet system instead of a presidential system. The experience was short-lived, though. On May 16, 1961, a military coup put an effective end to the Second Republic.

executives' box scores cannot be fully explained by the forms of government. Therefore, another way to examine the variation in chief executives'
legislative performance is to classify the observations according to the
partisan distribution of seats in the legislature.

5.3 GOVERNMENT STATUS AND PASSAGE RATES

For the reasons presented in this chapter, as well as those discussed
in Chapter 2, it is important to examine the relationship between the
legislative support of a chief executive and his or her legislative performance. Regardless of constitutional structures, the average box score of
democratically elected leaders with majority governments is 78.5 percent,
relative to an average passage rate of 72.7 percent in the case of chief executives under minority governments. When accounting for constitutional
structures, some interesting patterns emerge. Under parliamentarism,
majority and minority chief executives possess very similar box scores
(roughly 83 percent), but the average box score for majoritarian presidents
(67.5 percent) is higher than those in the minority (62.6 percent).

One important consideration is that chief executives under both types
of regimes may try to boost their legislative base of support by crafting
government coalitions. This is typically the case under parliamentarism,
but as Chiebub et al. (2004), Amorim Neto (2006), and others have
demonstrated, it is also a frequent practice under presidentialism. Therefore, the legislative performance of chief executives under minority or
majority governments could potentially be affected by the coalition status of their administrations. To analyze this possibility, I examine whether
a chief executive's government is (1) a single-party majority; (2) a single-
party minority; (3) a majority coalition; or (4) a minority coalition.
I consider a government to be a (portfolio) coalition when legislators
belonging to different political parties hold cabinet posts. Namely, I
assume that governments can be composed of a single party or be a coalition of parties depending on the cabinet composition. When the party
of the chief executive does not have a majority of seats in the legislature,
some type of coalition existed in 158 observations under parliamentarism.
Of these coalitions, 82 percent are majoritarian. Under presidentialism,
coalitions occur 55 percent of the time when the president's party is not
the majority in the legislature, and 63 percent are majoritarian.[9]

---

[9] An observation for Italy (1995), due to the transitional character of the existing administration, and all the observations for Lebanon because of lack of detailed information on
government composition and seat distribution, were excluded from the sample.

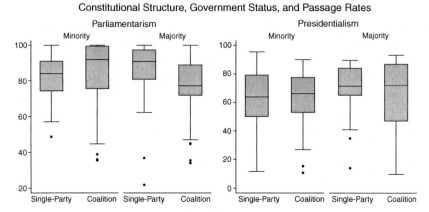

Figure 5.4. Box scores by government status.
Notes: The box score measure is calculated as the percentage of executive initiatives that are approved by the legislature over a period of time. The data are displayed using a boxplot. Each box extends from approximately the first to third quartiles. Observations more than the 1.5 interquartile range beyond the first or third quartile are plotted individually. The data reveal that prime ministers who lead single-party majority governments enjoy the highest average legislative passage rates, followed by those who rule under minority coalitions. Prime ministers who rule under a majority coalition are the least effective ones, followed by those leading single-party minority governments. In the case of presidentialism, single-party minority governments exhibit higher passage rates than do coalition majority and coalition minority administrations. The data also indicate that single-party minority presidents do not fare much worse than coalition governments. It is clear from this figure that legislative paralysis is a relatively rare phenomenon, even under presidentialism. Information about the composition of the sample and the sources from which the data were obtained are listed in Appendix B. I follow Przeworski et al. (2000) to classify countries' constitutional structures, and Cheibub et al. (2004) to determine a government's status (see main text). Data on constitutional structures reported in Przeworski et al. (2000) and Cheibub et al. (2010). Data on government status reported in Cheibub et al. (2004).

The question remains: Do chief executives in minority governments have lower box scores than those under majority governments? And also, does the coalition status of the government affect these scores? The distribution of chief executive's box scores presented in Figure 5.4, based on government status under parliamentarism versus presidentialism, can address these questions.

Prime ministers who lead single-party majority governments enjoy the highest average legislative passage rates (88 percent), followed by those who rule under minority coalitions (84 percent). Prime ministers who rule under a majority coalition are the least effective ones (with an average box score of 76 percent), followed by those leading single-party minority governments (with an average box score of 82 percent). Still, as the data indicate, even under parliamentarism, single-majority governments do suffer legislative defeats (including Westminster-type governments).

In the case of presidentialism, single-party majority governments exhibit higher passage rates (an average of 70 percent) than do coalition majority (66 percent) and coalition minority (62 percent) administrations. As Cheibub et al. (2004) note, government coalitions tend to form when the policy distance between a minority party in government and the rest of the parties in the legislature is large. Therefore, coalition governments are typically quite heterogeneous and have more players who could potentially veto a change.

Notice also that single-party minority presidents do not fare much worse than coalition governments. On average, 62 percent of single-party minority presidents' bills are approved by the legislature. Hence, it is clear that legislative paralysis is a relatively rare phenomenon, even under presidentialism. Moreover, it is apparent from these data that prime ministers posses higher legislative passage rates than presidents: The percentage of government bills approved in the legislature is higher under parliamentarism than under presidentialism, regardless of government coalition or majority status.

5.4 MULTIVARIATE ANALYSIS

The patterns presented in Figures 5.3 and 5.4 suggest that a relationship exists between chief executives' legislative passage rates, their country's constitutional structures, and the status of their governments. To evaluate the performance of chief executives in a multivariate setting, I estimate a statistical model with chief executives' box scores as my dependent variable and cross-country differences in institutional design as the primary correlates of interest.[10] I also control for some additional features, such as the share of seats held by the government, the government status, electoral rules, and the structure of the legislature.[11]

---

[10] Due to data limitations, the composition of the sample that I use to estimate the model is slightly different than the one in Appendix B.

[11] The variable *Electoral Rules* takes the value of 1 if plurality governs the majority/all of the seats in the lower house of the national legislature, 0 if proportional representation is used, and 0.5 if it is a mixed system. Source: Keefer (2005). The variable *Average*

The dependent variable, BOX_{ijt}, is the proportion of bills initiated by chief executive j and approved by the legislature of her respective country i in period t. Because this variable takes values between zero and one, a standard OLS regression is inappropriate, as its prediction equation will not be constrained between such values. To address this issue, I perform a logit transformation of the dependent variable, such that $LNBOX = ln\left(\frac{BOX_{ijt}}{1-BOX_{ijt}}\right)$, and then run an OLS regression. Table 5.2 presents two alternative specifications.[12]

The main findings discussed in this chapter remain unchanged. There is a strong relationship between a chief executive's passage rate and her country's constitutional structure. In particular, the results indicate that, relative to Westminster-style parliamentary systems, passage rates are lower in non-Westminster parliamentary countries, in semiparliamentary regimes, and especially under presidentialism.[13] Passage rates also appear to be lower when there is a multiparty coalition rather than a single-party government in power.[14]

One additional result is worth noting here. Both specifications in Table 5.2 reveal that, *ceteris paribus*, passage rates are higher under electoral systems in which legislators represent a national constituency. This finding buttresses my argument regarding the effect of the degree of predictability of legislators' behavior on chief executive's passage rates. Under conditions of more certainty, namely when legislators represent a *national* rather than a *local* constituency, chief executives can more accurately assess how the legislature will vote and thus achieve greater legislative success.

District Magnitude is calculated as the total number of seats allocated in the lowest tier divided by the total number of districts in that tier. Source: Golder (2005). The variable *Seats from a National District* indicate the proportion of legislators that are elected via a national tier to the lower house of the national legislature. Source: Wallack et al. (2003). The variable *Bicameral System* takes the value of 1 if the national legislature is bicameral; 0 otherwise. Source: Wallack et al. (2003).

[12] The first column reports the results of a model in which standard errors are robustly estimated and the disturbance terms for each country are allowed to be correlated, whereas the second column presents the results of a model with regional dummies.

[13] The following countries in the sample were coded as Westminster-style systems: Canada, Bangladesh, Ireland, Malta, United Kingdom, and New Zealand.

[14] The variable *Coalition Government* is a binary indicator that takes the value of 1 if the government is a multiparty coalition, and 0 otherwise. A government is considered to be a multiparty coalition if two or more political parties represented in the national legislature hold cabinet positions. Source: Cheibub et al. (2004).

Table 5.2. *Passage rates: Multivariate analysis*

	Country Clustered	Regional Effects
Non-Westminster Parliamentary	−1.896*** (0.531)	−1.941*** (0.252)
Semiparliamentary	−1.962*** (0.529)	−2.007*** (0.275)
Presidential	−2.645*** (0.533)	−2.379*** (0.388)
Government's Seat Share	1.595** (0.623)	1.785*** (0.446)
Coalition Government	−0.648*** (0.203)	−0.547*** (0.114)
Electoral Rules	0.795*** (0.261)	0.210 (0.208)
Average District Magnitude	0.004* (0.002)	0.004** (0.002)
Seats from National District	1.346** (0.618)	1.555*** (0.456)
Bicameral System	0.193 (0.283)	0.129 (0.144)
Asia		0.681** (0.296)
Latin America		−0.466 (0.372)
Eastern Europe		−0.289 (0.313)
Middle East		−0.729*** (0.249)
Intercept	2.249*** (0.563)	2.314*** (0.321)
N	272	272
R^2	0.473	0.52

Notes: This table examines the relationship between democratic chief executives' box scores, constitutional structures, and government status. The dependent variable, BOX_{ijt}, is the proportion of bills initiated by chief executive j and approved by the legislature of her respective country i in period t. It is expressed as $ln\left(\dfrac{BOX_{ijt}}{1-BOX_{ijt}}\right)$ to perform an ordinary least-squares estimation. Column 1 reports the results of a model in which standard errors are robustly estimated and the disturbance terms for each country are allowed to be correlated. Column 2 presents the results of a model with regional dummies. Variables listed as controls are described in the text. The omitted category in column 1 is Westminster-style system (for constitutional structure); in column 2, the baseline categories are Westminster-style system (for constitutional structure) and Western Europe (for region). Due to data limitations, the composition of the sample that I use to estimate the model is slightly different than the one in Appendix B. Standard errors are in parentheses. ∗ indicates significance at a 10% level; ∗∗ indicates significance at a 5% level; ∗ ∗ ∗ indicates significance at a 1% level. The results suggest that, relative to Westminster-style parliamentary systems, passage rates are lower in non-Westminster parliamentary countries, in semiparliamentary regimes, and especially under presidentialism. Passage rates also appear to be lower when there is a multiparty coalition rather than a single-party government in power. The results also reveal that, *ceteris paribus*, passage rates are higher under electoral systems in which legislators represent a *national* rather than a *local* constituency.

Overall, the multivariate analysis demonstrates that the comparative ability of chief executives to obtain legislative approval of their initiatives depends on the conditions under which they operate. And while some of these circumstances might be under their control, such as the government's partisan makeup, some others are structural features of the governance framework that cannot be easily changed by them.

5.5 BILL INITIATION AND PASSAGE RATES

One possible explanation for the patterns presented in this chapter is that the box score data are subject to a form of self-selection bias that favors chief executives under parliamentary systems. As Cheibub et al. (2004) note, because prime ministers risk losing the confidence of the legislature when they are defeated, they must be careful in proposing legislation. Presidents, as the argument goes, can be more reckless: If they are indifferent to the status quo, they can initiate bills expecting to be defeated to embarrass the opposition.

Is it really the case, however, that prime ministers are more careful when they propose legislation? According to my data, in a given year, the representative prime minister introduces 131 pieces of legislation, whereas the average president initiates 109 pieces of legislation. A difference of means test indicates that the null hypothesis cannot be rejected at conventional levels. Thus, there is no difference between the number of bills initiated by the two types of chief executives. In other words, at least with regard to the amount of legislation introduced by the executive to the legislature every year, the evidence indicates that presidents are not necessarily more reckless than prime ministers.

It might be argued that a chief executive's carefulness is reflected in the content rather than the amount of legislation. Unfortunately, I cannot put that argument to a test with my data. Nonetheless, I can still gauge how "strategic" chief executives are when it comes to bill initiation. In particular, the data allow me to answer the following questions: (1) Is it true that some of them can manage to fatten their "batting average" by withholding legislation? (2) What is the relationship between bill initiation and statutory achievements? Figure 5.5 shows the number of executive-initiated bills approved by the legislature as a function of the total number of proposals introduced by the chief executive in a given year (i.e., the box score's numerator and denominator, respectively).

The dashed line in Figure 5.5 represents the predicted number of executive-initiated laws obtained from a linear regression, where the number of executive-initiated laws is regressed on the number of executive bills. The shaded areas are the 95 percent confidence intervals around these estimates. The data clearly indicate that chief executives' legislative

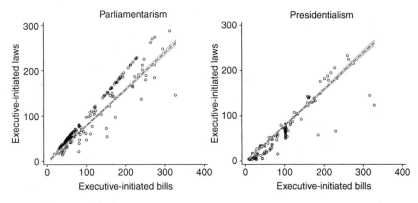

Figure 5.5. Bill initiation and statutory achievements.
Notes: Each graph shows the relationship between bill initiation and statutory achievements under parliamentarism and presidentialism. The y-axis of each graph is the number of executive-initiated laws and the x-axis of each graph is the number of executive-initiated bills. The dashed line represents the predicted number of executive-initiated laws obtained from a linear regression, where the number of executive-initiated laws is regressed on the number of executive bills. The shaded areas are the 95 percent confidence intervals around these estimates. The data clearly indicate that chief executives' legislative achievements and bill initiation have a linear relationship; the predicted number of executive-initiated legislation increases monotonically in the number of bills a chief executive sends to the legislature. As such, this evidence rejects the notion that chief executives can obtain higher passage rates by initiating less legislation. It also indicates that the difference between presidentialism and parliamentarism regarding passage rates is unrelated to bill initiation. Information about the composition of the sample and the sources from which the data were obtained are listed in Appendix B. I follow Przeworski et al. (2000) to classify countries' constitutional structures. Data on constitutional structures reported in Przeworski et al. (2000) and Cheibub et al. (2010).

achievements and bill initiation have a linear relationship; the predicted number of executive-initiated legislation increases monotonically in the number of bills a chief executive sends to the legislature. As such, these patterns suggest that the box scores remain somewhat constant irrespective of the number of bills an executive initiates.

In sum, this evidence rejects the notion that chief executives can obtain higher passage rates by initiating less legislation. It also indicates that the difference between presidentialism and parliamentarism regarding passage rates is unrelated to bill initiation. Finally, even though the data are not rich enough to test the claim directly, the patterns in Figure 5.5

suggest that chief executives under different constitutional structures do not necessarily adjust the content of their bills either.[15]

5.6 CONCLUDING REMARKS

The data presented in this chapter provides considerable evidence that chief executives do not always have all their of their proposals approved by the legislature. They also reveal that the relationship between chief executives' passage rates and the partisan makeup of the legislature is more complex than how it is currently depicted in the literature.

The analyses indicate that: (1) autocratic rulers have higher legislative passage rates than democratic chief executives, but they occasionally suffer legislative defeats, too; (2) the percentage of government bills approved in the legislature is higher under parliamentarism than under presidentialism, regardless of government coalition or majority status; (3) single-party minority presidents can often avoid "legislative impasse," "deadlock," or "stalemate"; (4) the notion that chief executives can manipulate their box scores by withholding legislation is not supported by the evidence; (5) chief executives display higher legislative passage rates when legislators' represent a national rather than a local constituency.

The aggregate nature of the data introduced in this chapter make them more suited to address the variation in chief executives' legislative passage rates rather than to account for the approval or rejection of particular pieces of legislation. The box scores, however, can inform expectations regarding legislative' behavior. For example, Calvo (2007) finds that aggregate-level factors tend to explain extremely well the fate of individual bills in Argentina between 1983 and 2001. More generally, by sorting out the conditions under which chief executives succeed or fail in the legislative arena, where constituency interests are often represented, the evidence presented in this chapter can helps us understand what institutional arrangements and practices work particularly well at combining the dual objectives of accountability and governability.

---

[15] To further explore the link between chief executives' bill initiation and legislative achievements, I used fractional polynomials to model their relationship. The results indicate that the relationship is linear. I also regressed the number of bills initiated by the executive on the share of seats held by the government using country-fixed effects and calculated the residuals. I used a similar model to predict the number of executive-initiated laws, and then I plotted the residuals of both executive bills and executive laws. Once again, the results support the conclusions presented in the main body of the text.

6

Political Prowess or "Lady Luck"?

Pelé or Maradona. Who was the better of the two? In the summer of 2000, the world soccer governing board, the Fédération Internationale de Football Association (FIFA), held an online poll to elect the Player of the Century. Maradona scored a resounding victory, obtaining 53.6 percent of the vote compared to 18.5 percent for Pelé. FIFA hastily set up another jury composed by its own officials to hand out another Player of the Century award, which, unsurprisingly, went to Pelé.

Regardless of FIFA's dubious practices, judging the worth of individual athletes is always a controversial matter. Similarly, ranking the performance of individual chief executives is a tricky affair. Statements such as "chancellor x is an effective ruler" or "president y is ineffective" are pervasive in both the scholarly and popular literatures. To assess "how well" or "how poorly" a chief executive performs as a lawmaker, however, one should have some reasonable *expectation* about how that particular chief executive should be doing.

The evidence presented in the previous chapter suggests that the comparative ability of chief executives to rule by statute depends to a great extent on circumstances that are not fully under their control. In this chapter, I take the analysis one step forward by examining the individual performance of chief executives once several contextual factors are taken into account. I focus specifically on chief executives' partisan support in the legislature, as well as other characteristics of their countries (such as constitutional structures, sociopolitical heterogeneity, culture, and history).

The chapter is organized in two sections. The first introduces a metric for measuring chief executives' legislative performance, which enables me to compare individual rulers against each other. The second section presents a standard to evaluate chief executives' lawmaking abilities when legislators' voting behavior is unpredictable. I examine the issue statistically, representing an uncertain world as one in which legislative outcomes are decided by chance. The results strongly support the notion that variations in legislative passage rates are the consequences of differences in uncertainty rather than partisan support. They also highlight the need to assess the relative performance of chief executives in conjunction with the particular informational environment under which they operate.

6.1 LEGISLATIVE PERFORMANCE: A SABERMETRIC APPROACH

Keeping records of players' achievements is a ubiquitous practice among coaches, the media, and fans alike. For example, numbers have always played a major role in baseball. Given the discrete nature of the events in a game, this sport lends itself to easy record-keeping and statistics. With every pitch, data can be collected and examined for trends, meaning, and significance. In March 1980, statistician Bill James revolutionized the analysis of baseball when he introduced "sabermetrics" to readers of his *Baseball Abstracts*. A combination of the acronym SABR (Society for American Baseball Research) and "metrics," the term was defined by James as "the mathematical and statistical analysis of baseball records" (Costa et al. 2008).

The influence of sabermetrics on baseball cannot be understated. Members of the Baseball Writers Association of America and others who report on baseball refer to sabermetrics and its metrics on a regular basis. Moreover, with the prospect of finding out who can be more valuable to their organization, many major league teams use sabermetrics statistics. Billy Beane, the hero of Michael Lewis's celebrated book, *Moneyball*, is a case in point. As the general manager of the Oakland Athletics, a Major League Baseball team, he pioneered the use of this approach to identify and evaluate amateur talent.

Sabermetric measures – such as runs created or on-base percentage – are usually more useful for measuring player performance in baseball than in other team sports. For instance, an offensive contribution in baseball can be measured for players independently of the rest of the team's contribution. This is not the case in soccer, where a forward's goal scoring may depend on the quality of service from the midfield (Duch et al. 2010). Moreover, offensive contributions in baseball can be measured identically for every player, regardless of their position or the team's "style of play."[1]

Turning back to the Pelé-versus-Maradona comparison, both players were brilliant. Yet, they competed in totally different eras. The rhythm of the game, the tactics on the pitch, and the make-up of their teams were widely different. In fact, as a Brazilian international, Pelé was usually the crown jewel of a team filled with talent: In 1958, he was surrounded by legends Nilton Santos, Garrincha, Didi, and Vava; and in 1970, he shared the team with the likes of Carlos Alberto, Jairzinho, Tostão, Gérson, and Rivelino. In contrast, when Maradona won the World Cup in 1986, the Argentine side was hardly a star-studded team. He also led SSC Napoli out of anonymity to two Italian championships and won a UEFA cup virtually single-handed. Hence, in terms of individual impact, Maradona was arguably the most dominant of the two.

The notion that players should not be given credit for events over which they have no direct control (such as the quality of their teammates) is well known to baseball sabermetricians, who have developed different methods for measuring the value of players. For example, the *total player rating* (TPR) developed by sabermetrician Pete Palmer intends to compare players against each other even if they played for different teams, in different leagues, and in different eras. Another example is the *equivalent average* (EqA). Invented by Clay Davenport, this metric expresses the production of hitters in a context independent of park and league effects. These measures of value are often used to compose lists of the best players in a certain season or of all-time.

Measuring chief executives' legislative prowess is as difficult as evaluating the individual performance of athletes who participate in team sports. As I discussed in Chapter 2, unlike ruling by decree, statutory policy making depends on the interactions of a diverse group of actors, including political parties, the legislature, and the executive. In other work (Saiegh 2009a), I introduced a sabermetric measure of chief executives' legislative performance. I estimated a statistical model with individual chief executives' box scores as my dependent variable and their legislative backing as the main explanatory variable of interest. For each chief executive, I calculated the amount of legislative support as the share of

---

[1] As ESPN star columnist Bill Simmons cleverly noted, "baseball is an individual sport disguised as a team sport" (Simmons 2010).

seats held by her copartisans and expressed as an offset in the average share of seats held in her country by the chief executive's party in all the periods in the sample. I thus considered a chief executive to be "lucky" if her party controlled more seats in the legislature than the norm in her country.[2] Beside the measure of legislative support, I also employed country specific constants, which allowed me to control for a potentially long list of otherwise unobserved fixed characteristics of each country (such as sociopolitical heterogeneity, culture, and history).[3]

Following the sports analogy, a good judgment of a player's quality depends not only on her individual characteristics, but also on those of both her team and the league where the team competes. The sabermetric measure proposed in Saiegh (2009a) offers a concrete indicator of the elusive concept of legislative *success*, as its allows one to distinguish the "quality" of a given league (i.e., the country), a certain team (i.e., the chief executive's party), and a particular player (i.e., an accomplished chief executive), and thus to evaluate the quality of a player as distinct from how good his team is, and how competitive the league is in which his team competes.

Using this measure, I now proceed to identify those individual chief executives who perform better or worse than their contextual factors (such as their country characteristics and the size of their legislative contingent) would suggest (i.e., the "overachievers" and "underachievers"). The sample includes 42 countries and covers the period between 1946 and 2006 for a total of 795 country-year observations.[4] To rank the performance of individual chief executives, I calculate the difference between a chief executive's actual box score in a given year and his or her predicted performance according to the statistical model described earlier (i.e., once their legislative backing and country characteristics are considered). Therefore, the most accomplished chief executive in a given country is one who exhibits the greater "unexpected" performance.

Table 6.1 displays a ranking of chief executives for a selected group of countries from my sample. The overachievers are listed in the top panel,

---

[2] For those observations in which there was more than one chief executive in charge – due to elections, or a change in government – I calculated the legislative support differential as a weighted average between the seats held by the parties of the different office holders.

[3] See Saiegh (2009a) for more details.

[4] Due to data limitations regarding the distribution of seats of the chief executive's party for several observations, the composition of the sample that I use to estimate the model is slightly different than the one in Appendix B.

Table 6.1. *Performance of individual chief executives*

Overachievers

Country	Year	Chief Executive	Box Score			Seats	Regime
			Predicted	Actual	Country Mean		
Argentina	1985	Raúl Alfonsín	60.54	80.10	58.77	50.98	Presidentialism
Uruguay	1997	Julio María Sanguinetti	65.13	78.00	66.32	32.32	Presidentialism
India	1956	Jawaharlal Nehru	92.03	98.38	85.94	74.43	Westminster
United Kingdom	1950	Clement Attlee	97.30	99.03	96.98	50.40	Westminster
France	1967	George Pompidou	72.63	90.73	77.34	8.72	Mixed
Portugal	1987–1990	Aníbal Cavaco Silva	78.64	94.89	68.92	59.20	Mixed
Germany	1976	Helmut Schmidt	75.60	82.80	76.32	43.14	Parliamentarism
Spain	1977–1978	Adolfo Suárez	86.23	91.05	85.71	47.14	Parliamentarism

Table 6.1. (cont.)

Country	Year	Chief Executive	Underachievers			Seats	Regime
			Box Score				
			Predicted	Actual	Country Mean		
Argentina	2001	Fernando de la Rúa	57.80	27.90	58.77	44.35	Presidentialism
Uruguay	1989	Julio María Sanguinetti	68.57	43.00	66.32	41.41	Presidentialism
India	1970	Indira Gandhi	89.14	63.16	85.94	54.11	Westminster
United Kingdom	1978	James Callaghan	97.30	93.24	96.98	50.23	Westminster
France	1983	Pierre Mauroy	85.74	72.32	77.34	56.54	Mixed
Portugal	1982	Francisco Pinto Balsemão	70.08	22.22	68.92	32.80	Mixed
Germany	1991–1993	Helmut Kohl	77.16	68.10	76.32	48.18	Parliamentarism
Spain	1981	Leopoldo Calvo Sotelo	86.40	69.30	85.71	48.00	Parliamentarism

Notes: This table presents a ranking of chief executives based on their individual performance. I calculate the difference between their actual box score and their predicted performance once their legislative backing and country characteristics are considered. The sample includes 42 countries and covers the period between 1946 and 2006 for a total of 795 country-year observations (the composition of the sample is slightly different than the one in Appendix B due to data limitations). The table displays those individual chief executives who perform better or worse than their contextual factors would suggest (i.e., the "overachievers" and "underachievers") for a selected group of countries. The table indicates the chief executives' names, along with their country, the year, their predicted box score, their actual box score, the average box score for their respective countries, the share of seats held by their copartisans, and their countries' constitutional structure.

whereas the underachievers are shown in the bottom panel. In both cases, the table indicates the chief executives' names, along with their country, the year, their predicted box score, their actual box score, the average box score for their respective countries, the share of seats held by their copartisans, and their countries' constitutional structure.[5]

A glance at the list of names included in Table 6.1 reveals that the sabermetric approach championed by Saiegh (2009a) can be used to settle questions regarding the relative legislative effectiveness of chief executives. Take the case of the United Kingdom throughout the postwar consensus era, which lasted from the end of World War II to the election of Margaret Thatcher as prime minister in 1979. According to the sabermetric analysis, Clement Attlee was the country's most accomplished chief executive during this period. Attlee, who lead the Labour party to a landslide election victory over Winston Churchill's Conservatives in 1945, is often considered one of the most effective of all the British prime ministers. In fact, he was voted as the most successful British prime minister in the twentieth century, according to a survey conducted in 2004 by the University of Leeds and MORI, one of the largest survey research organizations in the United Kingdom (Theakston and Gill 2006).[6]

The ranking of James Callaghan as Britain's least effective prime minister of the 1946–1979 period provides further validity to the sabermetric assessment. Callaghan, who became prime minister after the unexpected resignation of Harold Wilson in 1976, had no overall majority and was thus forced to make deals with minor parties in order to survive (including the Lib-Lab pact from March 1977 to August 1978). Despite Callahan's personal appeal, economic crisis, bad union relations, and a succession of strikes (known as the Winter of Discontent) led to a decline in his

---

[5] In the case of mixed systems, the chief executive is the prime minister and not the president. Also, I decided to exclude from the table those cases where there were multiple chief executives in a single year, and those countries that, due to scant data, do not exhibit enough variation across individual chief executives. The composition of the ranking would be very similar if these cases were included, but such ordering is less intuitive in terms of identifying the performance of a particular leader.

[6] The survey asked 139 academics specializing in modern British history and politics to indicate on a scale of 0 to 10 how successful or unsuccessful they considered each PM to have been in office (with 0 being highly unsuccessful and 10 being highly successful). For more details, see Theakston and Gill (2006). In 2006, Francis Becketta, a BBC History Magazine historian, also ranked Clement Attlee as as the greatest prime minister of the twentieth century. Additional rankings are included in http://en.wikipedia.org/wiki/Historical_rankings_of_Prime_Ministers_of_the_United _Kingdom

support. By the end of 1978, as Kingdom (2003) notes, the media and some academics proclaimed a crisis of governability. In March 1979, the government lost a no-confidence motion by 311 votes to 310, making Callaghan the first prime minister since 1924 to be forced into an election by the chamber. On May 3, 1979, Margaret Thatcher defeated Callaghan in the first of four consecutive general election victories for the Conservative Party.[7]

In addition to facilitating the task of rating chief executives in any given country, the sabermetric analysis presented in Table 6.1 also highlights three important points. First, it demonstrates that a country's institutional context matters. As the evidence in Table 6.1. indicates, an accomplished prime minister in the United Kingdom or India should be expected to get his/her initiatives approved almost all the time. Even underachievers in these countries are likely to obtain passage of the majority of their initiatives (93 percent of them in the case of James Callagham!). In contrast, the legislative passage rates of underachievers in presidential democracies, like Argentina or Uruguay, are typically below 50 percent. A box score in excess of 70 percent, in fact, would deem a leader in one of these countries as effective.

The second important point is that other contextual factors also matter. Many accomplished chief executives were operating under exceptional circumstances (such as regime transitions, or post-war experiences); therefore, it was a combination of their skills with the *spirit of the times* that boosted their individual performances. This is true, for example, of Argentina's Raúl Alfonsín in 1985 and of Spain's Adolfo Suárez in 1977-78; both took office as leaders of a democratic transition from authoritarian rule. Similarly, many ineffective chief executives fell prey to unfortunate circumstances. Argentina's Fernando de la Rúa who presided over the country's worst economic crisis of the 20th century is a good example. Or consider the case of Leopoldo Calvo Sotelo, Spain's Prime Minister between 1981 and 1982. His appointment was preceded by the *Tejerazo*, an attempted coup d' état that took place on 23 February 1981. The event benefitted Calvo Sotelo in the short term (he was confirmed

---

[7] The somewhat limited coverage of the data imposes a constraint on an "all-time" comparison within countries, as some of these leaders are absent from the sample altogether. It is an open question whether Callaghan in 1978 would have remained the least effective prime minister in Britain if more recent periods had been incorporated into the analysis. Unfortunately, the sample used in the analysis presented in this chapter does not cover the administrations of Margaret Thatcher, John Major or Gordon Brown.

two days later by a majority vote); but, the Socialist opposition as well as fractures within his own political party (Unión de Centro Democrático, or UCD), left him with insufficient support in the legislature.

Last, but not least, the sabermetric analysis indicates that legislative prowess (or lack thereof) can be a fleeting trait. As is often the case with professional athletes, chief executives tend to alternate good showings with bad ones. Take, for instance, Julio María Sanguinetti, who served twice as president of Uruguay (from March 1985 to March 1990 and from March 1995 to March 2000). He is listed in Table 6.1 as both an underachiever in 1989 (with an actual box score of 43 percent) and as an overachiever in 1997 (when he passed 78 percent of his legislative initiatives). Both performances were, to some extent, unexpected given the amount of support that he enjoyed in the legislature: 41 and 32 percent of the seats in 1989 and 1997, respectively. It would be fair to say that he had a bad year in 1989, the last year of his first term in office, and a good one in 1997.

6.2 LAWMAKING UNDER UNCERTAINTY

The box score introduced in Chapter 4 allows us to assess the relative number of "victories" in the legislature for chief executives. In addition, the sabermetric measure discussed in this chapter can be used to establish chief executives' comparative effectiveness. Evaluating the meaning and significance of these measures, however, remains problematic. In particular, the question that needs to be answered is to what extent a highly rated chief executive (or one with a certain number of victories) qualifies as a successful ruler.

Box scores are imperfect measures of chief executives' statutory abilities. As revealed by the sabermetric analysis, the comparative lawmaking ability of chief executives often depends on circumstances beyond their control. Put simply, in any given year, the actual legislative performance of a chief executive can be – at least in part – due to chance or luck. The implication is that we should expect legislative passage rates to *regress toward their mean*.

Regression toward the mean signifies that, left to themselves, things tend to return to normal, whatever that is. An intuitive way to look at this is to return to the sports analogy. Say that box scores are analogous to baseball players' batting averages. As Schall and Smith (2000) note, because baseball performances are an imperfect measure of underlying abilities, batting averages regress toward the mean: Outstanding performances exaggerate player skills and are typically followed by more mediocre performances. Indeed, regression toward the mean explains such clichés as the Cy Young jinx, sophomore slump, rookie-of-the-year jinx, and the *Sports Illustrated* cover jinx (Schall and Smith 2000).

The same can be said about chief executives. As the example of Julio María Sanguinetti indicates, they may have good and bad years. A chief executive's true accomplishments, therefore, need to be assessed by her own standards. The key question, of course, is what this expectation should be. In light of the argument presented in this book, it should be grounded not only in the individual abilities of a given chief executive, but also account for the unpredictability of legislators' behaviors. Namely, any judgment of how well a chief executive is doing as a lawmaker, depends on how well one *expects* her to do in a world fraught with uncertainty. It is not clear, however, how this expectation should be formed. One way to tackle this problem is to think about it in statistical terms; thus, I represent a completely uncertain world as one in which legislative outcomes are decided by chance (Hammond and Fraser 1983).[8]

Suppose that each member of the legislature decides her vote by flipping an unbiased coin (i.e., the probability of a "yes" vote by any legislator is 0.5). In this fully uncertain world, roughly half the time, a majority of legislators will vote with the chief executive and half the time against her; this results in an expected passage rate of 50 percent (Hammond and Fraser 1984b).

While this representation of uncertainty yields passage rates below 100 percent, it is still too unrealistic to accommodate the facts presented in previous chapters. A somewhat less uncertain situation is one in which legislators' preferences can be approximated by their partisan affiliations. One way to incorporate uncertainty in such a world is to assume that a majority of the chief executive's copartisans always have preferences identical to hers, and that her party majority will vote yes or no according to her wishes. Yet, just because a chief executive can count on the support of a majority of her party on a vote, it does not mean that she will actually win the vote. The outcome will depend on the number and size of legislative parties; the larger the share of seats of the chief executive's party, the greater the probability that a majority of her party will be on

---

[8] See also Hammond and Fraser (1984a, 1984b). Unlike the work of Hammond and Fraser, which focuses exclusively on the case of the United States, I explore the consequences of the unpredictability of legislators' behavior for legislative passage rates in a cross-national setting.

the winning side. Following Hammond and Fraser (1983), I identify this representation of the legislative process as the *party-augmented* model of uncertainty.

The probability that a majority of the chief executive's party, and therefore the chief executive, is on the winning side of a roll call is calculated using the assumption that legislators vote by flipping unbiased coins. To get an intuitive idea of how this concept works, consider the following thought experiment (Hammond and Fraser 1983). Suppose that the chief executive faces a three-member legislature (composed of legislators A, B, and C) operating under majority rule. Say that the chief executive belongs to the same party as legislator A. Each legislator flips an unbiased coin to decide her vote, so the probability that she will vote yes is $\frac{1}{2}$. There are eight possible voting combinations, and in six out of the eight combinations, the position of A prevails.[9] Therefore, the probability that the chief executive is on the "winning side" of a vote is $6 \times \frac{1}{8} = \frac{3}{4}$, or 75 percent. Similarly, if we restrict our attention to those situations where the chief executive likes the proposal, she will be on the "winning side" of a vote three times out of four, or 75 percent of the time.[10]

The logic behind the *party-augmented* model does not change if more structure is added to the representation of the legislative process (cf. Hammond and Fraser 1984). Assume that executive-initiated bills must be considered two separate times, once in committee and once on the floor. At each stage, each legislator makes a decision by flipping a coin. While a chief executive's proposal can be referred to committees that are likely

---

[9] When A likes the proposal, there are three events in which the chief executive is on the winning side $\{AB, AC, ABC\}$ (i.e., the proposal is passed); and when A dislikes the proposal, there are three events in which she votes against it along with at least somebody else $\{0, B, C\}$ (and the proposal is killed).

[10] More realistic models designed to accommodate different configurations of legislators' preferences and seat distributions (and departures from equiprobability) can yield predictions that are very similar to the ones obtained from this model. Following Barry (1980), consider a legislature composed of three parties, with weights of 3, 2, and 2 votes, and where a majority of 5 out of 7 votes is needed for the passage of a measure. Call the player with 3 votes A and the other two B and C. Assume also that the chief executive belongs to the party A. Therefore, her legislative contingent controls 42.8 percent of the seats in the legislature. Suppose that there is a random association between A's preferences and those of B and C, but that B and C always disagree (i.e., the chief executive faces a divided opposition). If this is the case, then the chief executive will always win. Suppose now that the preferences of B and C are associated at random with each other (and also with A's preferences). The outcome in this case will be a box score of $\frac{7}{8}$ for the chief executive. Finally, suppose that B and C always agree (i.e., the chief executive faces a united opposition). In this case, the chief executive will secure a victory $\frac{3}{4}$ of the time.

to vary in their size and partisan composition, the norm that most legislatures use to assign members to committees states that the composition of each committee shall proportionally reflect the partisan composition of the body as a whole. Therefore, although party ratios may vary somewhat from committee to committee, the effects of these differing ratios on expected passage rates would counterbalance each other almost exactly. In consequence, the average expected passage rate in a legislature's committee would be almost exactly equal to the expected passage rate on the floor. If the decisions made at each stage are statistically independent of each other, then the overall passage rate is just the product of the probabilities of passage at each point (Hammond and Fraser 1984). Decisions at each stage in the legislative process, however, may not be independent of each other (Cox and McCubbins 2005). For example, if some executive-initiated proposals never make it out of committee, but every bill that reaches the floor is subsequently enacted, then the calculation of a chief executive's legislative passage rate is the same as before (i.e., the *party-augmented* model with a single decision instance).

Finally, it is always possible to move back to a world of complete certainty. In this case, members of the chief executive's party should always vote in favor of her proposals, whereas members of the opposition will always vote against them. Per the *law of anticipated reactions*, if a chief executive has complete information, then she can strategically adjust for changes in legislative control. Therefore, in such a simple world, passage rates should be unrelated to the number of seats held by the chief executive's copartisans in the legislature.[11]

6.3 ACTUAL AND EXPECTED PERFORMANCE

The statistical exercises described earlier illustrate how chance affects chief executives' passage rates. These simulated outcomes would certainly be validated if different data-generating processes, analogous to repeating an experiment a large number of times, enables me to empirically observe

---

[11] Another way to think about the issue is to consider a situation with multiple pro-government parties, multiple opposition parties, and both committed and uncommitted legislators in the legislature. Hence, a chief executive will always be able to count with the votes of a group of "core" supporters and will never be able to muster support from "core" antagonists, yet he or she may also be able to collect votes from "uncommitted" pro-grovernment and opposition legislators. In this case, the probability that a chief executive will be on the winning side of a roll call could be calculated using the assumption that only the uncommitted legislators vote by flipping unbiased coins.

the relative frequency with which legislation tends to be approved. The basic idea can be illustrated by a simple example from probability theory: If a coin is tossed in the air, it can land heads or tails, but it is unknown which of these will occur in a single toss. Assuming the coin is perfectly balanced, one can arrive at the value $\frac{1}{2}$ deductively. That is, one side of the coin is as likely to occur as the other. Alternatively, suppose this experiment is repeated by tossing a coin several times. If the coin is perfectly balanced, then the coin will land heads approximately 50 percent of the time or, in other words, the relative frequency will approach $\frac{1}{2}$. Although the specific outcome on any one toss is unknown, the behavior over time is predictable.

Just as in the case of the coin toss, the passage rates of chief executives should become stable in the long run. Using the chance models discussed earlier, I can now ask the following question: How does the actual performance of chief executives compare with their expected performance when legislators' preferences are unknown? To answer this question, I compare the data introduced in Chapter 5 with the predictions of the *party-augmented* model. Specifically, to explore the relationship between party size and a chief executive's expected win rate, I employ the technology of the binomial distribution and Monte Carlo simulations. Implementation of this methodology is quite straightforward. For any given roll call, each individual legislator can either vote "yes" or "no". Following the convention, I call one of the two possible results a *success* (S) and the other a *failure* (F). Given this particular experiment has only two outcomes, let p denote the probability of success in such experiment and let $q = 1 - p$ denote the probability of failure (in this case, $p = .5$). Suppose now that the experiment is repeated and the trials are independent. In this case, I am interested in the expected number of yes votes from the members of a party of size n. The probability of exactly k successes is given by: $\binom{n}{k}p^k q^{n-k}$. Notice that the number of yes votes from a party in a series of coin flip roll calls will be binomially distributed. Therefore, I can simulate the results of a roll call by generating a series of binomially distributed random numbers.

Given a party size, these random numbers will produce a distribution of yes votes that approximates the binomial distribution. For each simulated roll call, a series of random numbers is produced, one for each party, and each of these random numbers represents the number of yes votes from each of these parties. Using these simulated roll calls, I can then determine which side a majority of the chief executive's party is on. If a majority of the chief executive's party is on the winning side, I count the roll call as a win for her; if a majority of her party is on the losing side, it is counted as a loss (Hammond and Fraser 1983).[12]

I simulated 5,000 roll calls for a 100-member legislature, using different sizes for the chief executive's party as inputs. For example, in a legislature where the party of the chief executive holds 45 seats and the opposition controls the remaining 55 seats, the chief executive won 3,705 of the roll calls, yielding an expected passage rate of 74.1 percent. The second column in Table 6.2 presents the simulated passage rates for the different sizes of the chief executive's party. As expected, a chief executive's passage rate should be somewhere between 50 and 100 percent, and does not drop below 50 percent. This is a logical consequence of equating a chief executive's position with that of a majority of her party in the legislature (Hammond and Fraser 1983).[13]

Armed with these numbers, I can evaluate the actual performance of chief executives worldwide. In doing so, I first classify the observations according to the share of seats held by the party of the chief executive (prime minister or president). The variable ranges from no seats (these are cases of caretaker governments, such as the one in place in Italy in 1995) to 80 percent of the seats controlled by the chief executive's party (in India between 1985 and 1988). Next, I calculate the average share of seats controlled by a chief executive's copartisans and the corresponding average passage rate. So, the average passage rate for a chief executive whose party controls, on average, 45 percent of the seats in the legislature amounts to 74.8 percent.

As the third column in Table 6.2 indicates, the actual passage rates are remarkably close to what is expected in a world where legislators' preferences cannot be fully predicted despite their partisan identities. These results, thus, are *prima facie* evidence that any sensible model of executive-legislative relations should incorporate incomplete information into the analysis. More importantly, the findings presented in Table 6.2

---

[12] If the chief executive's party is evenly split on a simulated roll call, I count it as a loss.

[13] As noted above, if legislation must be considered by committees that have a partisan composition similar to the parent chamber, and the decisions made at each stage are statistically independent of each other, then the overall passage rate is just the product of the probabilities of passage at each point. To calculate these probabilities, one needs only to compute the square of the simulated passage rates in column 2. So, if the party of the chief executive has 45 seats and the opposition controls the remaining 55, then the expected passage rate would be 55.94 percent.

Table 6.2. *Simulated and actual passage rates*

Seats	Simulated Values	Actual Values		
	Mean	Mean	Std. Dev.	Obs.
5	57.56	56.40	22.65	25
10	61.06	66.31	22.58	62
15	63.44	72.63	18.85	57
20	66.48	75.15	17.51	56
25	66.90	74.54	21.27	101
30	69.12	70.69	24.08	129
35	70.2	69.32	22.55	103
40	71.26	72.92	17.38	113
45	74.1	74.80	16.25	255
50	75.62	77.93	16.54	362
55	76.26	82.33	15.88	246
60	79.74	86.79	11.71	69
65	80.54	87.91	11.80	22
70	81.80	88.61	14.92	41
75	82.42	89.85	15.35	30
80	85.80	95.06	3.70	7
85	87.6	n/d	n/d	n/d
90	90.22	n/d	n/d	n/d
95	92.28	n/d	n/d	n/d
100	100	n/d	n/d	n/d

Notes: This table presents a comparison between simulated and actual legislative passage rates. The values in column 2 were generated by simulating 5,000 roll calls for a 100-member legislature, using different sizes for the chief executive's party as inputs. The number of observations reported in column 5 doubles the sample size because I used the full sample to calculate the average share of seats controlled by a chief executive's copartisans in multiples of 5 and 10 seats, respectively. The data reveal that the actual passage rates are remarkably close to what is expected in a world where legislators' preferences cannot be fully predicted despite their partisan identities. They also indicate that the *party-augmented* model of uncertainty constitutes the most appropriate benchmark to evaluate the actual statutory performance of chief executives.

indicate that the *party-augmented* model of uncertainty constitutes the most appropriate benchmark to evaluate the actual statutory performance of chief executives.[14]

---

[14] The chance models rest on the idea that legislative decisions are made "as if" they were like experiments in coin tossing, each legislator tossing a coin to decide whether to vote for or against an executive-initiated proposal. This is obviously an inadequate description of legislative behavior. However, the unrealism of these coin-tossing models do not make the results based on them inadequate, because all models use more or less unrealistic simplifying assumptions (Poole and Rosenthal 1987).

6.3.1 The "Three-Fourths" Rule

The results presented in Table 6.2 provide face validity to the idea of using a *chance* model of lawmaking to represent uncertainty. The findings also square well with some of the existing findings in the literature. Several studies focusing on the United States have used data generated by actual bills presented to Congress to estimate baseline models from which to assess relative presidential success (Peterson 1990; Covington et al. 1995; Fleisher et al. 2002)

For example, Hammond and Fraser (1984b) simulate 5,000 roll calls for each composition of the U.S. House of Representatives between 1947 and 1974. They use party and faction sizes from the year under consideration as inputs, and assume that any given legislator would vote yes with probability $p = 0.5$. They find that for the two-party version, the average expected passage rate for presidents (1947–1974) is 75.22 percent, and for the three-party version, the passage rate is 71.5 percent.[15]

Using a random sample of 229 presidential proposals between 1953 and 1984, Peterson (1990) notes that the most important bills received favorable action from Congress 58 percent of the time. He also finds that if Congress acted on a less important proposal, it was much more likely to provide some success to the president. In this case, the passage rate would increase to 76 percent (Peterson 1990; Cameron and Park 2007).

Covington et al. (1995) use probit analysis to predict presidential victories on each roll-call vote taken in the U.S. House of Representatives between 1953 and 1973. Their "presidency-augmented" model of success takes into account the distinction between "on agenda" and "off agenda" bills, and whether a particular bill under consideration was either supported or opposed by the president. To establish a basis for comparison, their baseline model is one in which presidents do not use their proposing power and do not express their support or opposition to bills. The authors find that the probability of a presidential victory in the *Congress-centered* model (i.e., when a bill is off the president's agenda and he opposes passage) is 75.2 percent (Covington et al. 1995).

In a more recent study, Fleisher et al. (2002) obtain similar results using data of presidential victories on roll-call votes in the U.S. Congress from 1953 to 2001. In this case, the authors estimate a baseline or naïve model

---

[15] In their 1984b paper, Hammond and Fraser also provide estimates of a more procedurally complete and realistic model of legislative behavior. They look at the composition of the House Rule Committee and calculate the expected presidential passage rates on proposals sent to the Committee. For the two-party faction, the probability is 74.95 percent.

as one in which presidential victory is predicted from party control alone. The model predicts that majority presidents should have a victory rate of about 76 percent in the House of Representatives (Fleisher et al. 2002).

Another rich source of evidence is provided by the Westminster Parliament between the Restoration and union with Ireland. A team lead by Julian Hoppit at University College in London compiled a history of parliamentary legislation between 1660 and 1800 (Hoppit et al. 1994; Hoppit 1996, 1997). In particular, the authors produced a detailed list of all failed attempts to pass an act of Parliament formally considered at Westminster. Some 7,025 failed legislative initiatives were identified. With 14,216 acts that were actually passed, it appears that about two thirds of all initiatives succeeded. Between the Glorious Revolution and the accession of George I, passage rates rose gradually: For the rest of the eighteenth century (between 1714 and 1800), the rate averaged 75.3 percent.

The authors not only identified these attempts to pass legislation, but also analyzed the types of legislation being considered. They produced a categorization of the initiatives in terms of their aims. The distinction is made between those acts that were general and had a national provenance and those that were essentially local, highly particular or personal in their concerns. Interestingly, various types of legislative initiatives generated different patterns of success and failure. Whereas just over half of attempts at general legislation succeeded through the whole period, for specific initiatives, it was nearly three quarters (Hoppit 1996: 117).

In sum, there are no general principles regarding how legislatures create statute law. Nonetheless, the evidence presented in Table 6.2 indicates that it seems like a good idea to use the "three fourths rule" as a baseline to evaluate the expected performance of an *average* chief executive in the legislative arena.

6.4 CONCLUDING REMARKS

Several of the arguments advanced in this book, such as the proposition that executive-initiated legislation will not always be approved by the legislature, may seem intuitive to the reader. Other assertions, such as the idea that variations in legislative passage rates are the consequences of differences in uncertainty rather than partisan support, challenge the conventional wisdom. Together with the empirical evidence suggesting that a complex connection between the legislature's partisan composition and chief executive's passage rates exists, my view of statutory policy making points legislative research in a new direction.

This chapter carefully examined the notion that legislative defeats are associated with situations where legislators' voting behavior is unpredictable. Indeed, all of the chief executives identified as underachievers in Table 6.1 had a plurality of seats in their respective legislatures (and some of them had an absolute majority). Still, their degree of partisan support did not necessarily translate into a distinguished legislative performance. Instead, in many cases, intense partisan infighting and factionalism forced these chief executives to operate in uncertain environments that ultimately undermined their efforts.

The conundrum faced by French prime minister Pierre Mauroy in 1983 after Francois Mitterand's so-called turn toward the right is a telling example of this phenomenon. With the election of Mitterrand as president in 1981, the Socialists obtained an absolute parliamentary majority for the first time in the country's history. Between 1981 and 1983, prime minster Mauroy nationalized the banks, as well as the insurance and defense industries, at the behest of Mitterrand. Other reforms included the reduction of working hours, retirement at sixty years of age, and a rise in workers' wages. Facing a declining economy, in March 1983, the president advocated a change in economic policies. Mauroy declared his opposition to the plan, but Mitterrand asked him to remain as prime minister. As Friend (1998) notes, the controversy signaled to the country that the government lacked a prime minister and was hesitating between two policies. Public support for Mauroy fell from 45 to 33 percent between March and May 1983 (Friend 1998). Whipsawed by the contradiction between his need to defend austerity policies and his own personal convictions, Mauroy steadily lost his credibility. As Table 6.1 indicates, despite having a solid parliamentary majority, his legislative performance was clearly below par. In 1984, after failing to pass a bill restricting the financing of private schools, he resigned.

As this example demonstrates, assessing a chief executive's level of success based exclusively on his level of parliamentary support is likely to produce erroneous answers. More generally, the evidence presented in this chapter highlights the role of uncertainty in statutory policy making. Table 6.2 reveals that, on average, chief executives' performances are not much different from what would be expected if legislators flip coins to decide how to respond to their proposals. Furthermore, the findings indicate that under complete uncertainty, chief executives will face significant difficulties in passing their agendas, regardless of their support in the legislature.

The main conclusion that emerges from this chapter is thus unequiv-ocal: Any sensible model of executive-legislative relations should incorporate incomplete information as part of the analysis. I examine this contention from an empirical standpoint in the next two chapters. Chapter 7 discusses one of the possible strategies that chief executives may use to pass their legislative agendas in the face of uncertainty: monetary payments. Next, in Chapter 8, I analyze the impact of candidate selection on legislative behavior. In particular, I study the relationship between ideologically cohesive parties and chief executives' legislative passage rates.

7

Buying Legislators

This book has thus far considered the different strategies that chief executives may use to induce cross-pressured legislators to adopt their preferred policy outcomes. It has also discussed how these strategies arise from the properties of statutes, and the manner in which they are produced: The content of a bill creates its own winners and losers, but the gains are not confined to those who voted on the winning side, nor are the losses confined to those on the losing side. A clever vote buyer can exploit this fact to her advantage. For example, a chief executive might be able to buy only a few votes and then benefit from "bandwagon" effects to obtain a majority of votes in support for her proposal. In fact, when legislators care about both policy and position taking, it might even be possible for the chief executive to get her proposal approved without having to offer any bribes.

Nonetheless, governments may sometimes need to incentivize legislators to support their policies, and may do so in a variety of ways. These incentives are ubiquitous in legislative policy making, and common terms such as "horse trading," "arm twisting," "influence peddling," "back scratching," and "deal making" are often used to describe the general phenomenon of vote buying. In many cases, votes are traded in exchange for favors, sinecures, or political rewards (e.g., better committee assignments). In particular, in countries with institutionalized party systems, party leaders can use the carrot of advancement and the stick of nonadvancement to impose a certain degree of organizational loyalty on their membership. In contrast, in countries with inchoate party systems, governments may have difficulty controlling individual legislators through a party machine. In these contexts, monetary payments may be the government's currency of choice.

This chapter presents evidence on legislative vote buying involving outright bribery. Of course, the illegal nature of these transactions presents a formidable obstacle when it comes to their empirical identification. Even though accusations of corruption and horse trading are ever-present in legislative policy making, it is rare to acquire such information. Nonetheless, I examine two historical cases where detailed records of monetary payments made to members of the legislature in exchange for their support do exist: England under George III and Peru under Alberto Fujimori. The empirical evidence confirms the main findings presented in Chapter 3 and reveals that the amount paid in bribes by the British and Peruvian governments were not excessively large. The pattern of bribes in these two countries also validates the idea that when governments engage in vote buying, winning coalitions will not be oversized.

7.1 THE WALLET OF KING GEORGE

Historians often refer to the period before the accession of George III and the aftermath of the American Revolutionary War as the era of *personal parties* in the British House of Commons. This characterization is a misleading guide to the political independence of Members of Parliament (MPs), given that many of them literally owed their seat to a patron. It still conveys some idea of the lack of party distinctions during this period. Up until the fall of Walpole, at least, party differentiation between Whigs and Tories remained intact because the issues that gave birth to this distinction were still very much alive (Hill 1976; Speck 1981). By 1754, as Namier and Brooke note, it was universally recognized "... that the old party denominations of Whig and Tory no longer corresponded to political realities and that the issues which formerly distinguished them were dead ..." (1964: 186).[1]

This epoch in British history (1754–1783) has been generally described as one of tight governmental control by an aristocratic clique (Judd 1972; Cannon 1984; Holmes and Szechi 1993). Although it is true that the system was "government by a few", it was not always the same few who were in power. Instead, power rotated among different factions that represented different interests within the elite. Occasionally, such differences were regionally based, and at other times they were associated with specialized activities, such as commerce. No faction achieved continuous

[1] For a very similar characterization, see Palmer (1959), pages 149–153.

predominance; the political environment was instead characterized by constant realignments between these factions. Temporary alliances were constantly made and broken as circumstance and advantage dictated (Namier 1957; Speck 1977). This situation was reflected in the House of Commons. The social backgrounds of the MPs were mostly homogeneous; yet, House membership included merchants, financiers, and land owners. These politicians usually identified themselves with some political current, such as *Court* or *Country*. No modern-day party organizations, however, existed until the onset of the twentieth century. Instead, political loyalties emerged mostly out of networks of personal relationships and the distribution of positions and sinecures in the national and provincial bureaucracies (Namier 1957; Palmer 1959; Speck 1977; Cox 1987).

The lack of programmatic parties was reinforced by the persistence of personalism in Britain. To be sure, this old political tradition continued with the *parliamentarization* of British politics. In fact, the preponderant role of prime ministers exacerbated the personalistic nature of political competition. The ascendancy of ministerial power was established by the premiership of Sir Robert Walpole. Seated in the House of Commons, as first lord of the Treasury and chancellor of the Exchequer, Walpole inaugurated the dual function of "minister with the King in the House of Commons," and "minister of the House of Commons in the Closet" (Sedgwick 1970). His influence in each place was strengthened by his influence in the other.[2] The appointment of the Duke of Newcastle in 1754 represented an attempt to revert to the pre-Walpole type of prime minister. Nonetheless, the norm that ministers should defend in the House of Commons all the actions of the government had been established by this time.

The extinction of party distinctions and the increasing role of parliamentary accountability posed a serious challenge for orderly and stable government in eighteenth-century England. In particular, these factors fueled the underlying tension between leaders of the House of Commons, who continuously attempted to force the King to take their advice, and the King, who would attempt to control the assembly directly (Cox and Morgenstern 2002). The lack of party divisions in the House of Commons also

---

[2] As Sedgwick (1970) notes, before Walpole, the King was still the effective head of the government. Ministers regarded and referred to him as their "Master" and themselves as his "servants". The "Closet", where the most important of them worked with him, was a higher level than the Cabinet. The sign of real ministerial power was "habitual, frequent, familiar access" to the King.

meant that the behavior of individual legislators was quite unpredictable. Namier and Brooke contend that the fact that an MP was "... classed as a Tory in 1754 or 1761 is no guide to what his subsequent conduct would be or what attitude he would take when the American problem came before Parliament ..." (1964: 188). It is thus unsurprising that in this era of personal parties, the most significant sources for the actual affiliations of MPs were parliamentary lists that either purported to show how individuals voted in a particular division, or else attributed to them a specific party label. Compilers were frequently frustrated by the elusiveness of MPs' political allegiances; even experienced parliamentary managers were incapable of gauging MPs' attitudes. This frustration was expressed by William Pitt on October 3, 1754, when he wrote about the newly elected House of Commons: "They are not disciplined troops, and he must be an able general indeed who can answer for them." (cited in Namier and Brooke, 1964: 194).

Dealing with the "whims and caprices" of Parliament required more than patience, however. The methods used by the King and ministry to secure a responsive legislature can be summarized in one word – *influence*. In Palmer's words, "... it was this influence that made possible the effective functioning of government under a constitution characterized by separation of powers ..." (Palmer 1959: 150). Influence meant primarily patronage, the award of honors, titles, promotions, pensions, and sinecures. And, as odd as it may seem by today's standards, the exchange of legislative support in return for these emoluments was amenable to the political class. Neither the House of Lords nor the House of Commons questioned the practice of providing for MPs at the public expense. In the eighteenth-century view, the executive, which was responsible for the business of the nation, consisted of the King and his Ministers, and the role of the legislature was to advise the King and control his servants. Right-minded MPs were expected to cooperate with the government so long as their conscience permitted (Namier 1957). Hence, it was viewed as perfectly reasonable that those who dedicated their time and fortune to service the government should be entitled of the rewards that were at its disposal.

On the other hand, it was widely accepted that such emoluments should not deprive MPs of their independence. As Namier (1957) notes, around 1750, even Cabinet ministers could speak and vote against government measures. The one factor that place or office precluded was systematic opposition. At present times, the analogous situation would be that of a legislator who accepts from her party organization payment of expenses incurred from her campaign. As a rule, such legislator must vote with her party, unless it would be unconscionable for her to do so.[3]

Although officeholders and pensioners represented a high proportion of the active MPs, these emoluments did not provide the government with an 'automatic majority' (Holmes and Szechi 1993). This view is supported by the evidence of division lists that indicate that the majority of MPs voting with the government held no office and did so through honest conviction (Namier and Brooke 1964: 125). In addition, governments during this period were frequently defeated: "... their majorities depended largely on the support of the independents, and that support could always be withdrawn ..." (Namier and Brooke 1964: 194). It was not officeholders and courtiers, but independents who almost invariably had the final say on the survival of failure of any ministry (Holmes and Szechi 1993). The data compiled by Julian Hoppit also supports the notion that patronage could not control the House of Commons on its own: Between 1760 and 1800, the passage rate of general legislative initiatives amounted to 74.8 percent (Hoppit 1996). As such, the use of influence was, first and foremost, a response to the unpredictability of legislators' behavior. In other words, in the absence of well-structured party organizations, the promise of places, pensions, and contracts to MPs, or threat of their termination, enabled the government to secure the additional votes it needed (Foord 1947; Namier 1957; Palmer 1959).[4]

Indeed, because the matter was essential for governments, it was handled in a systematic fashion. In the words of Sir Lewis Namier (1957: 213):

> ... eighteenth-century Administrations, not being able to control individual Members through a party machine and a party-trained electorate, had to bind their following by honours, places of profit, contracts, and pensions; in these, Ministers had to find the attractive and constraining force to satisfy the self-interest, to tame the exuberance, and restrain the consciences of individual Members, which otherwise would have produced a condition of permanent instability and uncertainty ....

---

[3] In the case of the House of Lords, the number of peers holding government office, court place, or pension gave administrations a majority in a legislative body, which, until the mid-1780s, numbered little more than 200, with far fewer normally attending (Cannon 1984). Still, peers were not particularly good attenders, and many MPs would often remain in opposition to the government while holding offices or positions of trust.

[4] As Holmes notes, the smooth working of the eighteenth-century constitution owed much to the "... lubricant of 'influence' in preserving good relations between executive and legislature ..." (Holmes, 1986: 56).

The Treasury played the part of a modern party machine. In addition to controlling public patronage, which was distributed to MPs and then to their constituents, the Treasury carried a further source of political power: the secret service money. These funds were entirely at the King's disposal and he was not held accountable to Parliament for their expenditure. Therefore no one, except the persons immediately concerned, knew how it was spent (Namier and Brooke 1964). A proportion of this money went to genuine secret service purposes, but the funds were also used to dole out pensions to MPs. A number of MPs held profitable government posts (e.g., a tellership in the Office of the Exchequer), and others held posts that either involved no work or could be performed by somebody else. All of these positions, though, provided decent retirement pensions. Secret service pensions were given in lieu of places to MPs who were in acute financial distress, and were treated in most cases as a temporary arrangement (Namier 1957).

The King's *private accounts*, the books containing the details on the allocation of secret service money, were usually returned to the King and apparently destroyed by him. However, these accounts survived for three periods: when Newcastle headed the Treasury (March 1754–November 1756 and July 1757–May 1762); Rockingham's first administration (July 1765–July 1766); and the last three years of the North Ministry, which lasted from 1779 to 1782 (Namier and Brooke 1964).[5] Thus, this material makes it possible to discern the nature of these pensions and the type of MP who receive them.[6]

According to Namier and Brooke, sixteen MPs were in receipt of secret service pensions in 1762, whereas ten MPs received pensions in 1780. These numbers were not exceeded at any time during this period, and by August 1782, only three MPs were left on the secret service list (Namier and Brooke 1964). The value of these pensions, according to Namier and Brooke, ranged from £500 and £1,000 per annum. The authors also note that these pensions were not paid automatically; instead, the recipients applied each quarter to the first lord of the Treasury. In addition, it was exceptional for an MP to be allowed to retain his pension after he left the

---

[5] According to Namier and Brooke (1964) there are also extant fragments of Grenville's secret service accounts, a list of secret service pensions compiled by Shelburne in August 1782, and one or two lists of similar kind.

[6] Unfortunately, a complete list of MPs who received secret service pensions during the whole era of *personal parties* cannot be compiled. It is also impossible to match the recipients of these pensions with how they voted in particular divisions with pinpoint accuracy.

House, and it was understood that he would cease to apply for the funds if he entered the opposition (Namier and Brooke 1964: 125).

A long-standing controversy surrounding the nature of these payments abounds. According to some descriptions, secret service money was used to buy votes in the House for specific divisions. For example, Horace Walpole referred to the buying of votes in connection to the divisions on the Peace Preliminaries in December 1762. By his account, Henry Fox,

... leaving the grandees to their ill humor ... directly attacked the separate Members of the House of Commons; and with so little decorum on the part of either buyer or seller, that a shop was publicly open at the Pay-Office, whiter the Members flocked, and received the wages of their venality in bank-bills, even to so low a sum as two hundred pound for their votes on the Treaty .... (cited in Namier, 1957: 181)

However, Namier is reluctant to take such allegations as proof of vote buying. In his interpretation, the fact that the "... vast fund of Parliamentary corruption called 'secret service money'... [was] ... surprisingly small, a mere supplement to places and other open favours ..." means that "... there was more jobbery, stupidity, and human charity about it than bribery ..." (Namier 1957: 234). It is beyond the scope of this book to resolve the controversy.[7] In light of the arguments presented in the previous chapter, however, it is precisely due to their limited scope and the modesty of their amounts that the secret service funds served the purpose of facilitating the passage of controversial legislation. The fact that these funds were disbursed with absolute discretion, and that their recipients were among the neediest of legislators, suggests that they were ideally suited to buy the support of potentially decisive legislators. In addition, as Chapter 3 demonstrates, if a government engages in a vote-buying strategy, it would need to buy just a few votes to craft a minimum winning coalition. Secret service payments should thus be concentrated in a few MPs and be relatively modest in monetary terms.

At the time of Newcastle's first term at the Treasury (March 1754–November 1756), the government's supporters in the House of Commons numbered as many as 368. Supporters included members of the court and treasury party, of whom 170 where employed by the crown, and some 198 independents. The opposition at that time could roughly be divided into two groups of Tories and Country Whigs. The former consisted of

---

[7] Readers interested in the controversy about the nature of these payments should consult Namier (1957), Palmer (1959), White (1968), Owen (1975), Cannon (1984), and Holmes and Szechi (1993).

approximately 106 members, whereas the latter numbered 42 at most. Finally, 26 MPs were classified as *uncertain* in Lord Dupplin's contemporary estimate (cf. Holmes and Szechi 1993: 362). Had the Minister's supporters held together like a well-organized party, they would have been an invincible majority. Because the votes of officeholders and courtiers could not be completely taken for granted, however, a parliamentary majority on paper was not enough to control the House of Commons.[8]

The Duke of Newcastle was certainly aware that government's supporters were a notoriously fickle lot. The general election of 1754 gave him a majority of more than 200 members. According to Newcastle, "... The Parliament is good, beyond my expectations, and I believe that there are more Whigs in it, and generally well dispos'd Whigs than in any Parliament since the Revolution ... The great point will be to keep our friends together, and that they should do right, when they are chose ..." (cited in Namier 1929: 590). Nevertheless, keeping the group of friends together proved to be challenging, as divisions on specific questions were not exactly partisan. As a case in point, on March 1756, a motion for the second reading of the highly unpopular Plate Bill carried an unexpectedly narrow majority of nine votes, 129 to 120 (Namier 1929). A straightforward way to assess the "cost" Newcastle paid to muster sufficient support for his measures is to examine the records of votes for each MP during his tenure in office. Whenever a division or roll-call vote was taken, a list of MPs who voted "aye" or "nay" was generated.[9] For the period between 1747 and 1762, the only complete analysis of a vote is the so-called *Mitchell Election* division list (Colley 1976). The list records the critical vote in the Commons on March 24, 1755, by which Robert Clive, elected to the borough of Mitchell in 1754, was disqualified. On March 12, the committee of elections decided in favor of sitting members, Clive and John Stephenson (who were supported by the Fox-Bedford-Sandwich group) by a vote of 158 to 141. Twelve days later, the two MPs

---

[8] As Speck notes, Pitt appreciated this when he warned Newcastle not to rely on a paper majority: "Indeed, my Lord, the inside of the House must be considered in other respects besides merely numbers, or the reins of government will soon slip or be wrested out of any minister's hands." (cited in Speck 1977: 264).

[9] These lists are a great source of information except for two caveats. First, divisions were not always taken for the votes on bills, even very important bills. A division was taken only if there was a challenge to the conclusion of the Chair as to a aye or nay voice vote. Second, the British Parliament did not start keeping an official record of MPs' votes until 1836. Therefore, before that date, all records were unofficial lists, usually published in newspaper accounts or in random letters and manuscripts.

were disqualified in favor of the treasury candidates, Richard Hussey and Simon Luttrell. As Colley (1976) notes, the list was compiled in and for the opposition interest. In fact, several MPs who did not support Clive and John Stephenson were described as "enemy."

The division list shows 209 MPs as having voted for Newcastle's candidates, whereas 185 members are listed as supporting Clive and Stephenson. The list also gives 164 absentees, but 22 of them were actually in the House of Commons during the session and only later decided to go home early before the division. Two additional MPs were listed as absent only in the sense that they could not vote: Sir Arthur Onslow in his capacity as Speaker and Robert Clive because the issue was put in his name (Colley 1976). Once these 24 MPs are appropriately accounted for, the number of legislators who did not attend the session was 140, roughly 25 percent of the House. This figure was a relatively low one for the 1750s: As Thomas (1971) notes, contemporaries regarded an attendance of more than 400 as a very full House.

The high attendance of MPs at the Mitchell debate reflects the great importance of the issue. It also indicates that when the House of Commons was in session on March 24, 1755, there were 416 MPs who were eligible to cast a vote. The Newcastle administration thus needed at least 209 to vote in favor of its preferred candidates. And this is exactly what took place: at the end of the session, Hussey and Luttrell received 209 votes.

More importantly, an examination of legislators' votes suggests that, as the theory presented in this book predicts, the government was able to create a minimum winning coalition by buying eight votes and then benefiting from the "bandwagon" effects. According to the Mitchell Election list, fourteen MPs who were present at the session were in receipt of secret service pensions. Still, these votes alone could not have mustered enough support for the government's proposal. In fact, only eight of these legislators voted with the government. On the other hand, the list also identifies twenty two legislators who changed their votes, when compared to the votes cast on March 12 in the committee on elections. Eight out of the 13 MPs who originally voted in favor of Clive and Stephenson supported Newcastle's candidates on March 24, while the remaining five abstained. Hussey and Luttrell also received seven votes from MPs who had not voted in the committee, and another legislator who also did not vote in the committee abstained from voting on March 24. Finally, one MP who voted against Clive and Stephenson in the committee abstained the day of the division. By this account, the government picked up 15 votes in favor of its preferred candidates from MPs who had previously supported Mr. Clive and Mr. Stephenson.

In terms of the discrepancy between attendance and voting, the list identifies not only those MPs who left the House but also their vote intention should they have decided to stay. Identifying their vote intentions was achieved through the custom of pairing–a practice that began as an informal way for MPs to be present at the debate and go home early before the division. According to the pairing norm, each MP who wished to leave the House before a question was put to a vote should form a "pair" with an MP on the opposite side and depart together (Thomas 1971). Therefore, the twenty-two MPs who were absent at the time of the vote included an equal number of supporters of the government's candidates and of Clive and Stephenson.

By the time the motion was presented to the House for a vote, the Newcastle administration secured eight votes from the group of legislators who were in receipt of secret service pensions, and another fifteen from MPs who changed their votes between the March 12 and March 24 sessions. But the motion passed by twenty four votes, indicating that the government swayed one additional vote away from the opposition. According to the list, which recall was compiled by the opposition, Edward Smith from Leicestershire "... came to town to vote for us ..." but voted for Hussey and Luttrell. Indeed, on March 25, the day after the division, Edward Digby noted that the opposition should have carried the measure "... if all who were there had voted according to promises and separate inclinations ..." (cited in Colley 1976: 91). As Colley notes, Smith was probably one of the defaulters that Digby lamented.

The analysis of the Mitchell Election division list thus corroborates the notion that when governments engage in vote buying, winning coalitions will not be oversized. With respect to the MPs included in the winning coalition, no historical evidence exists to suggest that members of the opposition received bribes to change their votes. Those legislators who received secret service pensions are nonetheless worthy of examination. Four MPs, Thomas Fane, Soame Jeyns, William A'court-Ashe, and George Mackay, casted votes against Newcastle's candidates, despite being government's pensioners. These recipients were hardly the neediest of legislators. Fane received a one-time £200 pension after his brother Francis relinquished a Commissionership on the Board of Trade in December of 1755. Jeyns received a pension between 1754 and 1756 (£600 per year) until he was appointed Commissioner for Trade and Plantations. Likewise, Mackay received a modest pension for two years (£300 per year) until he was appointed Master of the Mint of Scotland in 1756. While A'court-Ashe received an annual pension of £500 between 1756 and 1762, he seemed to be so indifferent to the money that "... sometimes for two years he did not trouble to draw it ..." (Namier 1957: 218). Coincidentally, the two pensioners casting absentee votes, Thomas Brerenton-Salusbury and Sir William Middleton, died shortly after the vote took place and thus did not receive multiyear pensions.[10] In contrast, the eight MPs who voted in favor of the government's candidates received secret service pensions throughout Newcastle's administration, and, with the exception of John Buller, these sums were not in exchange for salaries as a government's placeman. As such, these legislators received, on average, £2,712 between 1754 and 1762, compared to average payments of £1,720 made to the group of pensioners who did not vote in favor of Hussey and Luttrell.

Turning now to the case of Rockingham, few divisions took place during his first administration. According to contemporary lists, the government party was about 220 strong; the opposition was comprised of 150 members, and about 180 MPs were attached to neither government nor opposition (Namier and Brooke 1964). Consequently, the mass of uncommitted MPs usually held the balance in the House, which rendered secret service money useful. During the last years of the North Ministry, the uncommitted MPs gained even more prominence. Because the war in America united all the opposition parties, by the end of the administration, there were 241 MPs who supported the government, 237 who voted with the opposition, and only 31 uncommitted legislators (Namier and Brooke 1964). Not surprisingly, most of the divisions during this period were decided by very narrow margins.

Table 7.1 presents summary statistics for fifty five salient divisions that occurred during North Ministry's last three years (March 1779–March 1782).[11] The data indicate that the mean attendance at the time of casting a vote in a division (net of absentees and paired votes) consisted of roughly 205 MPs, including a minimum of 39 on June 28, 1780 and a maximum of 467 on March 15, 1782. Notice also that the average margin by which divisions were decided was thirty two votes, one more vote than the number of uncommitted legislators.

---

[10] Thomas Brerenton-Salusbury passed away on March 9, 1756. Sir William Middleton died on September 28, 1757; but the last yearly payment was made to him by Newcastle on May 21, 1756.

[11] These divisions are included in the databases compiled by Donald E. Ginter (1995) and by Julian Hoppit (1996).

Table 7.1. *Divisions in Commons (1779–1782)*

	Mean	Standard Deviation	Minimum	Maximum
Total Number of Votes	205.6	151.82	39	467
Margin	32.7	27.2	1	108

Notes: This table presents summary statistics for 55 salient divisions that occurred during North Ministry's last three years (March 1779–March 1782). The data indicate that the mean attendance at the time of casting a vote in a division (net of absentees and paired votes) consisted of roughly 205 MPs, including a minimum of 39 and a maximum of 467. They also reveal that the average margin by which these divisions were decided was 32 votes. Given that fewer than 5 active MPs were left on the secret service list by March 1782, this evidence suggests that the North government benefitted from "bandwagon" effects throughout the minister's tenure. Data reported in Ginter (1995) and Hoppit (1996).

Given that most divisions were decided by an average majority of thirty-two votes, even though fewer than five active MPs were left on the secret service list by March 1782, the evidence in Table 7.1 suggests that the North government benefitted from "bandwagon" effects throughout the minister's tenure. An examination of the divisions that took place in the last weeks of North's administration lends additional support to this view. On February 22, 1782, the government rejected a motion pertaining to mismanagement of naval affairs with a nineteen-vote majority. Two days later, in the vote of General Conway's motion against further prosecution of the war in America, the North administration survived again, but only with a one-vote majority. A second motion, however, took place on February 27, and the government's position was beaten by 19 votes (236 to 217). Encouraged by this defeat, the opposition proposed a motion of no confidence in the North administration on March 8, yet this initiative was defeated by 10 votes (220 to 218). Finally, on March 15, a motion of censure against North was also struck down, this time by 9 votes (238 to 229).[12] Although the measure was unsuccessful, North wished to avoid being defeated by a vote of no confidence and resigned as prime minister (Ginter 1995; Namier and Brooke 1964).

7.2 SAY CHEESE!

Despite the obvious differences between eighteenth-century Britain and twentieth-century Peru, several features charactering politics in the Hannoverian period can be applied to the Fujimori era. Most notably,

---

[12] The four legislators included in the list of MPs who were in receipt of secret service pensions during North's tenure – John Mayor, George Augustus Selwyn, James Macpherson, and Sir James Cockburn – voted with the government in all of these divisions.

both polities shared an inchoate party system; and in both cases, governments used public funds to bribe legislators in exchange for their support. Moreover, detailed records of the monetary payments given to members of the Peruvian legislature exist.

Under the rule of Alberto Fujimori, the Peruvian political landscape was almost entirely devoid of party organizations. As Roberts (2006) notes, although parties existed in the legal sense, their organizational development was minimal, informal, and ephemeral, as they lacked the central features associated with modern political parties. Most parties had no registered members or identifiable ideological position; parties, therefore, served as labels rather than political organizations. The inchoateness of the party system was far from accidental. Peru's pre-Fujimori parties were renowned for personalism, volatility, and a lack of institutionalization (Stokes 1995). Nevertheless, much of the party system's decomposition can be traced to the early 1990s and Fujimori's outsider attack on the Peruvian political establishment (Stokes 2001). Following his election on July 28, 1990, Fujimori quickly demobilized his Cambio 90 party, which he hastily assembled with his collaborators in the months preceding the election. He also fired the party's secretary-general, closed its central office, and resisted policy input from Cambio 90's parliamentary bloc (Roberts 2006). Fujimori's final attack on the *partidocracia* ("partyarchy") occurred in April 1992, as he mounted a coup against its own government (autogolpe) and dissolved the Peruvian Congress. Three years later, he contested the presidential elections as the candidate of a new "party" known as Nueva Mayoría (New Majority). Yet, after his successful reelection to a second term, Fujimori declared that democracy based on parties was officially dead in Peru (Conaghan 2005). In an an interview with the *Houston Chronicle*, he offered his philosophy on politics and democracy:

Mine is the politics of anti-politics. The priority is the national interest (with) management leaders, honorable people. Democracy no longer should include the participation of political parties. This (new Peruvian) model is going to be reproduced in other places because the people are fed up with the manipulations of the leadership of the political parties. They make deals between themselves behind the backs of the people. This (party-based) system is going to collapse like the Berlin Wall. It's already collapsed in our country.[13]

In spite of his disdain for political parties, Fujimori created a new electoral vehicle to compete in the the 2000 general elections, the Frente

---

[13] Interview by Dudley Althaus in the *Houston Chronicle*, April 16, 1995.

Independiente Perú 2000 (Independent Front Peru 2000). Fujimori failed to win 50 percent of the vote in the first round, but he ultimately prevailed when the opposition candidate, Alejandro Toledo, withdrew from the race prior to the runoff. The congressional elections, which run concurrently with the first round of the presidential contest, produced 52 seats for Perú 2000 out of the overall total of 120 seats in the unicameral congress. The number of seats held by Fujimori's supporters thus fell short of the absolute majority the government enjoyed since the postautogolpe political reconstruction (Roberts 2006). On the other hand, the opposition had a slim chance of securing a stable majority in the congress. As Conaghan (2005) points out, many of those elected were primarily motivated by their own ambitions and had no real commitments to the parties they affiliated themselves with in order to get on the ballot.

Devoid of a solid partisan organization to control individual legislators, and unwilling to govern under the constraints of political compromise, Fujimori resorted to what is now known as Operation Recruitment. He entrusted Vladimiro Montesinos Torres, the head of the country's intelligence service, the Servicio de Inteligencia Nacional (SIN), with the operation.

SIN's main goal was to entice legislators to support the government. Financial incentives, in the form of cash, served as the primary inducement in Operation Recruitment. Recruits were invited to a meeting at the SIN where Montesinos offered money and favors in return for promises that legislators would join the government caucus. Most legislators joined Fujimori's ranks as *transfugas* (turncoats), but a handful were recruited as *topos*, moles who provided information about the congressional opposition and who casted absentee votes when the opposition needed their support (Conaghan 2005). Operation Recruitment underscored the relative weakness of the opposition's political organizations. The deals were consummated in April and May of 2000, during the run-up to the presidential election. Montesinos usually offered "sign-up" bonuses to legislators ranging from reimbursements for campaign expenses to the cost of a new car or apartment. In addition to these initial payments, recruits also received monthly bribes that ranged from ten to twenty thousand dollars. Montesinos pledged that such bribes would continue until the end of Fujimori's term in 2005. In return for these payments, Montesinos asked the *transfugas* to sign three documents: a receipt for the bribe, a letter asking Fujimori to admit him or her into Perú 2000, and a *compromiso de honor* (an "honor pledge") written on official congressional letterhead. To ensure that legislators were not fudging the records, Montesinos had their signatures verified against other official documents. Also, as was later revealed, Montesinos videotaped the meetings (McMillan and Zoido 2004; Conahan 2005).

On September 14, 2000, Fernando Olivera, the leader of a small opposition party known as the Frente Independiente Moralizador (Independent Moralizing Front, FIM), released one of the videotapes. It displayed a negotiation between Montesinos and Alberto Kouri, a legislator who defected from the opposition and joined the government caucus. Montesinos could be seen handing out an envelope with money to Kouri, who then proceeds to place it in his pocket.[14] In the days following its release, the tape was played endlessly on Peruvian television, unleashing a scandal that precipitated the fall of the Fujimori's regime. On November 19, 2000, Fujimori used the excuse of a diplomatic trip abroad to abandon the presidency of Peru, and he faxed his resignation from Tokio's New Otani Hotel (Conahan 2005). Whether the *Valdivideos*, as the videotapes became known, were responsible for Fujimori's fall is still subject to debate among Peruvian scholars. Regardless, what matters here is that the existence of the *Vladivideos* and the bribes' receipts make it possible to identify those receiving payments to join the government ranks, and the "cost" paid by Fujimori to recruit these *transfugas*.

Based on McMillan and Zoido's (2004) estimates, 21 of the 120 members of the Peruvian Congress received monetary bribes. These payments ranged from US$3,000 to US$20,000 per month. Two exceptions were María del Milagro Huamán, a member of Toledo's opposition party who was recruited as a *topo*, received US$30,000 per month, and turncoat Ruby Rodríguez, received US$50,000 per month. Apparently, Rodríguez's bribe was higher than average since she bargained extensively. A Peruvian legislator's official monthly salary was approximately US$4,500 plus US$4,500 for expenses at the time. Therefore, with the exception of Huamán and Rodríguez, most bribes were equivalent to twice the amount of that a legislator would earn legally as an elected official (McMillan and Zoido 2004).[15]

The pattern of bribes, both in terms of those who received payments and their amounts, can be ascertained from Montesinos' testimony.[16]

---

[14] The video can be seen on YouTube: http://www.youtube.com/watch?v=HRfKA0XDYJc.

[15] According to Montesinos, "the conversations with the lady [Rodríguez] were slower, they lasted about three weeks, because she is a difficult person and because her husband, who is the mayor of Piura, was always counseling her" (cited in McMillan and Zoido 2004: 77).

[16] The testimony was given in Peru's Sixth Special Criminal court on July 13, 2001, and is reproduced in its entirety in the final report of the Peruvian Congress's investigation.

Table 7.2. *Factions and bribes under Fujimori*

Group	Size	Average Bribe
Unbribed Government Legislators	46	–
Unbribed Opposition Legislators	53	–
Bribed "Party Switchers" (to Gov.)	10	US$ 34,000
Bribed Government Legislators	6	US$ 17,000
Bribed Opposition Legislators	5	US$ 16,500

Notes: This table displays the pattern of payments made by Montesinos to 21 of the 120 members of the Peruvian Congress between April and May of 2000. It shows the number of bribed/unbribed government/opposition legislators as well as the average payments. At the time of the bribery acts, Fujimori's party held 52 seats. As the table shows, Fujimori bribed 10 members of the opposition to switch parties and join his legislative contingent. This evidence squares well with one of the main ideas of this book: The notion that in the presence of vote buying, winning coalitions will not be oversized (they will be either strictly minimal, or they will include a majority of legislators plus one). Data reported in McMillan and Zoido (2004).

The twelve *transfugas* (turncoats) identified by Montecinos included Ruby Rodríguez de Aguilar (APRA), José Luis Elías Alvaro (Avancemos), José Luis Cáceres Velásquez and Róger Cáceres Pérez (FREPAP), Juan Carlos Miguel Mendoza Del Solar Jorge Polack Merel, and Eduardo Farah Hayn of Partido Solidaridad Nacional (PSN). There were also five members of Perú Posible, Gregorio Ticona Gómez, Antonio Palomo Orefice, Edilberto Canales Pilaca, Mario González Inga, and Alberto Kouri. According to Montesinos, two of these legislators Jorge Polack Merel and Eduardo Farah Hayn, a vice presidential candidate on the ticket of Castañeda Lossio's PSN, did not receive any monetary compensations to join the government's ranks. The other ten legislators, according to Montecinos received an average monthly payment of US$ 34,000.

Montencinos also identified five legislators who were recruited as *topos* (moles). These bribed opposition legislators included José León Luna Gálvez (PSN), Jorge D'Acunha Cuervas and María del Milagro Huamán (PP), and two members of Frente Independiente Moralizador (FIM), Guido Pennano Allison and Waldo Enrique Ríos Salcedo. The average monthly bribe given to these legislators amounted to US$ 16,500. Finally, six members of Fujimori's party also received bribes; they included Rolando Reátegui, Luz Salgado, Carmen Lozada de Gamboa, Manuel Vara Ochoa, Martha Chavez Cossio de Ocampo, and Sobero Taira. Their average monthly bribe was US$ 17,000. Table 7.2 presents the number of bribed/unbribed government/opposition legislators, as well as the average payments.

The pattern of payments squares well with the model presented in Chapter 3. Recall that a main empirical implication of the model is that vote buying does not generate super-majority coalitions. Specifically, a corollary to Proposition 2 is that chief executives may be able to buy a minimum winning coalition, or even fewer votes than those needed to pass an initiative, and have it approved. Moreover, in the presence of vote buying, winning coalitions are either strictly minimal or include ($\frac{n+3}{2}$) legislators. Such assertions are reflected in these data. At the time of the bribery acts, Fujimori's party held fifty two seats in the Peruvian Congress. As Table 7.2 shows, Fujimori bribed ten members of the opposition to switch parties and join his legislative contingent. These *transfuga* legislators provided Fujimori's party the type of majority in the 120-member legislature predicted by the formal model (cf. Comment 2).

According to Montesinos' testimony, the six government legislators who received bribes were actually compensated for their recruiting efforts as opposed to their votes in the legislature. Nonetheless, even if the forty six unbribed government legislators were deemed as unconditional supporters,[17] as defined in the model, then the government bribed ten legislators from the opposition and six members of its own party to muster sixty two votes; this squares quite well with the model's predictions. The data in Table 7.2 are also consistent with the role played by the *topos* (moles) in Montesino's calculations. As previously mentioned, these legislators could be counted on to abstain when the opposition needed votes. Therefore, if the government could ensure a maximum of 115 votes, then it would only require the support of 58 legislators to hold a minimum winning majority. Once again, if one considers the forty six unbribed legislators as unconditional Fujimori supporters, then the government could reach such a majority by adding the votes of the twelve *transfugas* (of which only ten received bribes).

This interpretation can be further validated by examining the behavior of Peruvian legislators in the aftermath of the scandal. After the Kouri tape aired on television, several legislators left the Perú 2000 caucus and became independents. Some were disgruntled Fujimoristas and *transfugas*, others were suspected *topos* who became independents strategically, as a way to disguise their real allegiance and obtain access to opposition information (Aguayo 2004). The distribution of political forces in the legislature resulting from this realignment underscores the decisive role that the *transfugas* played in the preceding months. With fifty four seats, the

---

[17] Indeed, the analysis in Carey (2003) supports this view.

government party lacked sufficient votes to control the legislature. Likewise, the opposition parties needed to persuade the fifteen independents to take control of the Peruvian congress.

On October 13, 2000, the opposition sought to censure the Speaker, Perú 2000's Martha Hildebrandt. Despite the scandal, Perú 2000 secured its control of congress with the support of all its votes and a few from the independents. Only fifty six legislators voted in favor of the censure, whereas sixty voted against it. As Aguayo notes, the most likely explanation for this outcome is that several independents "... at the last minute decided to vote with their old colleagues. The fear of retaliation in case the opposition won this vote, was big among these legislators ... [who] ... knew that they would be the first victims of any witch-hunt ..." (Aguayo 2004: 176).

The influence of Perú 2000 begun to wane a month later. On November 13, 2000, a new censure vote took place. This time, sixty four legislators voted in favor and fifty one one against the censure of the Speaker. Likewise, on November 16, congress elected an opposition legislator, Valentin Paniagua, as Speaker with sixty four votes. The Perú 2000 candidate only obtained fifty one votes. Once again, the *transfugas* held the balance in the Peruvian congress. The headline from *Expreso*, the newspaper most aligned with the government, succinctly summarized the outcome: "*Transfugas* Elect Valentin Paniagua" (cited in Aguayo 2004: 243).

In the aftermath of the videotapes' release, Montesino's calculation that fifteen members of the legislature were needed to obtain a majority of votes was quite accurate. The theoretical model also correctly predicts the minimum amount of legislators that Fujimori needed to secure a legislative majority. Of course, both the need for and the opportunity to buy votes originated in Peru's extremely fickle party system. As in the case of seventeenth-century England, the lack of a party machine posed serious challenges for government control of legislators' behavior.

7.3 CONCLUDING REMARKS

The theory of statutory policy making advanced in this book states that legislators are concerned with both policy outcomes and the position aspect of their voting decisions. An important implication of this characterization of legislative behavior is the notion that vote buying should not be associated with super majority coalitions. The main goal of this chapter was to provide empirical evidence to support this argument. I focused on two historical cases where public records of monetary payments in exchange for legislative support exist.

It is clear from the findings in this chapter that a chief executive interested in obtaining a majority of votes may be able do so by spending as little as possible. In the case of eighteen-centrury England, most divisions were decided by razor-thin majorities, indicating that the votes of the MPs who were in receipt of secret service pensions alone could have not mustered enough support for government proposals. The evidence thus suggests that both the Newcastle and North administrations benefitted from "bandwagon" effects in legislative voting. The pattern of bribes in Peru under Fujimori provides additional support for the notion that a strategic chief executive should only buy enough votes to ensure that none of the cross-pressured legislators who dislike his proposals would be in a position to unilaterally change the outcome. The ten *transfuga* legislators recruited by Montesinos definitively gave Fujimori such reassurance.

The evidence presented in this chapter also buttressed my argument regarding the effect of the degree of predictability of legislators' behavior on chief executives' passage rates. In the two cases examined here, legislators' partisan identities were hardly good indicators of their ideal policies. Thus, this lack of programmatic parties was the main reason why these chief executives ultimately adopted monetary payments to incentivize legislators to support their policies. In contrast to England under George III and Peru under Fujimori, in countries with strong partisan organizations, chief executives can use partisan resources rather than outright bribery to obtain legislative support. This discussion is the focus of the subsequent chapter.

8

Electoral Rules and Lawmaking

The previous chapter examined how governments incentivize legislators to support their policies in inchoate party systems. Because individual legislators cannot be controlled through a party machine and a party-trained electorate, governments tend to use monetary payments to buy votes. In contrast, governments with institutionalized party systems can employ a variety of institutional tools to obtain party loyalty. Specifically, party leaders can exert influence on legislators' behaviors by two avenues: (1) the prospect of nomination; and (2) ideological screening (Londregan 2002). To understand how partisan resources can work as a substitute for outright bribery, this chapter focuses on candidate selection and ideological cohesion, seeking to understand the manner in which party leaders use the *carrot* of advancement and the *stick* of nonadvancement to impose a certain degree of "party unity" on their legislators (Carey and Shugart 1995; Mainwaring 1998; Morgenstern 2004).

I go on to examine the impact of selection rules on legislative behavior. The first section focuses on nomination rules and demonstrates that party leaders can use their control over ballot access to reward voting loyalty and punish legislative dissent. The evidence also indicates that lack of party unity may allow chief executives to form policy coalitions with dissenting opposition legislators, but may also deprive them of support from members of their own party. The aggregate, cross-national level of analysis lends external validity to these findings.

The formal model presented in Chapter 3 focused on individual legislators' voting decisions. To further explore the implications of *ideological screening* on statutory policy making, in the second section of this Chapter, I examine how candidate recruitment in Chile and Colombia affects legislators' preferences at the individual level. The findings suggest that party leaders can effectively use candidate selection rules to recruit individuals with similar preferences. They also indicate that chief executives who receive the support of ideologically cohesive parties enjoy higher legislative passage rates than those who deal with unwieldily legislative coalitions. These individual-level results not only offer support to the arguments presented in this chapter, but also buttress the internal validity of the theoretical model.

8.1 BALLOT ACCESS AND LEGISLATIVE BEHAVIOR

Political scientists have argued that the design of electoral systems can encourage legislators to favor the interests of parochial constituencies rather than those of their party leadership (Carey and Shugart 1995; Ames 2001; Nielson 2003; Wallack et al. 2003; Hallerberg and Marier 2004; Shugart, Valdini, and Suominen 2005). According to this view, national electoral laws that promote intraparty competition encourage candidates to cultivate personal reputations in their districts, whereas laws that preclude intraparty competition strengthen the role of party labels in elections. Electoral systems encouraging intraparty competition are thus also likely to create weak party loyalty, because legislators will challenge party leaders in order to protect their personal reputation when constituency interests conflict with the party line (Mainwaring and Pérez-Liñán 1997; Ames 2001).

The conventional wisdom identifies three institutional factors that bolster the role of national party leaders and reduce the incentives for legislative dissent: (1) strong leadership control over party labels; (2) vote pooling, where votes are counted, aggregated, and translated into legislative seats at the party level and not at the faction or individual level; and (3) a ballot structure that allows voters to cast only one vote for a party list (Carey and Shugart 1995; Nielson 2003; Wallack et al. 2003). This view has emphasized the effect of macroinstitutional variables (electoral rules at the national level) on legislators' incentives. As Mejía-Acosta et al. (2009) note, however, other important causal forces are salient. For example, at the district level, leadership control over the party label along with the district magnitude tend to shape electoral incentives: In closed-list systems, greater district magnitude creates fewer incentives to cultivate a personal vote, but the opposite is true under open lists or faction lists.[1] In the first case, large districts make it more difficult for voters to identify their legislators, and thus credit claiming can be more challenging. But, under open lists, large districts cast a greater number of candidates from the same party against each other, and thus place a stronger premium on personal reputations. Although the literature recognizes these multiple effects as part of the discussion of national systems (Carey and Shugart 1995; Crisp and Ingall 2002), legislators from disparate districts may face different incentives under the same national electoral rules.

At the party level, procedures for nominating candidates can vary across organizations. For instance, in some party organizations, the founder or top leader nominates all candidates and rank-orders the lists; other parties use a convention or a closed primary to settle the issue. In yet other parties, an open primary may define the ranking of the candidates (Alcántara 2004; Siavelis and Morgenstern 2008). As Siavelis and Morgenstern point out, open-list systems provide incentives for candidates to cultivate a personal vote. If district magnitude is small and parties wield significant control over nominations, however, much higher levels of party loyalty and less of a tie to constituents may result, with important consequences for legislative behavior (Siavelis and Morgenstern 2008). Conversely, closed lists may encourage dissent if competitive primaries require the organization of internal campaigns and promote the autonomous actions of legislators interested in building their own political machines.

8.1.1 Cross-National Analysis

How do these party-centered electoral rules affect statutory policy making? As these arguments demonstrate, the strength of party loyalties can be observed through several factors. Specifically, party unity is easier to achieve and maintain in countries where candidate selection and ballot access are in the hands of the party leadership. Chief executives who enjoy a majority of seats in the legislature may use these institutional tools to

---

[1] Following Mejía-Acosta et al. (2009), I use "closed lists" exclusively to refer to electoral systems where parties present a fixed ballot, votes are pooled across the whole party, and voters cast a single vote. If leaders do not control access to ballots, pooling takes place at the subparty level, and voters cast a single vote (e.g., Colombia before 2006), I refer to "faction lists" (even though lists are "closed" and the allocation of seats may follow a Hare procedure). The term "open lists" is reserved for systems in which parties present a single ballot that can be disturbed by voters, pooling takes place at the level of the party, and voters cast multiple votes (if voters cast a single vote, I refer to lists as "unblocked").

suppress legislators' propensity to dissent and thus get their bills approved. Party-centered electoral rules, however, can generate an opposite effect on passage rates when the chief executive's party is in the minority. If a chief executive faces a unified opposition in the legislature, she may find it difficult to achieve additional support for her initiatives by targeting individual legislators (Linz 1994; Shugart 1998).

Figure 8.1 presents the comparative performance of all democratic chief executives using the box score measure.[2] The data are presented using a boxplot to facilitate these comparisons.[3] The observations are classified according to the majority or minority status of the government and the type of electoral rules. Specifically, I used the data collected by Johnson and Wallack (2009) to assess the amount of party control over candidates' access to a competitive position on the ballot. If individual candidates face few or no legal impediments to appear on the ballot, I stipulate that they possess *unrestricted access* to a party label. These situations occur under single-member districts if parties allow independent candidates and/or use primaries to select candidates. In contrast, candidates face restrictions if: (1) parties control access to the ballot, even if they do not control the order in which candidates will receive seats. These situations arise under open lists where intraparty preference votes significantly influence candidate selection, and under single-member districts where parties control access to the list. (2) Parties control access to ballots as well as the order in which individuals fill the seats won by the party. These situations include closed-list multimember districts and open-list multimember districts with little or no de facto change in list order (Wallack, et al. 2003; Johnson and Wallack 2009).

Note that under majority governments, the observations do not exhibit as much variance as they do for minority ones. Moreover, under both parliamentarism and presidentialism, the box scores of majority governments tend to surpass the sample average of 75 percent, irrespective of the electoral rules. In contrast, a considerable difference emerges between the performance of minority chief executives facing legislators with unrestricted ballot access and those operating under party-centered electoral rules. Under minority governments, box scores are higher when parties have little control over individual candidates' access to a competitive

---

[2] See Chapter 4 for a discussion of how the measure is constructed and Chapter 5 for a description of the sample.

[3] Each box extends from approximate first to third quartiles, and observations more than 1.5 interquartile range beyond the first or third quartile are plotted individually.

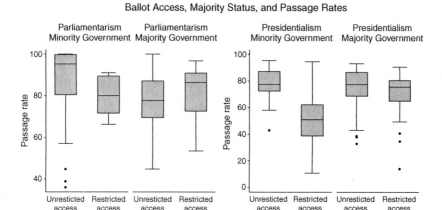

Figure 8.1. Electoral rules and passage rates.
Notes: Variation in chief executives' box scores under different constitutional structures, government status, and ballot access rules. The box score measure is calculated as the percentage of executive initiatives that are approved by the legislature over a period of time. The data are displayed using a boxplot. Each box extends from approximately the first to third quartiles. Observations more than the 1.5 interquartile range beyond the first or third quartile are plotted individually. The data reveal that box scores are higher under minority governments when parties have little control over individual candidates' access to a competitive position on the ballot. Information about the composition of the sample and the sources from which the data were obtained are listed in Appendix B. I used the data collected by Johnson and Wallack (2009) to assess the amount of party control over candidates' access to a competitive position on the ballot (see main text). Data on constitutional structures reported in Przeworski et al. (2000) and Cheibub et al. (2010). Data on government status reported in Cheibub et al. (2004).

position on the ballot. In fact, minority governments with restricted ballot access fare quite badly. The notion that party-centered electoral rules negatively affect passage rates when the chief executive's party is in the minority is thus supported by the evidence.

As previously shown, however, chief executives' box scores differ in parliamentary and presidential systems. The evidence from Chapter 5 indicates that chief executives under parliamentarism exhibit higher legislative passage rates than their presidential counterparts. It also suggests that, on average, chief executives possess higher box scores when cabinet posts are controlled by a single party rather than by a coalition of parties. These findings are buttressed by the multivariate analysis presented in the same chapter. The results indicate that, *ceteris paribus*: (1) a strong relationship exists between a chief executive's passage rate and his or her country's constitutional structure; (2) passage rates are lower when a multiparty coalition rather than a single-party government is in power; (3) chief executives' box scores are higher under electoral systems in which legislators represent a "national" rather than a "local" constituency. To properly evaluate how party-centered electoral rules affect chief executives' lawmaking abilities, it is thus necessary to account for these possible confounding effects.

Figure 8.2 presents the estimated effects of seat shares on box scores in a multivariate context. To generate these results, I used the following approach. First, as in Chapter 5, I performed a logit transformation of my dependent variable, the proportion of bills initiated by chief executives and approved by the legislature of their respective countries. Next, I regressed these box scores on several explanatory variables using ordinary least squares (OLS). These explanatory variables include the government's seat share and its coalition status, as well as the country's constitutional structure and its electoral institutions (see Appendix C for more details).

The dashed line in Figure 8.2 indicates the conditional effect of seat shares when individual candidates face few or no impediments to appear on the ballot. The solid line in Figure 8.2 illustrates the marginal effect of restricted ballot access across the observed range of government seat shares. The dotted lines represent 95 percent confidence intervals around these estimates.

Ballot access produces no discernible effect on a chief executive's legislative passage rates when the government controls a majority of seats in the legislature.[4] The effect of party-centered electoral rules, however, is both clear and pronounced when the chief executive's party is in the minority: (1) when individual candidates instead of parties control access over the ballot, chief executives' passage rates depend little on government's seat shares; (2) in contrast, when ballot access is more restrictive, legislators are more beholden to their parties, with resulting difficulty for chief executives in the legislative arena.

The results presented in Figure 8.2 lend credence to the notion that party leaders can use institutional carrots and sticks to reward voting loyalty and punish dissent. As an additional check, I conduct another test to ensure that the findings are not an artifact of parliamentary democracies

---

[4] It should be noted, though, that box scores are much higher when the government controls more than 90 percent of the seats in the legislature and candidates face significant impediments to appear on the ballot.

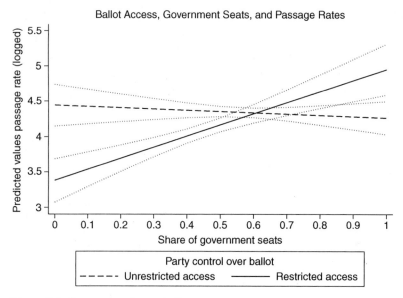

Figure 8.2. Party control over ballot.

Notes: This graph presents the estimated effects of seat shares on box scores in a multivariate context. The y-axis shows a chief executive's predicted legislative passage rate, and the x-axis represents the share of seats held by her party · in the legislature. The dashed line indicates the conditional effect of seat shares when individual candidates face few or no impediments to appear on the ballot. The solid line illustrates the marginal effect of restricted ballot access across the observed range of government seat shares. The dotted lines represent 95 percent confidence intervals around these estimates. The data indicate that ballot access produces no discernible effect on a chief executive's legislative passage rates when the government controls a majority of seats in the legislature. The effect of party-centered electoral rules, however, is both clear and pronounced when the chief executive's party is in the minority: (1) when individual candidates instead of parties control access over the ballot, chief executives' passage rates depend little on government's seat shares; (2) in contrast, when ballot access is more restrictive, legislators are more beholden to their parties, with resulting difficulty for chief executives in the legislative arena. To generate these results, I regressed the logit transformation of the box scores on several explanatory variables using ordinary least squares (see Appendix C for more details). Data on constitutional structures reported in Przeworski et al. (2000) and Cheibub et al. (2010). Data on government status reported in Cheibub et al. (2004). Data on ballot access reported in Johnson and Wallack (2009).

possessing more unified parties. According to the conventional wisdom, under parliamentarism, the authority of the executive to offer legislative proposals as matters of confidence explains why parties are more unified in parliamentary than in presidential systems (Huber 1996; Diermeier and

Feddersen 1998; Carey 2007).[5] Figure 8.3 presents the effects of party-centered electoral rules, interacted with constitutional structure, on chief executives' legislative passage rates.[6]

The findings suggest that the impact of ballot access on chief executives' box scores is negligible under parliamentarism when the government is in the minority.[7] The passage rates of majority governments under parliamentarism, however, are considerably higher when individual candidates have restricted access to party labels. On average, prime ministers who are backed by a parliamentary majority under unrestricted ballot access rules, tend to obtain passage for 75 percent of their bills. In contrast, when parties possess control over candidates' access to the ballot, the average box score of a majoritarian prime minister increases to 82 percent. This difference is not only statistically significant but also substantively important. Recall that the average legislative passage rate for presidents is 65 percent. Therefore, even if they are ruled by majority governments, parliamentary democracies resemble presidential ones when parties lack control over candidates' access to the ballot.

Turning to presidentialism, the impact of ballot access is more pronounced when the president is in the minority. In this case, though, chief executives appear to enjoy higher passage rates when candidates have unrestricted access to the ballot. The average box score for minority presidents with unrestricted ballot access is 78 percent, compared to only 50 percent when party-centered electoral rules exist. Thus, minority presidents seem to have less difficulty in mustering additional support for their initiatives when partisan control over ballot access is weak. When partisan control is high, in contrast, minority presidents are substantially hindered. Finally, under the scenario of the government controlling a majority of seats, ballot access produces an insignificant effect on presidents' legislative passage rates.

---

[5] In its barest form, as Kam (2009) notes, the argument is that the confidence convention suppresses dissent because government backbenchers do not want to bring down their government and deprive themselves of the privileges of power. Yet, as he also points out, the confidence convention is a heavy-handed instrument, ill-suited for securing members loyalty on an on going basis (and of no use whatsoever to leaders of opposition parties). For another critical assessment of the view that the confidence provision elicits party *discipline*, see chapter 5 in Cheibub (2007).

[6] The models used to generate these results are presented in Appendix C.

[7] A simple comparison of means shows that the average passage rate is almost the same regardless of the electoral rules.

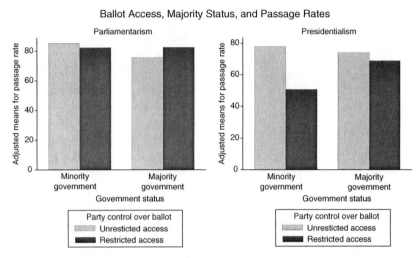

Figure 8.3. Majority status and passage rate.
Notes: This graph presents the effects of party-centered electoral rules, interacted with constitutional structure, on chief executives' legislative passage rates. The findings suggest that the impact of ballot access on chief executives' box scores is negligible under parliamentarism when the government is in the minority. The passage rates of majority governments under parliamentarism, however, are higher when candidates have restricted access to party labels. Turning to presidentialism, minority presidents seem to have less difficulty in mustering additional support for their initiatives when partisan control over ballot access is weak. When partisan control is high, in contrast, minority presidents are substantially hindered. Under the scenario of the government controlling a majority of seats, ballot access produces an insignificant effect on presidents' legislative passage rates. The models used to generate these results are presented in Appendix C. Data on constitutional structures reported in Przeworski et al. (2000) and Cheibub et al. (2010). Data on government status reported in Cheibub et al. (2004). Data on ballot access reported in Johnson and Wallack (2009).

Overall, the cross-national analysis underscores the importance of electoral rules and the relationship between ballot access and chief executives' legislative passage rates. These findings have important implications for the study of statutory policy making. Namely, party leaders can effectively use candidate selection and ballot access to impose a certain degree of "party unity" on their legislators. Moreover, majority governments in parliamentary democracies can use these institutional tools to pass their bills.

The results also indicate that minority presidents face greater difficulty in obtaining support for their legislative initiatives when partisan control over ballot access is restrictive. Another important implication of these findings is that "strong" political parties are a hardly the *sine qua non* of successful governance. Instead, strong parties are like a double-edged sword: They can be helpful in passing legislation when the government is in the majority, but not when the government is in the minority. Hence, a common assertion in the literature stating that new democracies, particularly new presidential democracies, need strong political parties to improve their performance seems to be unwarranted.

8.2 IDEOLOGICAL COHESIVENESS AND LEGISLATIVE BEHAVIOR

As the preceding section demonstrates, party leaders use their control of candidate nominations to reduce the incentives for legislative dissent. Nonetheless, as discussed at the onset of this chapter, voting unity within legislative parties may also be driven by ideological cohesiveness. A group of legislators is *cohesive* when they vote together as a result of common beliefs or ideological affinity (Özbudum 1970; Morgenstern 2004; Carey 2007; Kam 2009). Parties may thus be able to head off dissent before it becomes a problem. In particular, leaders can use the party's candidate selection rules to recruit individuals who share their preferences and to weed out uncongenial candidates before they get to the legislature (Londregan 2000; Siavelis and Morgenstern 2008; Kam 2009). As Siavelis and Morgenstern (2008) note, legislative parties comprised of like-minded individuals are likely to be more united, thereby enabling chief executives to anticipate more accurately their legislative support and boost their passage rates.

To test this hypothesis, I turn my attention to the political systems of Chile and Colombia, two Latin American countries with very different candidate selection processes. In Chile, candidate selection procedures lead to political parties with high levels of ideological cohesion. Colombian legislators, on the other hand, typically rely on their own personal traits to further their careers; therefore, they often see themselves as legislative free agents rather than members of an ideologically cohesive party (Moreno and Escobar-Lemmon 2008; Navia 2008; Siavelis and Morgenstern 2008). Comparing the dynamics of these two countries makes it possible to examine the relationship between ideological cohesiveness and statutory policy making.

8.2.1 Measuring Ideological Affinity

Successfully evaluating the effects of ideological screening on legislative behavior depends heavily on one's ability to measure legislators' preferences. Recovering politicians' ideological positions from recorded votes (i.e., roll-call data) is a frequently used practice not only in the study of the U.S. Congress, but also in comparative politics (e.g., Voeten 2000; Figueiredo and Limongi 2000; Londregan 2000; Ames 2001; Hix 2001; Carey 2002; Desposato 2003; Morgenstern 2004; Rosenthal and Voeten 2004; Jones and Hwang 2005; Poole 2005; McCarty, Poole, and Rosenthal 2006; Alemán and Saiegh 2007). Despite its merits, the use of roll-call data is not without problems. For example, if agenda manipulation and strategic voting exist, then votes may fail to accurately reveal legislators' preferences (Ames 2002; Cox and McCubbins 2005). Other scholars argue that using actions (votes) to impute policy positions can be problematic (Krehbiel 2000). These skeptics do not doubt the role of ideology in influencing legislative behavior, but are concerned over how these ideological predispositions can be measured (Jackson and Kingdon 1992).

These criticisms have led researchers to consider alternative indicators of legislators' preferences. One particularly useful instrument for measuring legislators' ideological positions are interviews with political elites (Katz and Wessels. 1999; Norris 2001; Wessels 2004; Morgenstern 2004; Rosas 2005; Zoco 2006; Alcántara 2008). In previous work, I analyzed data from nine Latin American countries included in the Universidad de Salamanca's Parliamentary Elites of Latin America (PELA) survey (Saiegh 2009b).[8] Specifically, I examined the responses to questions where legislators were presented with the task of locating themselves and other relevant political actors on a ten-point left/right ideological scale.[9]

The data generated by the survey responses can be reliably used to locate legislators' ideological positions in a low-dimensional space in a manner analogous to roll-call-based methods.[10] This approach, however,

---

[8] The PELA project included four waves of surveys in the lower chambers of eighteen Latin American countries since 1994. For a more detailed description of the project, see García and Mateos (2001) and Alcántara (2008), or go to http://americo.usal.es/oir/elites/

[9] The typical format of these questions is: "When we talk about politics, the expressions left and right are usually used. Where would you place < yourself > on a scale where 1 is left and 10 is right?" The questions containing political *stimuli*, such as the country's main political parties or its leading politicians, were phrased in the same way.

[10] I estimated the respondents' location in a low-dimensional ideological space using Aldrich-McKelvey's (1977) scaling procedure to correct for interpersonal incomparability, or *differential item functioning* (DIF). The use of DIF to refer to interpersonal incomparability originated in the educational testing literature: a test question is said to have DIF if equally able individuals have unequal probabilities of answering the question correctly (cf. King et al. 2004). Using the raw data provided by the PELA responses can thus be problematic due to DIF. Fortunately, as King et al. (2004) note, the

has an important advantage. Unlike roll-call votes, legislators' responses to surveys are unrelated to their voting behavior. Therefore, this instrument is not contaminated by the effects of legislative or party institutions, including party discipline, agenda setting, log rolls, and the like (Kam 2001; Morgenstern 2004).

Another issue in measuring spatial preferences using roll-call data pertains to the ability to compare the preferences of decision makers across the different branches of government (the presidency, the legislature, the courts). Addressing various propositions regarding executive-legislative relations, such as the ones advanced in this book, requires that different political actors be placed in a common spatial map. The problem of estimating a common map for a legislature and an executive, however, can be quite challenging (Poole 2005). As Bailey notes, "... no matter how well preferences are estimated within an institution, they are not comparable across institutions without clear points of reference ..." (Bailey 2007: 434).[11] Thus, an additional advantage of measuring spatial preferences using elite data is in its ability to make such comparisons. The representation of each country's ideological configuration obtained using the PELA surveys contains two main elements: the location of key political actors (such as the country's main political parties or its leading politicians), and the locations of the legislators. Therefore, as long as the incumbent president is included among these actors, this information can be used to estimate his or her preferences and legislators' ideal points in a common ideological space.

Aldrich-McKelvey (1977) scaling procedure is one of the most satisfactory approaches to correcting for DIF. The basic Aldrich-McKelvey model assumes that the actual positions of the political stimuli (i.e., key political actors) are the same for all respondents; as such, they can be used as anchors to adjust both actor and legislator ideological positions. Since these actual positions are unobserved, one must assume that legislators have unbiased perceptions of each actor's positions, but that the reported positions are linearly distorted in an unknown, yet estimable, manner. For a more detailed description of their methodology, see Aldrich and Mckelvey (1977); see also Poole (1998) and King et al. (2004)

[11] In spite of some important difficulties, previous research demonstrates that it is technically possible to make such comparisons. Still, the corresponding prerequisite, namely a common policy space for all actors analyzed, can only be estimated if the appropriate ancillary information, such as interest groups' ratings of legislators, is available. For example, Poole and Rosenthal (1997) use interest groups and some common roll calls to combine the two chambers in the U.S. congress. In a similar fashion, Bailey (2007) employs the positions taken by U.S. presidents and members of congress on Supreme Court cases to "bridge" across institutions. Unfortunately, these additional informational requirements are unlikely to be met in most cases outside the United States, rendering these technical innovations generally unusable for comparative research.

8.2.2 Screening and Ideological Cohesiveness: Chile and Colombia

In their cross-national analysis of candidate selection and recruitment in Latin America, Siavelis and Morgenstern (2008) identify four categories of legislators: *party loyalists, constituent servants, entrepreneurs,* and *group delegates.* These legislators are primarily responsive to party elites, constituents, the legislators themselves, or particular corporate groups, respectively. According to Navia (2008), Chilean legislators fit the profile of the party loyalist most closely. In contrast, as Moreno and Escobar-Lemmon (2008) note, legislators in Colombia are, first and foremost, entrepreneurs. Most importantly, these different types of legislators should exhibit varying degrees of ideological cohesion. In particular, party loyalists in Chile should display higher levels of ideological cohesion, whereas the ideological cohesivenss of Colombian entrepreneurs should be distinctively lower.

8.2.2.1 Chile

Legislative elections in Chile are conducted using an open-list proportional representation, commonly referred to as the binomial system.[12] Deputies are elected for renewable four-year terms. Two legislators are elected in each of the sixty Chamber of Deputies districts using the d'Hont seat-allocation method. Seat allocation goes first to parties, then parties allocate seats to candidates according to their individual vote share (Navia 2008). As Navia (2008) notes, this system, which was adopted under Pinochet, helped consolidate an electoral duopoly in legislative elections. Because the threshold to secure the first seat is rather high (about one-third of the vote), Chilean parties have an incentive to form electoral coalitions to pool their votes and obtain half of the seats in every district. Hence, it is impossible to understand Chile's party loyalists without considering the role of coalition politics.

Since Chile's return to democracy in 1990, two legislative coalitions have captured virtually all seats in the chamber of deputies. The *Concertación,* comprised of the Socialist Party (PS), the Party for Democracy (PPD), the Christian Democrats (DC), and the smaller Radical Social-Democratic Party (PRSD), held the majority in the lower chamber of congress and the presidency between 1990 and 2010. The opposition, made up of the Independent Democratic Union (UDI), the National

---

[12] The following description of Chile's candidate selection procedures is based on Navia (2008).

Renewal Party (RN), and the smaller Centrist Union (UCC), also coalesced into a formal alliance, known as the *Alianza por Chile*.[13] Over the the past twenty years, the two coalitions have generally split the two seats in most districts, irrespective of their electoral support. In fact, as Navia (2008) points out, the more competitive the election, the more likely it is that the seats are spilt between the coalitions. As a consequence, strong institutional incentives arise for candidates to be party loyalists. Because party leaders negotiate within their coalitions for the slate of candidates, aspirants must curry favor to secure their party's endorsement. The combination of the electoral rules and the centralized characteristics of Chile's partisan organizations also offer party leaders an incentive to intervene in selection, both to secure good deals from the coalition and to ensure the election of their preferred candidates (Navia 2008). Thus, in some important ways, the Chilean political system allows party leaders to use candidate selection procedures to recruit like-minded politicians.

As previously noted, the implications of *screening* for ideological cohesiveness are clear. Legislative parties full of like-minded individuals should behave in a more unified fashion. In addition, as Morgenstern (2004) points out, the effects of ideological agreement on party unity are often magnified when parties stand firmly in opposition to other parties (i.e., more polarized groups should be more unified than centrists). Centrists, by definition, are pulled in multiple directions and thus may exhibit less well-defined platforms. Ideological cohesiveness, in contrast, usually rises as parties move toward well-defined, noncentrist, positions (Palfrey and Poole 1987; Morgenstern 2004).

The current ideological location of Chilean parties was molded by their reaction to the military government of General Augusto Pinochet. The traditionally centrist DC entered into an alliance with most parties on the left and shared an opposition to Pinochet's regime. Interestingly, these groups had been previously at odds; leftist leaders belonged to parties that, in the early 1970s, endorsed Marxist ideals and supported deposed president Salvador Allende, who was opposed by the DC (Cohen 1994). By the late 1980s, however, programmatic differences between the center and the left were subordinated to achieve a common front in a yes/no referendum on regime change called by the military regime (Siavelis 1997). After Pinochet's defeat in the plebiscite, these parties renewed agreements to support a single presidential candidate and establish a multiparty

---

[13] The opposition coalition was named *Unión por el Progreso* and *Democracia y Progreso* in prior years. The junior partner, the UCC, joined the alliance in 1993.

coalition government. The two main parties that supported a continuation of the Pinochet regime (RN and UDI) also entered into a formal electoral coalition and fielded a common presidential candidate.[14] In addition to partisan positions over the military regime, broader policy goals also factored into the selection of political partners: Both Chilean coalitions, the *Concertación* and the *Alianza*, consist of parties with contiguous ideological positions (connected coalitions).

Figure 8.4 displays the ideological position of Chilean legislators. These measures were estimated using the responses to the PELA interviews conducted in 2002. Legislators' preferences were normalized such that those with more "leftist" views have negative scores and those with more "rightist" positions have positive scores. The data indicate that legislators in Chile are ideologically cohesive. The distribution of preferences for each coalition is unimodal, with peaks to the center-left for the *Concertación* and to the center-right for the *Alianza*.

The pattern in Figure 8.4 further reveals that the center of the distribution is relatively empty and that ideal points of legislators from different coalitions have little overlap. In other words, the ideological makeup of the Chilean legislature consists of two noncentrist coalitions with very cohesive memberships. Therefore, candidate selection rules in Chile do allow party leaders to successfully recruit individuals who share their ideological preferences.

8.2.2.2 Colombia

For most of Colombia's modern history, legislators were elected in proportional-representation districts congruent with departmental boundaries. Deputies were elected using closed-lists and the largest-remainder Hare method (also known as the simple quota).[15] Colombian law, however, placed no restrictions on the number of lists submitted by the parties. This allowed them to present multiple lists, and because votes were not pooled to the party, the system can actually be characterized as a personal-list proportional representation, or more accurately a single nontransferable vote (SNTV) system (Cox and Shugart 1995;

---

[14] The only relevant national party excluded from either coalition was the Communist party.

[15] The description of Colombia's candidate selection procedures is based on Moreno and Escobar-Lemmon (2008). Under the largest-remainder method, the number of votes for each party is divided by a quota representing the number of votes required for a seat. The quota, according to the Hare formula, is given by the number of valid votes cast in the election, divided by the total number of seats to be filled.

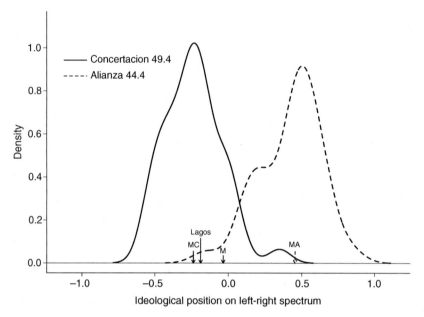

Figure 8.4. Chilean legislators (2002).

Notes: This graph displays the ideological position of Chilean legislators. The y-axis represents the quantity of legislators in a given ideological location and the x-axis shows legislators' ideological positions in the left-right spectrum. The data indicate that legislators in Chile are ideologically cohesive. The distribution of preferences for each coalition is unimodal, with peaks to the center-left for the *Concertación* and to the center-right for the *Alianza*. The evidence also suggests that President Lagos faced a predictable legislature, and that his ideological preferences were close to the location of the median legislator. The measures were estimated using the responses to the PELA interviews conducted in 2002. Legislators' preferences were normalized such that those with more "leftist" views have negative scores, and those with more "rightist" positions have positive scores. The numbers next to the labels of the Concertación and the Alianza indicate the percentage of legislators from each coalition who participated in the PELA survey. The graph also shows the estimated ideological position of president Lagos, as well as the relative locations of the legislator with the *median* position in: (1) the legislature (M); (2) the Concertación (MC); and (3) the Alianza (MA).

Moreno and Escobar-Lemmon 2008).[16] Reforms enacted in 2003 introduced important changes to the electoral system and limited the number

---

[16] In single nontransferable vote (SNTV) system, each voter casts a single vote for one of the candidates competing in a multiseat race with multiple candidates. The *k* highest vote getters are elected, where *k* is the number of seats to be filled per district (Shepsle and Bonchek 1997).

of lists per party. Nonetheless, for nearly forty years, the electoral rules prior to the electoral reform largely shaped the selection of Colombian legislators. Therefore, understanding Colombia's *entrepreneurs* would be impossible without considering the role of personal list proportional representation.

Since the 1840s, two traditional political parties, the Liberals and Conservatives, have dominated Colombian politics. In 1958, after ten years of political violence and four years of a military government, the two parties agreed to alternate power during the four presidential terms between 1958 and 1974; this was known as the *Frente Nacional*. The pact also ensured legislative parity of representation for Liberals and Conservatives (Cárdenas et al. 2008; Moreno and Escobar-Lemmon 2008).

Parity in legislative bodies reduced interparty conflict. However, because partisans competed with one another for a limited number of seats, it actually increased intraparty competition. In order to resolve these internal conflicts and to avoid difficult choices at the nomination stage, Colombian party leaders adopted the practice of submitting multiple lists of candidates for the same race. As Moreno and Escobar-Lemmon (2008) note, this strategy, known as *operación avispa*, promoted *entrepreneurial* behavior among candidates for national legislative bodies.

Under the Hare quota, the formula of largest remainders provided no advantage to lists with either a large or a small proportion of the votes. It thus generated incentives for parties to present multiple lists under the same party label.[17] In fact, parties that submitted multiple lists won a disproportional number of seats, especially in contrast to single-party lists. On the other hand, because a candidate's success was not tied to partisan efforts and intraparty competition was high, partisan affiliation became irrelevant. As such, parties increased the number of lists over time, maximizing their seat share while enhancing the proliferation of so-called electoral microenterprises (*microempresas electorales*) (Moreno and Escobar-Lemmon 2008).

Given the combination of incentives created by the electoral system and the absence of formalized rules regarding nominations, ballot access procedures in Colombia were mostly guided by self-selection. This weakened

---

[17] As Levin and Nalebuff (1995) note, a distinctive feature of the Hare quota is that in a multiwinner election, a united minority can elect candidates in proportion to the size of the minority. For example, in a district with six seats to be filled, any candidate who can obtain 17 percent of the vote will win. Beyond that, however, a candidate ranked second or third by a majority may or may not defeat a candidate with a small but loyal minority base (Levin and Nalebuff 1995).

national-party leaders and resulted in legislative parties with low degrees of ideological cohesiveness. Moreover, as candidates seek to capture "moderate" voters, they usually present themselves as "centrists." Given that centrists often possess ill-defined platforms, these electoral strategies further reinforced the lack of ideological cohesiveness of Colombian parties. Figure 8.5 displays the ideological locations of Colombian legislators based on their partisanship.

Legislators' preferences were estimated using the responses to the PELA interviews conducted in 2002. As before, their ideological positions were normalized such that those on the left of the political spectrum have negative scores and those on the right have positive ones. The ideological heterogeneity of Colombian parties is readily apparent in Figure 8.5. Moreover, a substantial overlap can be discerned in the ideal points of legislators belonging to the two factions of the Liberal party (PLO and PLU) and the Conservative party (PC). Another noteworthy pattern emerging from Figure 8.5 is that Colombian legislators tend to locate themselves at the center of the political spectrum. Most importantly, the evidence presented in Figure 8.5 supports the notion that electoral systems encouraging intraparty competition are likely to create parties with low ideological cohesiveness.

8.2.3 Ideological Cohesiveness and Passage Rates

Having demonstrated the link between candidate selection and legislators' preferences, I now examine how ideological cohesiveness affects chief executives' statutory performance. The analysis focuses on the two distinct contexts discussed above: (1) high cohesiveness (Chile), and (2) low cohesiveness (Colombia).

In Chile, the legislature is primarily made up of *party loyalists*, and levels of voting unity among parties are very high (Carey 2002; Morgenstern 2004; Alemán and Saiegh 2007; Toro 2007). Because Chilean legislators' partisanship is highly correlated with their ideological positions, presidents can anticipate quite accurately their legislative support. In contrast, Colombian presidents face a more unpredictable legislature. The previous analysis reveals a poor correlation between legislators' partisan identities and their ideological positions. Therefore, *ceteris paribus*, the legislative passage rates of Colombian presidents should be much lower than those of their Chilean counterparts. The passage rates of executive-initiated bills in Chile and Colombia lend support to these propositions. Of the 1,113 bills proposed by Chilean presidents

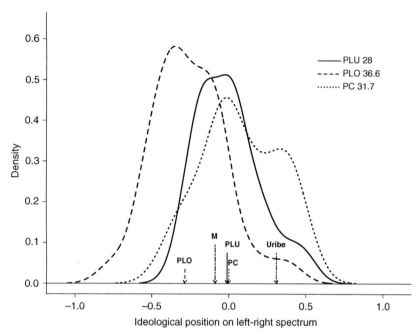

Figure 8.5. Colombian legislators (2002).
Notes: This graph displays the ideological position of Colombian legislators. The y-axis represents the quantity of legislators in a given ideological location and the x-axis shows legislators' ideological positions in the left-right spectrum. The data indicate that parties in Colombia exhibit low ideological cohesiveness. Legislators tend to locate themselves at the center of the political spectrum, and their ideal points have substantial overlap regardless of their partisan identities. The evidence also suggests that President Uribe faced a very unpredictable legislature, and that his ideological preferences were far from the location of the median legislator. The measures were estimated using the responses to the PELA interviews conducted in 2002. Legislators' preferences were normalized such that those with more "left-ist" views have negative scores, and those with more "rightist" positions have positive scores. The numbers next to the labels of the two factions of the Liberal party (PLO and PLU) and the Conservative party (PC) indicate the percentage of legislators from each party who participated in the PELA survey. The graph also shows the estimated ideological position of president Uribe, as well as the relative locations of the legislator with the *median* position in: (1) the legislature (M); (2) the "officialist" faction of the Liberal party (PLO); (3) the "Uribist" faction of the Liberal party (PLU); and (4) the Conservative party (PC).

between 1990 and 2005, 75 percent were approved by the chamber of deputies. In contrast, of the 494 bills presented by Colombian presidents between 1991 and 2003, only 51 percent were enacted by the house of representatives.

An examination of these two countries in greater depth confirms this view. At the time when the PELA survey was conducted in Chile, president Ricardo Lagos faced the most adverse Chamber of Deputies since the country's return to democracy. The ruling coalition and the opposition forces held the same number of seats in the lower house.[18] Many perceived that the government would have to overcome serious obstacles in order to fulfill its legislative agenda (Toro 2007). Nonetheless, the passage rate of the bills introduced by President Lagos in 2002 was roughly 80 percent, which is comparable to those of his predecessors: Patricio Aylwin (75 percent) and Eduardo Frei Ruiz-Tagle (79 percent).

The three *Concertación* administrations negotiated their most important legislative initiatives with opposition party leaders before sending them to the legislature (Navia 2008). As Navia (2008) notes, because the Chilean legislature is comprised of *party loyalists*, presidents could be confident that these deals would be carried out. This account is certainly borne out by the evidence presented in Figure 8.4, where the locations of (1) the median legislator within each coalition, (2) the overall median legislator in the legislature, and (3) president Lagos are identified. It is clear that for Lagos, it was not excessively onerous to craft a cross-alliance majority in favor of change. Given the predictability of Chilean legislators' behavior, and the particular location of the median voter, he could easily avoid legislative gridlock by proposing centrist policies to the legislature (i.e., a policy located at point M in Figure 8.4).

Turning to the Colombian case, as Cárdenas et al. (2008) observe, the meager passage rates of executive-initiated bills in Colombia can be explained by the expansion in the number of candidates following the enactment of a new constitution in 1991. In particular, their analysis indicates that an increase in the number of lists competing in previous elections and a higher effective number of legislative parties lowers the probability of legislative passage by 4.5 and 16.1 percent, respectively (Cárdenas et al. 2008).

The representation of Colombian legislators' ideological positions are shown in Figure 8.5 and illustrate why the proliferation of the *microempresas electorales* made the legislative process so difficult. The scaled positions of (1) the median legislator within each party, (2) the overall

---

[18] The *Concertación* suffered a loss of seats from 70 to 62 versus the 58 seats won by the *Alianza*. In addition, 4 legislators of the governing coalition were suspended due to judicial inquiries, which left the government with the support of only 58 legislators (Toro 2007).

median legislator in the legislature, and (3) the president of Colombia, Alvaro Uribe, are also identified in Figure 8.5. Notice that, unlike Chile, there is a considerable distance between the location of the median legislator and that of the president. As Pachón (2002) notes, Alvaro Uribe's candidacy in 2002 became the axis of a partisan realignment. The previously dominant Liberal Party (PL), of which Uribe was a member before contesting the presidential election as an independent, became fractured. The "officialist" leadership of the Liberals (PLO) openly opposed Uribe's government and his policies. However, he retained the support of a substantial minority within the party, including a majority of the elected Liberal congressmen (classified as "Uribist" Liberals [PLU] by the media). In addition, the Conservative Party (PC) turned into a close political ally of the president (Pachón 2002). Therefore, Figure 8.5 clearly captures the difficulties faced by Uribe in 2002, as an independent tasked with the responsibility of dealing with an unwieldily multiparty coalition in the house of representatives. Not only did Uribe face a very unpredictable legislature, but his ideological preferences were clearly to the "right" of the political spectrum, far from the location of the median legislator.

8.3 CONCLUDING REMARKS

Overall, the evidence presented in this chapter indicates that nomination rules and ideological cohesiveness possess important consequences for statutory policy making. My findings suggest that electoral ballot access is a significant factor shaping party unity. Lower degrees of party unity in the legislature act in two ways: by depriving the chief executive of support from members of her own party, and by allowing the formation of policy coalitions with dissenting opposition legislators.

The analysis in this chapter also underscores the importance of *ideological screening* for statutory policy making. As I argued throughout this book, an accurate prediction of the ideological location of legislators is critical for all chief executives. My spatial representation of Chilean and Colombian legislators in an underlying left-right continuum clearly illustrates the problem confronted by chief executives. By examining these figures, it is possible to appreciate chief executives' vantage point when seeking to predict legislators' voting behavior. In the case of Chile, president Lagos could successfully identify legislators' policy preferences using the partisan distribution of the legislature. However, president Uribe in Colombia was not as fortunate; legislators' partisan identities offered little help in identifying their ideological inclinations.

PART IV

NORMATIVE IMPLICATIONS

9

The Political Gap

More than forty years have passed since the late Samuel P. Huntington argued that Great Britain, the United States, and the Soviet Union belonged to the same category of political systems. According to his landmark expression, in "... all three systems the government *governs* ..." (Hungtington 1968: 1). What he meant was that in these countries, the Cabinet, the President, or the Politburo could successfully enact policy changes. The issue of *governance* or *governability* has been a central concern for both political scientists and policy makers. Yet, scholars also generally focus their attention on the other side of the coin: The question of whether government decisions are attuned to citizens' preferences (Przeworski et al. 1999). Indeed, one of the most important challenges related to the quality of democracy is how to improve governability while simultaneously protecting government *responsiveness* or *accountability*.

Back to Huntington's observation, how can one determine if a government actually governs? In the notorious report to the Trilateral Commission on the "crisis of democracy," Huntington links the notion of governability with the effectiveness of the political system (Crozier, Huntington, and Watanuki 1975). Effectiveness is understood as actual performance and defined as the extent to which the political system satisfies the basic functions of government as perceived by the public (Lipset 1960). Therefore, governability indicates whether "... governments can cope with what they have on their plate ..." (Dahrendorf 1980: 398). In contrast, a society is deemed ungovernable if it cannot preserve itself as a polity due to its inability to protect its integrity, satisfy the needs and expectations of its citizens, and accommodate change.

In the mid-1990s, the scholarly literature emphasized governmental ability to enact policy changes, and the discussion of governability was recast in terms of veto players, legislative deadlock, and democratic stability. A number of studies claimed that extreme executive-legislative conflict inevitably leads to government deadlock, with such state of affairs being dangerous for democracy. For example, Tsebelis (1995:321) argues that "... in regimes where government change is impossible (except for fixed intervals like in presidential regimes), policy immobilism may lead to the replacement of the leadership through extra-constitutional means ..."

Most of this literature, however, was primarily inferential. It did not offer much evidence of governmental performance, and the term was vaguely defined via constitutive referents, such as stability or viability. Thus, the bulk of the research inferred performance from probable causes, like constitutional structures and political fragmentation.[1] As Di Palma (1977) notes, *performance* is closely related with the execution and accomplishment of an intended task. It refers to "... what is rendered, given back, returned, yielded, in short, to outputs ..." (Di Palma 1977: 7). Rules represent one of the most significant outputs of a political system; therefore, rule making epitomizes political performance. I draw on Di Palma's conceptualization to examine the relationship between stalemate, governmental action, and political instability.

I am specifically concerned with the following set of questions: Is it true that polities unable to accommodate change are brittle? How does popular mobilization affect a government's chances of survival in office? And does a high concentration of power over the policy making process lead to protest and dissent? This chapter addresses these questions. Its ultimate goal is to identify what institutional arrangements and practices work particularly well (or poorly) at combining the dual objectives of governability and accountability.

---

[1] The argument concerning the alleged inferiority of presidential systems in generating effective governance goes as follows: (1) Parliamentarism and presidentialism are different: The former is a system of *mutual dependence* and the latter of *mutual independence* between the executive and the legislature. (2) Institutions shape incentives: Presidentialism generates fewer or weaker incentives to form coalitions. (3) Coalitions are difficult to form and only exceptionally do form under presidentialism. (4) When no coalition is formed under presidentialism, a long-term legislative impasse ensues. In consequence, presidential systems that consistently fail to provide the president with sufficient legislative support are unlikely to prosper. As Cheibub et al. (2004) note, however, these assertions are often offered as inductive generalizations while being accompanied by exhortations to collect the data. These are generalizations from observations yet to be made.

9.1 GOVERNMENT PERFORMANCE AND POLITICAL INSTABILITY

As discussed earlier, much of the comparative politics literature has considered legislative impasse as a source of political instability (cf. Third and Fourth French Republics, Italy during the Cold War), and even as a precondition of regime breakdown (Linz 1990, Mainwaring 1990, Stepan and Skach 1993, Linz 1994, Mainwaring and Scully 1995; Linz and Stepan 1996, Huang 1997; Valenzuela 1994). Yet, others have challenged this view. Lupia and Strom (1995), for instance, demonstrate that under parliamentarism, opportunistic parties with favorable electoral prospects will not necessarily dissolve parliament to enhance their power. In the case of presidentialism, critics of Linz's perspective have argued that the reasons offered for the poor survival record of presidential democracies have neither sound theoretical foundations nor any empirical support (Shugart and Carey 1992, Power and Gasiorowski 1997, Foweraker 1998; Cheibub et al. 2004; Cheibub 2007).[2]

Moreover, in Latin America, the military often intervened against a ruling party controlling both the executive *and* the legislature (Pérez-Liñan 2007). Therefore, as Cheibub (2007) notes, presidential democracies are more fragile than parliamentary ones because they typically emerge in countries with a strong military, which places any type of democracy at risk. The nexus between military intervention in politics and democratic breakdown is further buttressed by several incidents that took place in Latin America during the 1980s and 1990s. After 1978, international and domestic factors reduced the incentives for military intervention in politics; as such, the vast majority of presidential crises have not been related to any form of regime breakdown (Pérez Liñan 2007). Instead, a combination of executive-legislative conflict and street protests led to the activation of constitutional mechanisms, such as impeachment, or unleashed unconstitutional actions (e.g., a legislative coup against the president). More importantly, Pérez-Liñan's (2007) analysis of presidential crises in Latin America indicates that the ability of the legislature to remove the president from office ultimately depends on the level of popular mobilization against the government. When presidents are unchallenged by mass mobilization, their chances of survival in office increase. But when a broad social coalition takes the streets to demand the resignation of the president, the fall

---

[2] In Linz's view, presidential democracies tend to be more brittle because they are prone to deadlocks, offer no incentives for coalition formation, and fragment decision making.

of the administration is usually inevitable. Public unrest thus plays an important role in determining which presidents are ousted (Hochstetler 2006; Negretto 2006; Pérez-Liñan's 2007).[3]

Social conflict, turmoil, and even violence can be the direct result of extraordinary problems. Yet, they can also be the product of a government's inability to address such challenges. A government's capacity to solve urgent societal problems usually takes center stage during times of crisis. External or domestic threats may require immediate action by the authorities, and failure to do so may lead to social and political chaos. Similarly, engaging in partisan squabbling during times of economic crisis could generate social and political unrest. The degree of popular mobilization against a government may vary with the number, variety, and severity of these challenges. Nonetheless, a poor performance by the incumbent administration during critical times can incite popular discontent. In practical terms, there should be a correlation between chief executives passage rates and observable manifestations of social unrest such as protests, demonstrations, riots, strikes, road blockages, and so on. In particular, chief executives with higher passage rates should be less likely to face popular protests than chief executives unable to accommodate change.

Political upheaval may also be the product of unpopular policies. As Przeworksi notes, majority rule generates winners and losers, and authorizes the winners to impose their will on the losers, even if within constraints (Przeworski 2009). The losers may try to persuade the government to modify its views, or they may be able to exercise their institutional prerogatives to block some legislation. Suppose, however, that the government is certain that its preferences will triumph in the policy-making process. Then, the political losers might graciously accept their short-term destiny and hope to do better in the future, or they may turn to violence out of desperation. Should the losers engage in the latter, the government can decide to persevere and repress the protests, wait for the protests to subside while tolerating a breakdown of order, or accommodate the demands of its opponents. So, if governments are too powerful within the institutional framework, they may achieve the paradoxical effect of undermining political stability (Przeworski 2009; Scartascini and Tommasi 2009).

---

[3] According to Pérez-Liñan (2007: 187–188), mass mobilization can weaken an elected president in three ways. First, extensive protests may indicate that he or she has lost popular support and thus is an easy target. Second, social turmoil may acquire a violent character. If this is the case, then important political actors may fail to support the president in order to avoid an escalation of social conflict. Third, if mass mobilization is met with repression and human tragedies take place, the government may see its legitimacy eroded, accelerating the president's downfall.

Of course, powerful governments will attempt to control oppositional violence. Both accommodation and repression of opponents will, to some extent, reduce violence (an intended consequence), but at the same time they will also increase policy immobilism (an unintended consequence). Thus, as Lichbach (1984) notes, the goals of political decision makers to simultaneously minimize both violence and policy immobilism are inconsistent with one another. In principle, governments should select an optimal level of political performance by trading off the costs and benefits that come from accommodating and repressing their opponents. This optimal level would depend on the degree of violence and immobilism that the government considers acceptable to its polity. Democratic regimes, for example, tolerate a higher level of opposition than do autocratic ones (Przeworski et al. 2000)

In sum, political instability can be the product of the government's incapacity to solve urgent societal problems, but it can also be attributed to unpopular policies. To effectively cope "with what they have on their plate," governments usually need to make decisions about the form and degree to which they accommodate and/or repress popular demands. However, dilemmas and trade-offs are inevitable because policies tend to affect all aspects of the governability of a polity.

9.2 CROSS-NATIONAL ANALYSIS

To establish how policy immobilism and governability are related, it would be ideal to know if regime stability is threatened when governments are unable to successfully enact policy changes. Unfortunately, endogeneity problems and the lack of appropriate data pose significant barriers to answering this question directly. Nonetheless, I can address this issue indirectly by examining the relationship between chief executives' legislative passage rates and social or political unrest. The arguments developed in the previous section suggest that governability is best served when the government can pass some of its agenda through the legislature and, at the same time, the opposition can realistically object to some of its proposals.[4]

A nonlinear relationship should thus be observed between a chief executive's legislative passage rate and social unrest. Specifically, chief

---

[4] Note that these arguments do not contradict the veto player literature (cf. Tsebelis 2002). As Franzese notes, the veto players approach cannot make any predictions about specific policy outcomes without information about the identity, powers, and preferences of agenda setters, and about the location of the status quo in particular policy-making instances (Franzese 2010: 5).

executives' statutory performance should incite popular discontent when: (1) passage rates are extremely low (i.e., stalemate); and (2) passage rates are extremely high (i.e., lack of accommodation of opposition's demands). In contrast, social turmoil should decrease when chief executives passage rates are at moderate levels.

To evaluate these propositions, I use the box score measure and data on social upheaval collected by Banks (1996). The main variable of interest, *riots*, measures the number of violent demonstrations or clashes of more than 100 citizens that involve the use of physical force. I restrict my attention to democratic countries with a per capita income below $6,055 (measured in 1985 purchasing power parity dollars), as no democracy ever fell in a country with a per capita income higher than that threshold (Przeworski 2005). The sample consists of 292 observations on 32 countries for the 1950–1995 period.[5]

Statistical models commonly use polynomials to describe curved relationships. Hence, I model the relationship between chief executive's legislative passage rates and social unrest by fitting a second-order polynomial on the data.[6] The predictor for a polynomial of order $M = 2$ for covariate x can be defined as

$$\beta_0 + \sum_{m=1}^{M} \beta_m x^{p_m}$$

where the powers p_m are chosen from the set $\{1, 2\}$, x is my box score measure, and the βs are the parameters to be estimated (see Appendix D for more details).[7]

---

[5] The choice of these countries is dictated by data availability. Appendix D provides a list of countries included in the sample.

[6] Polynomial regression may present a number of drawbacks, including undue influence of particular points on certain parts of the curve. In addition, poor fitting models may result if there are a number of turning or flex points (Lambert et al. 2005). Alternatives include regression splines and fractional polynomials. The latter were were first introduced by Royston and Altman (1994) as a method for determining the functional form of a continuous covariate from a flexible range of candidate models. Their use has been advocated as the analysis is no longer dependent on the number and choice of cut points when categorizing continuous variables (Lambert et al. 2005). I used fractional polynomials to model the relationship between my box score measure and social unrest. The results indicate that a second-order polynomial is sufficient.

[7] Given the nature of the dependent variable, the number of violent demonstrations, a count model analysis may be appropriate. I estimated the relationship between box scores and riots using both Poisson and negative binomial models. The estimated number of riots obtained from these models is virtually identical to the one presented in Figure 9.1.

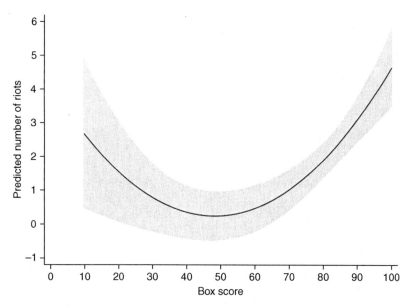

Figure 9.1. Riots and passage rates (democracies).

Notes: This graph shows the relationship between passage rates and social unrest. The y-axis indicates the predicted number of demonstrations and the x-axis shows the box scores of democratic chief executives. The solid line represents the predicted number of demonstrations as a function of the box scores, whereas the shaded areas denote the 95 percent confidence intervals around these estimates. The data indicate that chief executives' legislative passage rates and levels of social unrest exhibit a nonlinear relationship. The predicted number of demonstrations first diminishes and then increases in statutory performance. To generate these results, I regressed riots on my box score measure. The dependent variable measures the number of violent demonstrations or clashes of more than 100 citizens involving the use of physical force. The box score measure is calculated as the percentage of executive initiatives that are approved by the legislature over a period of time. I fitted a second-order polynomial to the data and restricted my attention to democratic countries with a per capita income below $6,055 (measured in 1985 PPP dollars). The sample consists of 292 observations on 32 countries for the 1950–1995 period (see Appendix D for more details). Data on regime type reported in Przeworski et al. (2000). Data on violent demonstrations reported in Banks (1996).

The solid line in Figure 9.1 presents the predicted number of violent demonstrations as a function of chief executives' box scores, whereas the shaded areas denote the 95 percent confidence intervals around these estimates. Chief executives' legislative passage rates and levels of social unrest exhibit a nonlinear relationship. The predicted number of violent demonstrations first diminishes and then increases in statutory performance. Since observations of extremely ineffective governments (i.e., legislative paralysis) are few, the standard errors are large. The relationship between passage rates and social upheaval, however, is pronounced when the opposition poses little chance of blocking the executive's proposals. As Figure 9.1 indicates, developing countries governed by chief executives whose legislative passage rates are above 85 percent are statistically more likely to experience a larger number of riots than those ruled by chief executives with lower passage rates.

This last finding begs the following question: Why would powerful governments fail to control oppositional violence through accommodation? There is strong reason to believe that governments consider the costs and benefits associated with accommodating and repressing their opponents in different ways. Specifically, the level of social unrest considered acceptable by the government likely depends on the consequences of those violent acts. As Przeworski et al. (2000) note, political upheavals affect the economic performance of democracies and autocracies differently. Riots are almost twice as frequent in democracies than in autocracies. Yet, democracies somehow live with social unrest without any economic consequences. In contrast, strikes, antigovernment demonstrations, and riots pose serious economic costs in autocracies. Because autocrats need to rely more heavily on economic performance to give legitimacy to their rule than do democratically elected leaders, autocracies should tolerate lower levels of opposition. However, as Gandhi and Przeworski (2006) demonstrate, it is not unusual for authoritarian leaders to use policy concessions to prevent a rebellion.

To further examine this issue, I perform the same analysis as before, but focus only on autocratic regimes. I include all autocracies in my analysis, regardless of their income level. In contrast to developed democracies, which can survive wars, riots, scandals, and economic and governmental crises, autocracies die at all levels of economic development (Przeworski 2005). The sample consists of eighty four observations on fourteen countries between 1965 and 1995.[8] Figure 9.2 illustrates how the predicted number of violent demonstrations changes across the observed range of box scores under autocracy.

Once again, the relationship between chief executives' legislative passage rates and social unrest is nonlinear. In the case of autocracies,

---

[8] As before, the choice of these countries is dictated by data availability (see Appendix D for a list of countries included in the sample).

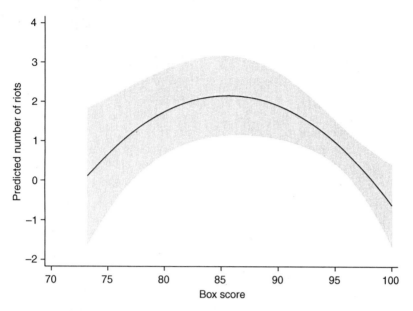

Figure 9.2. Riots and passage rates (autocracies).

Notes: This graph shows the relationship between passage rates and social unrest. The y-axis indicates the predicted number of demonstrations and the x-axis shows the box scores of autocratic chief executives. The solid line represents the predicted number of demonstrations as a function of the box scores, whereas the shaded areas denote the 95 percent confidence intervals around these estimates. The data indicate that chief executives' legislative passage rates and levels of social unrest exhibit a nonlinear relationship. The predicted number of demonstrations first increases and then decreases in statutory performance. To generate these results, I regressed riots on my box score measure. The dependent variable measures the number of violent demonstrations or clashes of more than 100 citizens involving the use of physical force. The box score measure is calculated as the percentage of executive initiatives that are approved by the legislature over a period of time. I fitted a second-order polynomial to the data, and included all autocracies in my analysis, regardless of their income level. The sample consists of 84 observations on 14 countries between 1965 and 1995 (see Appendix D for more details). Data on regime type reported in Przeworski et al. (2000). Data on violent demonstrations reported in Banks (1996).

however, the predicted number of violent demonstrations first increases and then declines in statutory performance. Under autocracies, legislative defeats are extremely rare; as such, the standard errors of the predicted number of riots when the chief executive's passage rate is below 80 percent are large. Still, these findings support the view that autocrats can use legislative institutions to either cement their support or divide potential opposition movements. The link between the box scores and unrest is much clearer when the former are above 80 percent. Social turmoil is highest when chief executives' passage rate is roughly 85 percent, suggesting that autocrats also face the trade-off between social mobilization and legislative defeats. Intermediate levels of statutory policy-making authority may signal to the opposition that the autocracy has lost control. In contrast, above-average box scores (i.e., higher than 93 percent) can be viewed as part of a sustained clampdown on opposition.

9.3 GOVERNING WITHOUT SURVIVING?

The cross-national evidence suggests that governmental performance, defined as the ability of chief executives to enact policy changes through statutes, affects the governability of a polity in complex ways. The findings also lend indirect support to the notion that regime stability is not threatened by ineffective governments. Furthermore, the analysis shows that in the developing world, popular discontent is higher when chief executives' passage rates are extremely high than when they are extremely low. And, if popular uprisings are a necessary condition for regime breakdown, then even deadlocked governments maybe able to survive without governing (Di Palma 1977; Pérez-Liñan 2007).[9] Di Palma's account of the Italian legislative process in the 1970s, as being governed by a political system that simply survived without in fact governing, illustrates this phenomenon. The Italian syndrome Di Palma referred to was a peculiar combination of policy paralysis and political stability. Chief executives were systematically unable to control their own majorities in the assembly, giving de facto legislative veto power to each of Italy's main parties. As a result, lawmaking was limited to those projects that were backed by ample bipartisan supermajorities. This situation, as Capano and Giuliani (2001) note, led to paralysis in the lawmaking process. Nonetheless, neither the political system per se nor the leaders of Italy's major parties suffered much from this lack of effectiveness. In fact, the frequent turnover of Italian prime ministers ensured the persistence of centrist administrations led by the Christian Democrats and the survival of Italian democracy.

[9] Indeed, Pérez-Liñan (2007) concludes that popular uprisings were the only condition necessary to remove an elected president from office in Latin America between 1978 and 2005.

Likewise, Pérez-Liñan (2007) offers a similar account of Colombia under Ernesto Samper's administration. Shortly after his presidential victory on June 19, 1994, Samper was accused of having received campaign donations from the Cali cartel. In December 1995, a congressional committee concluded that the president's direct involvement in the events of the campaign could not be proven. A month later, however, Samper requested that the Colombian congress reopen the investigation after new allegations arose. The president's party, the Liberals, argued that the opposition's insistence on incriminating the chief executive created a "governability crisis." But, without strong public mobilization against the president, the House of Representatives voted 111-43 and acquitted him of all charges on June 12, 1996. The administration's focus on survival thwarted its ambitious initiatives for social and political reform. The economy entered a period of stagnation, and political violence by both guerillas and paramilitaries remained steady. While his administration could hardly be considered a model of policy success, Samper was able to complete his term in office (Pérez-Liñan 2007).

These cross-national findings have another important implication for the study of regime breakdown. Most clearly, they demonstrate that governability is best served in developing countries when the chief executive passes some of its agenda through the legislature but not when the opposition has no possibility of blocking any government proposals. Therefore, democracy is possibly threatened when the government tries to do too much rather than too little. Although the data are inappropriate to test this hypothesis in a statistical fashion, the logic of the argument can be illustrated with historical accounts. These are cases in which chief executives likely perceived legislative activism as a necessary precondition for survival, but soon discovered it to be insufficient. The two historical episodes I use to illustrate governing without surviving highlight the differences between my view and other scholarly interpretations.

9.3.1.1 Allende's Fall

The minority coalition governing Chile from 1970 to 1973 is generally cited as a prime example of legislative impasse. Salvador Allende's attempt at a "constitutional" transition to socialism was beset by executive-legislative conflict. In January 1971, Allende sent congress a proposal replacing "bourgeois justice" with a system based on "socialist legality," in which neighborhood tribunals could rule on issues ranging from petty crimes to land-confiscation issues. The opposition clearly expressed their disdain for the neighborhood tribunals, and to avoid a certain defeat,

Allende withdrew the bill (Horne 1972). Allende's second major act of legislation, a proposal to expropriate copper from the Gran Minería, generated a different reaction in congress. It was ratified unanimously by both chambers of the National Congress in July 1971. Later in the same year, however, negotiations to nationalize several important economic activities turned sour, and the opposition's rather passive resistance in congress evolved into more aggressive action.

The rightist Christian Democrats were confident that economic hardship, anarchy, and instability would favor them in the 1973 congressional elections (Valenzuela 1978). Hence, between 1972 and 1973, opposition parties attempted to block all bills, even the most harmless ones, presented by the government (De Vylder 1976). In addition, the opposition tried to enforce completely new legislation. But Allende vetoed these proposals knowing that the opposition lacked the votes to override them. A combination of all these factors resulted in an almost constant deadlock between the executive and legislative powers (Cohen 1994; Valenzuela 1994; Siavelis 2000).

According to some scholarly interpretations, this episode exemplifies how policy immobilism leads to a breakdown of democracy (Linz 1990; Valenzuela 1994). Still, despite facing a hostile congress, Allende passed more than 100 pieces of legislation in 1971 (Alemán 2009). His passage rate fell precipitously in 1972 (he passed fewer than thirty laws), but as Alemán (2009) notes, he hardly faced complete and absolute gridlock. During his tenure in office, Allende obtained passage of more than 40 percent of all of his initiatives and close to 80 percent of his most important bills (Alemán 2009).

The notion that Allende stood idle in face of congressional opposition also seems unwarranted. Without the passage of any new legislation, and using an obscure law dating from 1932, Allende managed to nationalize 187 firms (including industrial establishments, banks, and media companies) by the end of his first year in office. In addition, a constitutional amendment adopted under Allende's predecesor, Eduardo Frei, allowed the president to appeal directly to the public via a *plebiscito* (referendum) should his legislation be thwarted by a hostile legislature. Hence, even though the conflict with congress increased the illegitimacy of Allende's social reforms in the view of the opposition parties who withheld their consent, it was not enough to block them (Cohen 1994).

As opposition forces found themselves increasingly limited in stopping Allende's agenda in the legislative arena, they took the struggle to the streets. Mass protests, first by middle- and upper-class housewives of

Santiago, and then by merchants, small businessmen, professionals, and white-collar employees, called for Allende's resignation. By September 1973, a truckers' confederation strike that had started a few months earlier finally strangled Chile's flow of supplies, making a major contribution to the crisis atmosphere in which the coup took place (Goldberg 1975).

9.3.1.2 The Fall of Sánchez de Lozada

The deadly rioting in Bolivia and the toppling of the country's government in October 2003 illustrates how an active chief executive may not survive in office, even if the element of executive-legislative conflict plays no central role. After a difficult coalition-building process, Gonzalo Sánchez de Lozada, also known as Goni, was elected president of Bolivia in August 2002. The government coalition included the Revolutionary Nationalist Movement (Movimiento Nacionalista Revolucionario, or MNR) and the Revolutionary Left Movement (Movimiento de la Izquierda Revolucionaria, or MIR). An advocate of free-market policies and one of Washington's most stalwart allies in South America, Sánchez de Lozada faced the opposition of a leftist indigenous movement led by Evo Morales of the Movement to Socialism (Movimiento al Socialismo, or MAS).

Sánchez de Lozada undertook a series of landmark social, economic, and constitutional reforms during his first term as Bolivia's president (1993–1997). He sought to resume his ambitious reformist plan, and in December 2002, completed the first piece of unfinished business from his first administration. Despite opposition from parties outside the government and the MIR – the key partner in the ruling coalition – his proposal to use the proceeds of privatization to assist elderly Bolivians was approved by congress. The honeymoon, however, was short-lived. In January 2003, after a stand-off that saw roads blocked and seven people killed, coca growers gave Sánchez de Lozada an ultimatum. The protesters demanded that the government halt the eradication of coca plants.[10] Sánchez de Lozada rejected the ultimatum and accused Evo Morales (the coca growers' leader) of conspiring to overthrow the government. A month later, in the midst of a grim fiscal situation, the government proposed a tax increase. The *impuestazo*, as it became known, was met with stark opposition from Evo Morales. Acknowledging that Sánchez de Lozada could check his forces in the legislature, Morales promised to take his cause to

---

[10] Coca growers and their supporters also opposed the Free Trade Area of the Americas (FTAA), called for higher workers salaries, and a reduction in congressional pay.

the streets.[11] On February 12, protests by several hundred striking policemen demanding a pay raise and the repeal of the *impuestazo* escalated into a situation of full-scale rioting. Furious demonstrators sacked businesses and government buildings in the cities of La Paz and El Alto. By the end of the day, seventeen people were dead and more than twenty were injured.

Sánchez de Lozada responded to these events with a cabinet reshuffle and also called off the *impuestazo*. Nonetheless, he kept his finance minister, sending a strong signal that he intended to continue with the economic policies that triggered the violent unrest. To make up the revenue shortfall, Sánchez de Lozada proposed an ambitious plan to export natural gas to the United States using Chilean ports in July. The government hoped to use the gas profits to bolster the sagging economy and claimed the money would be invested solely in health care and education.

The gas proposal galvanized the opposition. Figure 9.3 presents the ideological location of (1) the median legislator in each of Bolivia's main parties, (2) the overall median legislator in the legislature, and (3) President Sánchez de Losada in mid-2003.[12] The data demonstrate the isolation of Sánchez de Lozada's political existence during those turbulent times. As a member of congress put it, the government was "... in the cross-fire, from extremists on the right, extremists on the left ..."[13]

Nonetheless, although the government and the opposition had been bickering relentlessly in Congress, with opponents seeking to prod the president into resigning, the biggest threat to Sánchez de Lozada came from the streets. In September, a new wave of heightened protests began. Main roads were blocked and towns and cities were brought to a standstill. Protesters demanded that the government reverse the policy to export natural gas. With popular revulsion growing, the leaders of the parties in the precarious governing coalition announced that they were thinking of leaving the government. On October 6, the demonstrations brought La Paz to a halt. Several days later, the government announced that it would call a referendum on the export of gas. However, this attempt to regain the initiative proved to be "too little, too late." Two days

---

[11] In Morales' words: "They can block us in congress; we are going to block the highways." Quoted in *Latin America Weekly Report* (February 11, 2003, p. 69).

[12] The estimates were recovered with data generated by PELA interviews conducted between July and September 2003 using the procedure described in Saiegh (2009b). Legislators' ideological positions were normalized such that those with more "leftist" views have negative scores and those with more "rightist" positions have positive scores.

[13] These were the words of Luis Eduardo Siles, quoted in the *New York Times* on March 10, 2003.

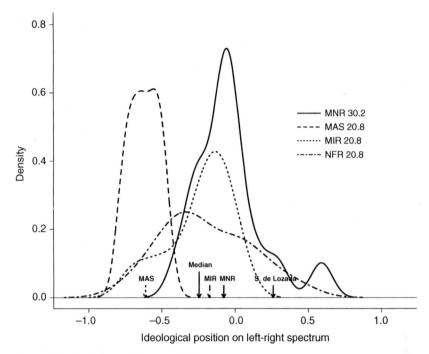

Figure 9.3. Bolivian legislators (2003).

Notes: This graph displays the ideological position of Bolivian legislators. The y-axis represents the quantity of legislators in a given ideological location and the x-axis shows legislators' ideological positions in the left-right spectrum. The data reveals that President Sánchez de Lozada's ideological preferences were on the fringes of Bolivia's political spectrum. The measures were estimated using the responses to the PELA interviews conducted in 2003. Legislators' preferences were normalized such that those with more "leftist" views have negative scores and those with more "rightist" positions have positive scores. The numbers next to the labels of Bolivia's major parties indicate the percentage of legislators from each of them who participated in the PELA survey. The graph also shows the estimated ideological position of president Sánchez de Lozada, as well as the relative locations of the legislator with the *median* position in: (1) the legislature (Median); (2) the Movimiento al Socialismo (MAS); (3) the Movimiento Nacionalista Revolucionario (MNR); and (4) the Movimiento de la Izquierda Revolucionaria (MIR).

later, Sánchez de Lozada presented his resignation to congress and went into exile.

What these two historical episodes show is that unpopular policies rather than policy immobilism brought these governments down. Neither Allende in Chile nor Sánchez de Lozada in Bolivia stood idle. In contrast, both of them pursued bold economic and social reforms – a transition to socialism in one case, market-oriented policies in the other. Both presumably thought that their activism would ensure their survival. It was this persistence, however, that ultimately led to their demise.

9.4 CONCLUDING REMARKS

In his classic treatise on the social bases of politics, Seymour Martin Lipset argues that the stability of any democracy depends not only on economic development but also "... upon the effectiveness and the legitimacy of its political system ... ." (Lipset 1960: 64) From an empirical standpoint, this statement begs the following question: How do we measure effectiveness and legitimacy?

It is tempting to emphasize general consent and participation as a condition of effectiveness. Yet, as Dahrendorf (1980) points out, participation is nice, but it is not indispensable. Instead, it is the possibility of participation to veto developments, to express dissent that should be of concern. Moreover, legitimacy should be measured "... not in terms of the active will of all, or even some fictitious general will, but in terms of doubt, of a perceived dissociation of government action and basic as well as cultural values ... ." (Dahrendorf 1980: 397) When governments violate fundamental societal values, they may no be met with doubts by the majority, but are likely to face dissent from some minorities. Therefore, according to Dahrendorf, it seems that "... the absence of effective protest is good enough ... ." (Dahrendorf 1980: 397)

The evidence presented in this chapter indicates that polities are more stable when the chief executive passes some of its agenda through the legislature. At the same time, however, the opposition must have a reasonable chance of defeating some government proposals. As such, these results lend support to the view that, in terms of governability, some intermediate degree of control of the executive by the legislature (i.e., accountability) is optimal. They are also consistent with the notion that placing limitations on a government's scope of action can be conducive to socially beneficial policy outcomes (North and Weingast 1989; Henisz 2000). More broadly, the findings suggest that at least part of the answer to the question of what makes democracies endure lies in the willingness of the relevant political actors to process their conflicts through the system of representative institutions and to accept the outcomes these institutions generate (Przeworski 2009).

In previous chapters, I identified conditions under which chief executives succeed and fail in the legislative arena. For example, the evidence presented in Chapter 8 indicates that high degrees of party loyalty in the legislature enable chief executives to form policy coalitions with members of their own parties, but can also deprive them of support from opposition legislators. Thus, as the Allende example indicates, minority presidents who face a unified opposition need to treat the legislature carefully. On the other hand, when party loyalty in the legislature is low, chief executives may be tempted to achieve additional support for their initiatives by targeting individual legislators. Yet, the case of Fujimori discussed in Chapter 7 indicates that such temptation is not without its drawbacks. Governments who buy votes in the legislature in the pursuit of effectiveness can easily lead to doubts regarding their legitimacy.

In light of the arguments and the evidence presented throughout this book, it is thus appropriate to conclude with Dahrendorf's sage reflections on the issue of governability: "... A free society does not need a strong government. It may indeed fare better if government is fairly inactive and quiet. But a free society needs an unworried government, and that means one which is effective where necessary and legitimate throughout ...." (Dahrendorf 1980: 409–410)

PART V

CONCLUSIONS

10

Conclusions

The general who wins the battle makes many calculations in his temple before the battle is fought. The general who loses makes but few calculations beforehand.

— Sun Tzu

Shortly after the end of the summer of 2008, as I was working on this book, I received an e-mail from Adam Przeworski. It was Monday, September 29, 2008 at 2:24 P.M. EST, and the U.S. House of Representatives had just rejected the Bush administration's $700 billion economic rescue plan. As a long-time friend and mentor, Adam was keenly aware of the event's overlap with this research project. His message read:

... Bombshell! The president and the majority opposition party support the bill and it fails. You must be happy theoretically, although perhaps less so financially ...

As it is often the case, he was correct. The bill's rejection validated the theoretical underpinning of statutory policy making discussed in this book.

The fact that a piece of legislation sponsored by the White House failed in Congress was not particularly noteworthy. After all, U.S. presidents typically achieve less than 70 percent of their legislative agenda approved by Congress. And Bush himself had failed on 22 percent of the roll calls where his administration had adopted a clear position. What made this event so notable was its tremendous financial and political consequences. The bill's rejection wiped out $1.2 trillion in stock market wealth – eclipsing the size of the proposed bailout package. The vote, which defied a full-court press from the president, the Treasury Secretary, and House leaders, also highlighted one of the main points made in this book: the unpredictability of legislative voting behavior.

The vote was expected to be a tight one. But, on the morning of Monday, September 29, the day the House would consider the bill, few foresaw the possibility of defeat. Twenty-four hours earlier, House Speaker Nancy Pelosi and Minority Whip Roy Blunt joined Treasury Secretary Henry M. Paulson, Jr. in hailing the merits of the bill in a news conference. Democrats promised to deliver between 125 to 140 votes; thus, the votes of approximately 80 to 100 Republicans were needed to pass the bill. By Sunday evening, after a nearly three-hour meeting with Republican lawmakers, Blunt and House Minority Leader John A. Boehner declared their support and began gathering additional Republican votes. On Monday, Paulson and Bush himself called numerous lawmakers, trying to round up last-minute support. Vice President Dick Cheney and senior aides, including chief of staff Josh Bolten and counselor Ed Gillespie, also joined in the effort. Less than an hour before the voting began, White House spokesman Tony Fratto predicted that the votes would be there (Kane and Montgomery 2008; Lueck et al. 2008).

When markets opened on September 29, 2008, the Dow Jones Industrial Average stood at 11,143. As lawmakers began to vote at 1:28 P.M., the Dow had already dropped below 11,000. A few minutes later, leaders of both parties realized they were behind. When the voting clock hit zero at about 1:43 P.M. with the "no" votes in the lead, the stock market lurched downward. In the span of one minute, the Dow lost 100 points, extending its loss to 414 points. The voting clock was kept open, as House leaders tried to cajole members into switching their ballots. By 1:45 P.M., the loss increased to 580 points; two minutes later, it widened to 673 points. At their high-water mark, just before 2:00 P.M., House leaders had 207 "aye" votes to 226 "nays." Only ten vote switchers were needed to pass the bill. At 2:06 P.M., however, lawmakers ran out of time, and no additional votes could be found. A few legislators switched their votes to no, making the final vote 228-205 against the bill. Just 65 House Republicans– less than one-third of Boehner's members– and 140 Democrats supported the bill. Hours later, at the end of the trading day, the Dow closed down 778 points, plunging to 10,365 (Kane and Montgomery 2008; Lueck et al. 2008; Lynch 2008).

So, what went wrong? As I have argued throughout this book, in deciding how to cast a vote, legislators must account for a variety of influences, including their personal values, the preferences of their party leadership, and the views of their supporters. The bill authorized the Treasury to purchase $700 billion of mortgage-related assets from U.S. financial firms. In Paulson's view, the federal government's massive and immediate infusion of capital was essential to stabilize the national and global economy. Still, the public expressed much concern over the proposal. Some believed it rewarded wealthy Wall Street risk takers while ignoring the economic plight of ordinary citizens. Others rejected the idea of a large, taxpayer-funded intervention into the free market. As a result, in the weeks leading to the final vote, legislators were flooded with e-mails and phone calls from angry constituents opposing the bill (Huse and Herszenhorn 2008).

From the onset, House leaders faced an uphill battle. Cross-pressured legislators struggled to appease their parties and constituents at the same time. With the November elections only five weeks away, supporting the bill would jeopardize lawmakers' political futures (Calmes 2008; Huse and Herszenhorn 2008). In the words of Representative Scott Garrett, a Republican from New Jersey who voted against the bill, "... [Democrats] saw the same problems we did ... they didn't want to go home and explain this thing ..." (cited in Lueck et al. 2008). Or as Representative David Obey, a Wisconsin Democrat, bitterly stated, "some guys were willing to lose the economy rather than lose the election" (cited in Lueck et al. 2008).

Indeed, analyzing legislators' vote decisions indicates that the vote failed due to a defection from ideologically moderate legislators in both parties. These lawmakers represented swing districts where constituents strongly opposed the proposal. Legislators facing tight reelection races were especially likely to oppose the bailout bill. Of the eighteen Demo-cratic and Republican incumbents in such races (classified as "tossup" contests by the Cook Political Report), just three voted for the bill. All six freshmen Democrats in tossup races opposed the bill (Aigner, Cox, Hossain and Tse 2008; Epstein and O'Halloran 2008; Green and Hudak 2008; Kane and Montgomery 2008).[1] These are precisely the *potentially decisive* legislators discussed in my theory and in the formal model. Unless a vote is "close enough" (i.e., there is a tie), these legislators favor their constituency rather than their party when casting a vote. And this is the reason why, unless rewards are appropriately dispensed, these "narrow victory" coalitions tend to unravel.

The aftermath of the failed bailout vote also illustrates the role of vote buying in statutory policy making. Determined to get statutory approval of the financial rescue plan, the Bush administration urged Congress to

---

[1] According to Epstein and O'Halloran (2008), going from a safe seat to one that leaned his or her way, and then from leaning to tossup, translated into about 20 percent likelihood of a legislator voting against the bill at each step.

reconsider the issue. By now the veil of uncertainty was removed. Once the bailout opponents were identified, political leaders used this information to effectively count "noses" and draft a version of the bill that included "face-saving measures" to insulate legislators from constituents' complaints (Epstein and O'Halloran 2008). On October 1, 2008, the U.S. Senate considered a new version of the bill. The revised proposal contained a variety of "sweeteners," including tax credits for alternative fuel production, a tax write-off for the National Association for Stock Car Auto Racing (NASCAR), and even an excise tax exemption for certain wooden arrow manufacturers (Green and Hudak 2008; Kang 2008). The revised plan passed with seventy four votes in favor and twenty five against (these came from ten Democrats and fifteen Republicans). Two days later, on October 3, 2008, the House considered the bill. This time fifty eight legislators (thirty three Democrats and twenty five Republicans) switched their votes to "aye." By packaging the bill with several popular things, the president, the Treasury, and congressional leaders secured 263 votes in support of the proposal and finally passed the rescue plan.

10.1 RULING BY STATUTE: A SUMMARY

This book advances a new theory of statutory policy making. I develop and test a theory explaining why governments suffer legislative defeats. I also examine the role and influence of the executive and legislative branches in creating law, and the capacity of different political systems to produce policy change. The analysis indicates that the unpredictability of legislators' voting behavior is key in shaping a chief executive's ability to successfully enact policy changes through statutes.

This research makes an important contribution to the comparative research on democratic governance. First, my emphasis on the unpredictability of legislators' behavior highlights the inadequacy of traditional (complete-information) models (Chapters 2 and 6). The theory presented in this book clearly transcends existing arguments about the effect of interbranch bargaining on the policy-making process and provides a more nuanced explanation of the conditions under which chief executives can win legislative majorities in support of their initiatives (Chapters 2 and 3).

Moreover, the existing work on chief executive's policy making suffers from several shortcomings. These include the lack of an adequate standard to evaluate the relative performance of chief executives and the scarcity of truly cross-national studies on this topic. My introduction of such a standard (Chapter 4), and the use of time-series cross-national data (Chapters 5–8), addresses these limitations. The data, which were specially collected for this project, and the standard also constitute an important contribution to the comparative study of democratic governance. For instance, they can be used in the future to test theories regarding the conditions under which chief executives adopt statutory versus nonstatutory policy-making strategies.

Finally, most studies of governability are primarily inferential. They offer little evidence of governmental performance and fail to properly define the term. By linking the notion of governability to chief executives' ability to enact policy changes, the analysis presented in this book overcomes these limitations. Therefore, the evidence presented in Chapter 9 provides another important improvement to the existing research .

10.2 DIRECTIONS FOR FUTURE RESEARCH

The theory of statutory policy making that I present in this book represents an initial attempt to account for the variation in chief executives' legislative passage rates. As with any stylized model, the issues discussed in this book are more complex than the model conveys. And although generalization and abstraction in thought and science is important, I am also keenly aware that the utility of modeling stems from useful simplification.[2] It is in this spirt that I would like to propose an outstanding theoretical issue calling for future research.

A contribution of this book is to highlight the plight of chief executives who consistently have to face legislators' strategic behavior. Central to the analysis is the idea that in deciding how to cast a vote, legislators take into account a variety of influences, including their personal values, the preferences of their party leadership, and the views of their supporters. This view guided my choices when modeling legislative behavior. I assumed that individual legislators have Euclidean preferences and that, absent any of those pressures, they would vote in favor of the chief executive's proposal if and only if the proposal is closer to their party's ideal policy than the status quo. I also stipulated that, in any given vote, each legislator chooses her own optimal action holding the choices of all other legislators fixed.

---

[2] Using Henry Theil's felicitous expression, "It does require maturity to realize that models are to be used, but not to be believed" (Theil 1971: vi).

Although I think this is an appropriate way to represent how legislators make their voting decisions, the "right" choice always depends on the issue under consideration. It is thus possible that these assumptions do not capture certain important complexities of legislative behavior. For example, an alternative characterization of the legislative process would be one in which (1) executive-initiated bills have a quality dimension (such as their technical merit, or their appropriateness for a given situation); and (2) legislators have access to different pieces of information about the quality of these proposals (cf. Austen-Smith and Banks 1996; Feddersen and Pesendorfer 1997). Adding common values and descentralized information to the analysis implies that legislators could potentially use the information from the voting decisions of other legislators to shape their own decision on how to vote (Dekel and Piccione 2000; Piketty 2000; Razin 2003; Iaryczower 2008). This departure from the standard sincere-voting spatial model may have important consequences for the study of lawmaking. Nonetheless, it would also require a novel approach to the empirical analysis of legislators' voting decisions (i.e., roll-call data). To date, with the exception of a few efforts (e.g., Battaglini et al. 2007; Iaryczower 2008; Iaryczower, Katz, and Saiegh 2010), little research in political science addresses these issues. Additional research on this subject matter would be most welcome.

Regarding the book's empirical findings, it is clear that the empirical tests are more systematic in Latin America than in other parts of the world. These choices primarily reflect my research interests. In this respect, the greater emphasis on these cases enhanced the quality of analysis presented in the book. On the other hand, because most countries in Latin America are presidential regimes, an individual-level analysis of legislators' policy preferences and the dynamics of parliamentarism were not fully explored. Expanding some of the analyses presented in this book to areas of the world other than Latin America is thus another very promising area of research.[3]

10.3 FINAL REMARKS

To conclude, I would like to point out the main implications posed by this research. The study of lawmaking, of course, can be viewed

---

[3] Kam's resarch on Westminster parliamentary politics is a case in point. His analysis of the underlying structure of party unity in Britain, Canada, Australia, and New Zealand is quite consistent with the findings presented in this book (Kam 2009).

from both positive and normative perspectives. The conventional positive view deems both agenda-setting powers and partisan support as essential to chief executives' statutory policy-making abilities. The conventional normative view is that chief executives unable to accommodate change through statutory policy making are at risk.

As a positive matter, constitutional arrangements and partisan configurations certainly influence statutory policy making. These features, however, are not the key to understanding why governments suffer legislative defeats. To reiterate, the fact that the agenda-setter model predicts that proposers should never be defeated underscores the importance of uncertainty. The formal model and the empirical evidence together highlight the subsidiary role of vote buying and of partisan sticks and carrots. The availability of these resources only becomes salient in situations where chief executives cannot fully predict legislators' voting behavior.

From a normative standpoint, I offer an important recommendation. In terms of *governability*, some intermediate degree of control of the legislature by the executive (i.e., *accountability*) is optimal. A *strong* government, however, is hardly a precondition for political stability. Instead, societies fare better when the government is proactive only when necessary, thereby providing a sense of legitimacy.

PART VI

APPENDICES

Appendix A

Proofs (Chapter 3)

Proof of Proposition 1. It is obvious that if $n_1(C) + n_6(C) \geq \frac{n+1}{2}$, then the chief executive offers no bribes and x^* becomes the new policy. To prove proposition 1, when $n_1(C) + n_6(C) < \frac{n+1}{2}$, I first prove the following lemmas:

Lemma 1 *Suppose that $k + n_1(C) + n_6(C) \geq \frac{n+1}{2}$, $n_2(C) = 0$, and $n_5(C) \geq k$. Then, there are two types of pure strategy equilibrium outcomes:*

1. *where $k - 1$ legislators in $N_5(C)$ vote for x^* and the rest of them vote against it;*
2. *where all legislators in $N_5(C)$ vote in favor of x^*. This equilibrium outcome, however, will only exist if there are "surplus" votes, that is, if $n_5(C) > k$.*

Proof of Lemma 1. I first prove that an equilibrium outcome where x^* is defeated always exists. Then I prove that an equilibrium outcome where x^* wins also exists if and only if $n_5(C) > k$.

Suppose that $k + n_1(C) + n_6(C) \geq \frac{n+1}{2}$, $k = 2$, $n_5(C) = 3$, and $n_2(C) = 0$. Consider the situation faced by the three potentially decisive legislators. There are eight possible voting profiles. Each legislator simultaneously casts a vote $v_i \in \{yes, no\}$. In the absence of bribes, each one of these legislators will vote in favor of x^* whenever the outcome is already decided. Otherwise, if a legislator finds herself in a decisive situation, she will vote in favor of x^{sq}. Define p_i to represent the probability that a legislator $i \in N_5(C)$ votes in favor of x^*.

For, say, legislator 1 in $N_5(C)$, the expected payoff when voting "*yes*" is $s_1 + \theta[1 + 2p_2(p_3 - 1) - 2p_3]$, whereas the expected payoff if she votes "*no*" is $\theta - 2p_2p_3\theta - s_1$. Legislator 1 in $N_5(C)$ will therefore vote "*yes*" whenever $s_1 > \theta[p_2(1-p_3)+p_3(1-p_2)]$. The strategies of the other two players are characterized analogously. Suppose that all three of them vote with the party. Then the following shall be true: $s_1 < \theta[p_2(1-p_3)+p_3(1-p_2)]$, $s_2 < \theta[p_1(1-p_3)+p_3(1-p_1)]$, and $s_3 < \theta[p_1(1-p_2)+p_2(1-p_1)]$.

I am looking only at pure strategies, therefore $p_i \in \{0,1\}$. In this case, $p_i = 0$ for all three legislators. We know that the sanction/rewards given by principals are always nonnegative quantities different from zero ($s_i > 0$). Therefore, such voting profile, $[n,n,n]$, cannot be an equilibrium outcome. The voting profile $[n,y,y]$ cannot be an equilibrium outcome either (and the same applies to $[y,y,n]$ and $[y,n,y]$). The voting profile $[n,n,y]$ constitutes an equilibrium outcome. By symmetry, the voting profiles $[y,n,n]$ and $[n,y,n]$ are also equilibrium outcomes. The voting profile $[y,y,y]$ also constitutes an equilibrium outcome.

Suppose now that there are only two potentially decisive opposition legislators. Everything else remains the same. Consider the situation faced by the two potentially decisive legislators. There are four possible voting profiles: $[y,y]$, $[y,n]$, $[n,y]$, and $[n,n]$. In this case, for legislator 1 in $N_5(C)$, the expected payoff when voting "*yes*" becomes $s_1 + \theta(1-2p_2)$, while the expected payoff if she votes "*no*" is $\theta - s_1$. Legislator 1 in $N_5(C)$ will therefore vote "*yes*" whenever $s_1 > \theta p_2$.

The strategies of the other player are characterized analogously. If both of them vote in favor of x^*, then the following shall be true: $s_1 > \theta p_2$ and $s_2 > \theta p_1$. In this case $p_1 = p_2 = 1$. This would imply $\theta < s_i$. Therefore, the voting profile $[y,y]$ cannot be an equilibrium outcome. The same logic can be extended to any situation where $k + n_1(C) + n_6(C) \geq \frac{n+1}{2}$, $n_2(C) = 0$, and $n_5(C) \geq k$. ∎

Lemma 2 *Suppose that* $k+n_1(C)+n_6(C) \geq \frac{n+1}{2}$, $n_5(C) = 0$, *and* $n_2(C) \geq k$. *Then, there are two types of pure strategy equilibrium outcomes:*

1. *where k legislators in* $N_2(C)$ *vote in favor of* x^* *and the rest of them vote against it;*
2. *where all legislators in* $N_2(C)$ *vote against* x^*. *This equilibrium outcome, though, will only exist if more than one vote is needed to change the outcome, that is, if $k > 1$.*

Proof of Lemma 2. I first prove that an equilibrium outcome where x^* wins always exists. Then I prove that an equilibrium outcome where x^* is defeated exists only if $k > 1$.

Suppose that $k + n_1(C) + n_6(C) \geq \frac{n+1}{2}$, $k = 2$, $n_2(C) = 3$, and $n_5(C) = 0$. Consider the situation faced by the three potentially decisive legislators. Let p_i now represent the probability that a legislator $i \in N_2(C)$ votes in favor of x^*.

For, say, legislator 1 in $N_2(C)$, the expected payoff when voting "*yes*" is $s_1 + \theta[1 + 2p_2(p_3 - 1) - 2p_3]$, while the expected payoff if she votes "*no*" is $\theta - 2p_2p_3\theta - s_1$. Legislator 1 in $N_2(C)$ will therefore vote "*yes*" whenever $s_1 < \theta[p_2(1 - p_3) + p_3(1 - p_2)]$. The strategies of the other two players are characterized analogously. Given that $s_i > 0$, the voting profile $[y, y, y]$ (all legislators vote with the party) cannot be an equilibrium outcome. By the same logic, the voting profile $[y, n, n]$ (one legislator votes with her party and the other two vote with their principals) cannot be an equilibrium outcome either (and the same applies to $[n, y, n]$ and $[n, n, y]$).

Suppose now that two of them vote with the party and the third one votes with her principal. We know that for every legislator in $N_2(C)$, $\theta > s_i > 0$. Therefore, the voting profile $[y, y, n]$ constitutes an equilibrium outcome. By symmetry, the voting profiles $[y, n, y]$ and $[n, y, y]$ are also equilibrium outcomes. The voting profile $[n, n, n]$ (all legislators vote their principals) also constitutes an equilibrium outcome.

Suppose now that only one additional vote is needed (i.e., $k = 1$). Everything else remains the same. Consider the situation faced by the three potentially decisive legislators. In this case, for legislator 1 in $N_2(C)$, the expected payoff when voting "*yes*" becomes $\theta - s_1$, while the expected payoff if she votes "*no*" is $s_1 + \theta[2p_3 - 2p_2(p_3 - 1) - 1]$. Legislator 1 in $N_2(C)$ will therefore vote "*yes*" whenever $s_1 < \theta[(p_2 - 1)(p_3 - 1)]$. The strategies of the other players are characterized analogously. The voting profile $[n, n, n]$ (all legislators vote with their principals) would imply that $\theta < s_i$, and therefore, it cannot be an equilibrium outcome. The same logic can be extended to any situation where $k + n_1(C) + n_6(C) \geq \frac{n+1}{2}$, $n_5(C) = 0$, and $n_2(C) \geq k$. ∎

Lemma 3 *Suppose that* $k + n_1(C) + n_6(C) \geq \frac{n+1}{2}$, $n_2(C) > 0$, *and* $n_5(C) > 0$. *Then, one of the following cases holds:*

1. *if* $n_5(C) \in \{k - 1, k\}$, *then no equilibrium outcome exists in pure strategies;*
2. *if* $n_5(C) < k - 1$ *or* $n_5(C) > k$, *then all legislators vote with their principals.*

Proof of Lemma 3. I first prove that an equilibrium outcome does not exist in pure strategies when $n_5(C) \in \{k - 1, k\}$. Then I prove that an equilibrium outcome where all legislators vote with their principals always exist in pure strategies when $n_5(C) < k - 1$ or $n_5(C) > k$.

Suppose that $k + n_1(C) + n_6(C) \geq \frac{n+1}{2}$, and $k = 2$. Suppose also that there are two potentially decisive government legislators (legislators 1 and 2) and one potentially decisive opposition legislator (legislator 3). Let p_i now represent the probability that a legislator $i \in N_2(C)$ or $i \in N_5(C)$ votes in favor of x^*. The following voting profiles cannot be equilibrium outcomes: $[y, y, y]$, $[y, y, n]$, $[y, n, y]$, $[y, n, n]$, $[n, y, y]$, $[n, y, n]$, $[n, n, y]$, and $[n, n, n]$. Suppose now that there is only one potentially decisive government legislator (legislator 1) and two potentially decisive opposition legislators (legislators 2 and 3). Everything else remains the same. The following voting profiles cannot be equilibrium outcomes: $[y, y, y]$, $[y, y, n]$, $[y, n, y]$, $[y, n, n]$, $[n, y, y]$, $[n, y, n]$, $[n, n, y]$, and $[n, n, n]$.

Suppose now that $k + n_1(C) + n_6(C) \geq \frac{n+1}{2}$, and $k = 3$. Suppose also that there are two potentially decisive government legislators (legislators 1 and 2) and one potentially decisive opposition legislator (legislator 3). In this case, legislator 1 in $N_2(C)$ will vote "*yes*" whenever $s_1 < \theta p_2 p_3$. In this case, the voting profile $[n, n, y]$ (all legislators vote with their principals) constitutes an equilibrium outcome. Suppose now that $k + n_1(C) + n_6(C) \geq \frac{n+1}{2}$, and $k = 1$. Suppose also that there is one potentially decisive government legislator (legislator 1) and two potentially decisive opposition legislators (legislators 2 and 3). In this case, legislator 1 in $N_2(C)$ will vote "*yes*" whenever $s_1 < \theta[(p_2 - 1)(p_3 - 1)]$. In this case, the voting profile $[n, y, y]$ (all legislators vote with their principals) also constitutes an equilibrium outcome. The same logic can be extended to any situation where $k + n_1(C) + n_6(C) \geq \frac{n+1}{2}$, $n_2(C) > 0$, and $n_5(C) > 0$. ∎

Given the conditions in lemma 2, it is proven that there are $\binom{n_2(C)}{k}$ equilibrium outcomes where enough legislators in $N_2(C)$ vote in favor of the chief executive government proposal, and some other ones get a "free ride" and vote with their principals. Still, it is also proven that if more than one additional vote is needed to change the outcome, the chief executive may not be able to pass the new policy x^* without offering bribes. Given the conditions in lemma 1, we know that the chief executive may be able to pass the new policy x^* while making no bribes. However, this is just one equilibrium outcome among $\binom{n_5(C)}{k-1} + 1$ possible ones. There are $\binom{n_5(C)}{k-1}$ equilibrium outcomes where x^* is defeated. We also know by lemma 3 that for any given measure of $n_2(C) > 0$, as long as $n_5(C) \in \{k - 1, k\}$, an equilibrium outcome does not exist in pure strategies. It is also proven that an equilibrium outcome where all legislators vote with their principals always exist in pure strategies when $n_5(\mathbf{C}) < k - 1$ or $n_5(\mathbf{C}) > k$. This means that x^* is defeated for sure when the conditions in lemma 3 are met and $n_5(\mathbf{C}) < k - 1$. Hence, under the same conditions, x^* wins for sure when $n_5(\mathbf{C}) > k$. ■

Proof of Proposition 2. To prove proposition 2, I first prove the following lemmas.

Lemma 4 *If neither unconditional supporters nor unconditional opponents constitute a majority, and there are no potentially decisive government legislators, the executive will have to buy any combination of legislators such that* $n_1(\mathbf{C}) + n_6(\mathbf{C}) + n(\mathbf{B}) = \frac{n+1}{2}$.

Proof of Lemma 4. Suppose that there are some potentially decisive opposition legislators, but $k + n_1(\mathbf{C}) + n_6(\mathbf{C}) \geq \frac{n+1}{2}$. Suppose also that there are no potentially decisive government legislators. By lemma 1, we know that when $N_2(\mathbf{C})$ is empty and $n_5(\mathbf{C}) \geq k$, all potentially decisive opposition legislators may vote in favor of x^* unbribed. However, we also know that without payments, another equilibrium outcome is possible: $k - 1$ legislators in $N_5(\mathbf{C})$ vote in favor of x^* and the rest of them vote against it.

To illustrate this situation, suppose that $k = 2$ and $n_5(\mathbf{C}) = 3$. Consider the situation faced by these legislators. Without bribes, there are four possible equilibrium outcomes: $[y, y, y]$, $[y, n, n]$, $[n, y, n]$, and $[n, n, y]$. Suppose now that the chief executive buys the vote of an unconditional opponent. Now, only one additional vote will be needed to pass x^*, and there are still three potentially decisive opposition legislators who have not been bribed. There are two possible equilibrium outcomes in this case: $[y, y, y]$ and $[n, n, n]$. Suppose that instead of bribing an unconditional opponent, the chief executive decides to bribe a potentially decisive opposition legislator. Given the bribed legislator, only one additional vote will be needed to pass x^*, but now there are two remaining potentially decisive opposition legislators. In this case, two equilibrium outcomes are possible: $[y, y]$ and $[n, n]$. The LEBM strategy for the chief executive is to buy one more vote. Therefore, he will have to buy two votes.

In a LEBM, the chief executive will have to buy any combination of legislators such that $n_1(\mathbf{C}) + n_6(\mathbf{C}) + n(\mathbf{B}) = \frac{n+1}{2}$. ■

Lemma 5 *If neither unconditional supporters nor unconditional opponents constitute a majority, and there are some potentially decisive* *government legislators but no potentially decisive opposition legislators, the chief executive only needs to buy $k - 1$ votes.*

Proof of Lemma 5. By lemma 2, we know that a potentially decisive government legislator will only cast a vote against her principal without receiving a bribe if she is decisive. Therefore, the LEBM strategy consist of buying any combination of legislators such that one and only one additional vote is needed to change the outcome.

To illustrate this situation, suppose that $k = 2$ and that $n_2(C) = 3$. Consider the situation faced by these legislators. Without bribes, there are four possible equilibrium outcomes: $[y, y, n]$, $[y, n, y]$, $[n, y, y]$, and $[n, n, n]$. Suppose that the chief executive buys a potentially decisive government legislator so that one additional vote will be needed to pass x^*. There are two remaining potentially decisive government legislators who have not been bought. In this case, two equilibrium outcomes are possible: $[y, n]$ and $[n, y]$. In both of them, x^* wins for sure. Suppose that instead of buying a legislator in $N_2(C)$, the chief executive decides to buy an unconditional opponent so that only one additional vote will be needed to pass x^*. There are now three potentially decisive government legislators who have not been bribed. In this case, there are three possible equilibrium outcomes: $[y, n, n]$, $[n, y, n]$, and $[n, n, y]$. In all three of them, x^* also wins for sure. The chief executive in this case has to buy only one additional vote. ∎

Lemma 6 *If neither unconditional supporters nor unconditional opponents constitute a majority, and there are some potentially decisive government legislators and some potentially decisive opposition legislators, then one of the following cases holds:*

1. *if $n_5(C) = k = 1$, then the chief executive has to buy one additional legislator and $n_1(C) + n_6(C) + n(B) = \frac{n+1}{2}$;*
2. *otherwise, the chief executive does not need to buy all k additional votes needed to pass x^*.*

Proof of Lemma 6. Suppose that $k + n_1(C) + n_6(C) \geq \frac{n+1}{2}$ $n_2(C) > 0$, and $n_5(C) > 0$. If $n_5(C) = k = 1$, by lemma 3 we know that no equilibrium outcome exists in pure strategies. In this case, the chief executive will have to buy one additional vote, and $n_1(C) + n_6(C) + n(B) = \frac{n+1}{2}$. We also know by lemma 3 that if $n_5(C) < k - 1$ or $n_5(C) > k$, then all legislators vote with their principals. Then, if $0 < n_5(C) < k + 1$, the chief executive has to buy any combination of legislators such that every one of them votes with her principal, and x^* wins for sure. For this to happen, there should be some potentially decisive government legislators, and the number of potentially decisive opposition legislators would have to surpass the number of additional votes needed to pass x^*. Therefore, the chief executive has to buy any combination of legislators such that:

$$n_1(C) + n_6(C) + n(B) < \frac{n+1}{2}, n_5(C) > k, \text{ and } n_2(C) > 0.$$

Alternatively, he can buy all potentially decisive opposition legislators such that one and only one additional vote is needed to change the outcome and there are some available potentially decisive government legislators:

$$n_1(C) + n_6(C) + n(B) < \frac{n+1}{2}, n_5(C) = 0, n_2(C) \geq k, \text{ and } k = 1.$$

Under either LEBM, it is true that:

$$n_1(C) + n_6(C) + n(B) < \frac{n+1}{2}.$$

Given lemmas 4-6, we know that for all cases, $n(B) \leq \frac{n+1}{2} - n_1(C) - n_6(C)$. As the cost of a winning coalition increases in $n(B)$, this is the cheapest way to secure passage for x^*. ∎

Proof of Comment 1. By lemma 4, we know that if $k + n_1(C) + n_6(C) \geq \frac{n+1}{2}$ and $n_2(C) = n_5(C) = 0$, the chief executive will buy enough legislators to meet simple majority. In case $k + n_1(C) + n_6(C) \geq \frac{n+1}{2}, n_2(C) > 0$ and $n_5(C) = 0$, by lemma 5, we know that the chief executive will buy $k - 1$ legislators. As one potentially decisive government legislator votes in favor of x^*, the proposal is supported by a minimum winning majority.

When $k + n_1(C) + n_6(C) \geq \frac{n+1}{2}, n_2(C) > 0$, and $n_5(C) > 0$, we known that the chief executive has three alternatives: (1) she may have to buy one additional vote (e.g., when $n_5(C) = k = 1$), and in this case the coalition in support of x^* would be minimum-winning; (2) she can choose to buy all potentially decisive opposition legislators such that one additional vote is needed to pass x^*, and there are some available potentially decisive government legislators; (this would also lead to a minimum winning coalition.) (3) she can buy enough legislators such that $n_5(C) > k$ and $n_2(C) > 0$. In other words, no opposition legislator should actually be decisive. Therefore, the cheapest voting coalition in support of x^* would have to include $(\frac{n+3}{2})$ legislators.

Proof of Proposition 3. To prove proposition 3, I first prove the following lemma:

Lemma 7 *Suppose the chief executive's estimate of the total cost of bribes is $\hat{Y} > \theta_E$. Then, he does not send a bill to the legislature.*

Proof of Lemma 7. Once the chief executive sends a bill to the legislature, she may need to spend $\sum_{i=1}^{n} \tau_i(v)$ resources to secure its passage. If we substitute $\sum_{i=1}^{n} \tau_i(v)$ for $\hat{Y}$, then the chief executive will derive utility $u_E(x^*) + \Pi(v) - \hat{Y}$ if the bill passes. An estimated total cost of bribes $\hat{Y} > \theta_E$, implies that $u_E(x^*) + \Pi(v) - \hat{Y} < u_E(x^{sq}) + \Pi(v)$. Therefore, $s(\hat{Y}) = 1$ cannot be a dominant strategy.

Proof of Proposition 4. Suppose the chief executive sends a bill to the legislature. With some probability q, he may be able and willing to pay the necessary compensations to achieve x^*. With probability $(1 - q)$, his budget will not be large enough, and/or the total cost of buying legislators will not make it worthwhile to make any payments. The chief executive should adopt a strategy $s(\hat{Y}) = 1$ if and only if:

$$q[u_E(x^*) + \Pi(v) - \hat{Y}] + (1 - q)[u_E(x^{sq}) + \Pi(v) - c] > u_E(x^{sq}) + \Pi(v)$$

Let $q \equiv Pr(\{Y \leq \min \Pi, \theta_E + c\}) = F(\Pi)$. Then, the chief executive will send a bill to the legislature if and only if:

$$F(\Pi) \geq \frac{c}{\theta_E - \hat{Y} + c}$$

By lemma 7, we know that the chief executive will not adopt a sending strategy $s(\hat{Y}) = 1$ if $\hat{Y} > \theta_E$, therefore the denominator is always some positive quantity, and $0 < F(\Pi) < 1$. In consequence, the game has an equilibrium where the chief executive sends a bill x^* and is defeated with positive probability. ∎

Appendix B

Data and Sources

Country	Period	Region
Argentina	1983–2003	Latin America
Australia	1974–1979, 1997–2006	Oceania
Austria	1974–1979, 1985	Western Europe
Bangladesh	1973–1979, 1991–1999	South Asia
Belgium	1968–1987, 1989–1991, 1993–1996	Western Europe
Bolivia	1995–2000	Latin America
Brazil	1946–1963, 1968–1981, 1983–2006	Latin America
Canada	1946–1967, 1969–1976, 1994–2006	North America
Chile	1990–2005	Latin America
Colombia	1982–1983, 1986–1987, 1992, 1995–1999	Latin America
Costa Rica	1958–1969, 1975, 1986–2003	Latin America
Czechoslovakia	1969–1973	Eastern Europe
Denmark	1953–2001	Western Europe
Ecuador	1979–2001	Latin America
Fiji	1974–1979	Oceania
Finland	1962–1965, 1975–1979	Western Europe
France	1946–1983	Western Europe
Germany	1949–1994	Western Europe
Greece	1978–1982	Western Europe
Honduras	1990–1996	Latin America
Hungary	1990–1993	Eastern Europe
Iceland	1951, 1961, 1971, 1977–1981	Western Europe
India	1955–1971, 1976–2007	South Asia

(*cont.*)

Country	Period	Region
Ireland	1974–1979, 1985–1987, 1989–1991, 1998–2008	Western Europe
Israel	1957–1969, 1974–1982	Middle East
Italy	1948–1957, 1960–1961, 1963–1973, 1975–1996	Western Europe
Ivory Coast	1965–1970	Africa
Japan	1947–1980, 1988–1997	East Asia
Jordan	1974–1979	Middle East
Kuwait	1974–1979	Middle East
Lebanon	1953–1972	Middle East
Malaysia	1974–1979	South-East Asia
Malta	1974–1982	Western Europe
Mexico	1982–2002	Latin America
Netherlands	1974–1982	Western Europe
New Zealand	1974–1982	Oceania
Pakistan	1972–1973	South Asia
Panama	1994–2001	Latin America
Paraguay	1989–2002	Latin America
Peru	1995–2002	Latin America
Poland	1991–1995	Eastern Europe
Portugal	1976–2001	Western Europe
Russia	1996–1999	Eastern Europe
South Africa	1974–1979	Africa
South Korea	1960, 1988–1999	East Asia
Spain	1974–1999	Western Europe
Sri Lanka	1974–1979	South Asia
Switzerland	1974–1979	Western Europe
Turkey	1983–2000	Middle East
United Kingdom	1946–1979, 1997–2005	Western Europe
Uruguay	1985–2002	Latin America
Venezuela	1959–1988	Latin America

SOURCES

Published Works

Ágh, Attila and Sándor Kurtán. 1995. *The First Parliament (1990-1994): Democratization and Europeanization in Hungary.* Budapest: Hungarian Centre for Democracy Studies.

Ahmed, Nizam. 1999. "In Search of Institutionalisation: Parliament in Bangladesh," in Philip Norton and Nizam Ahmed (eds.). *Parliaments in Asia.* London: Frank Cass.

Alemán, Eduardo, and Ernesto Calvo. 2010. "Unified Government, Bill Approval, and the Legislative Weight of the President," *Comparative Politics*, Vol. 43, No. 4: 511–534.

Amorim Neto, Octavio, and Eric Magar. 2000. "Veto Bargaining and Coalition Formation: A Theory of Presidential Policymaking with Application to Venezuela," paper delivered at the XXII International Congress of the Latin American Studies Association, Miami, March 16–18, 2000.

Andeweg, Rudy B., and Lia Nijzink. 1995. "Beyond the Two-Body Image: Relations Between Ministers and MPs," in Herbert Döring (ed.). *Parliaments and Majority Rule in Western Europe.* New York: St. Martin's Press.

Arter, David. 2003. "From the 'Rainbow Coalition' Back Down to 'Red Earth'? The 2003 Finnish General Election," *West European Politics* Vol. 26 No. 3: 153–162.

Baaklini, Abdo I. 1976 *Legislative and Political Development: Lebanon, 1842-1972.* Durham, NC: Duke University Press.

Baaklini, Abdo I. 1992. *The Brazilian Legislature and Political System.* Westport, CT: Greenwood Press.

Baaklini, Abdo, Guilain Denoeux, and Robert Springborg. 1999. *Legislative Politics in the Arab World.* Boulder, CO: Lynne Rienner.

Bergara, Mario, Andrés Pereyra, Ruben Tansini, Adolfo Garcé, Daniel Chasquetti, Daniel Buquet, and Juan André Moraes. 2006. "Political Institutions, Policymaking Processes, and Policy Outcomes: The Case of Uruguay," Research Network Working Paper #R-510. Research Department, Inter-American Development Bank, Washington, DC.

Blondel, Jean. 1977. *Comparative Legislatures.* Englewood Cliffs, NJ: Prentice-Hall.

Burbano de Lara, Felipe, and Michel Rowald García. 1998. "Pugna de Poderes, Presidencialismo y Partidos en el Ecuador: 1979-1997," Quito: Proyecto CORDES-Gobernabilidad.

Campbell, Colin. 1977. *Canadian Political Facts 1945–1976.* New York: Methuen.

Cárdenas, Mauricio, Roberto Junguito, and Monica Pachón. 2004. "Political Institutions, Policymaking Processes, and Policy Outcomes: The Case of Colombia," Latin American Research Network, Inter-American Development Bank, Washington, DC.

Cárdenas, Mauricio, Roberto Junguito, and Monica Pachón. 2008. "Political Institutions and Policy Outcomes in Colombia: The Effects of the 1991 Constitution," in in Ernesto Stein and Mariano Tommasi (eds.). *Policymaking in Latin America: How Politics Shapes Policies*. Washington DC: IDB – Harvard University Press.

Casar, María Amparo. 2002. "Executive-Legislative Relations: The Case of Mexico (1946–1997)," in Scott Morgenstern and Benito Nacif (eds.). *Legislative Politics in Latin America*. New York: Cambridge University Press.

Chandler, William, Gary W. Cox, and Mathew D. McCubbins. 2006. "Agenda Control in the Bundestag, 1987–2002," *German Politics*, Vol. 15, No. 1: 89–111.

Chasquetti, Daniel. 2001. "Multipartidismo, coaliciones y estabilidad democratica en America Latina," Master's Thesis, Universidad de la Republica, Montevideo, Uruguay.

Cheibub Figueiredo, Argelina. 2000. "Government Performance in Multiparty Presidential Systems: The Experiences of Brazil," paper delivered at the XVIII IPSA World Congress, Quebec City, August 1–5, 2000.

Cheibub Figueiredo, Argelina, and Fernando Limongi. 2000. "Presidential Power, Legislative Organization, and Party Behavior in Brazil," *Comparative Politics*, Vol. 32, No. 2: 151–170.

Crisp, Brian. 2000. *Democratic Institutional Design*. Stanford, CA: Stanford University Press.

Damgaard, Erik. 1992. *Parliamentary Change in the Nordic Countries*. New York: Scandinavian University Press.

Della Sala, Vincent. 1998. "The Italian Parliament: Chambers in a Crumbling House?" in Philip Norton (ed.). *Parliaments and Governments in Western Europe*. London: Frank Cass.

de Winter, Lieven. 1998. "Parliament and Government in Belgium: Prisoners of Partitocracy," in Philip Norton (ed.). *Parliaments and Governments in Western Europe*. London: Frank Cass.

Elder, Neil, Alastair H. Thomas, and David Arter. 1988. *The Consensual Democracies?* Oxford: Blackwell.

Esaiasson, Peter, and Knut Heidar. 2000. *Beyond Westminster and Congress: The Nordic Experience*. Columbus: Ohio University Press.

Farrell, Brian. 1994. "The Political Role of Cabinet ministers in Ireland," in Michael Laver and Kenneth Shepsle (eds.). *Cabinet Ministers and Parliamentary Government*. Cambridge: Cambridge University Press.

Field, Bonnie. 2000. "Frozen Democracy?" paper delivered at the XXII International Congress of the Latin American Studies Association, Miami, March 16–18, 2000.

Herman, Valentine, 1976. *Parliaments of the World: A Reference Compendium*. New York: DeGruyter.

Hughes, Steven W., and Kenneth J. Mijeski. 1973. *Legislative-Executive Policy-Making: The Cases of Chile and Costa Rica*. London: Sage Publications.

Inter-Parliamentary Union. 1986. *Parliaments of the World. A Comparative Reference Compendium*. 2nd Edition. Aldershot: Gower House.

Kim, Chong Lim, and Seong-Tong Pai. 1981. *Legislative Process in Korea*. Seoul: Seoul National University Press.

Kreppel, Amie. 1997. "Impact of Parties on Legislative Output in Italy," *European Journal of Political Research*, Vol. 31, No. 3: 327–349.

Lehoucq, Fabrice, Gabriel Negretto, Francisco Aparicio, Benito Nacif, and Allyson Benton. 2008. "Policymaking in Mexico Under One-PartyHegemony and Divided Government," in Ernesto Stein and Mariano Tommasi (eds.). *Policymaking in Latin America: How Politics Shapes Policies*. Washington DC: IDB – Harvard University Press.

Leston-Bandeira, Cristina. 1998. "Relationship between Parliament and Government in Portugal: Expression of the Maturation of the Political System," in Philip Norton (ed.). *Parliaments and Governments in Western Europe*. London: Frank Cass.

Leston-Bandeira, Cristina. 2001. "The Portuguese Parliament During the First Two Decades of Democracy," *West European Politics*, Vol. 24, No. 1: 137–156.

Leston-Bandeira, Cristina. 2004. *From Legislation to Legitimation*. London: Routledge.

Leston-Bandeira, Cristina and André Freire. 2003. "Internalising the Lessons of Stable Democracy: The Portuguese Parliament," *Journal of Legislative Studies*, Vol. 9, No. 2: 56–84.

Magar, Eric, and Juan Andres Moraes. 2007. "Of Coalition and Speed: Passage and Duration of Statutes in Uruguays Parliament, 1985-2000," unpublished manuscript, ITAM.

Mejía-Acosta, Andrés. 2000. "Weak Coalitions and Policy Making in the Ecuadorian Congress (1979-1996)," paper delivered at the Annual Meeting of the Latin American Studies Association, Miami, March 16-18 2000.

Mejía-Acosta, Andrés, María Caridad Araujo, Anibal Pérez-Liñán, and Sebastian Saiegh. 2008. "Veto Players, Fickle Institutions and Low-Quality Policies: The Policymaking Process in Ecuador (1979-2005)," in Ernesto Stein and Mariano Tommasi (eds.). *Policymaking in Latin America: How Politics Shapes Policies*. Washington DC: IDB – Harvard University Press.

Mezey, Michael L. 1979. *Comparative Legislatures*. Durham, NC: Duke University Press.

Miyoshi, Akira. 1999. "The Diet in Japan," in Philip Norton and Nizam Ahmed (eds.). *Parliaments in Asia*. London: Frank Cass.

Molinas, José, Anibal Pérez-Liñán, Sebastian Saiegh, and Marcela Montero. 2008. "Political Institutions, Policymaking Processes, and Policy Outcomes in Paraguay," in Ernesto Stein and Mariano Tommasi (eds.). *Policymaking in Latin America: How Politics Shapes Policies*. Washington DC: IDB – Harvard University Press.

Molinelli, N. Guillermo, M. Valeria Palanza, and Gisela Sin. 1999. *Congreso, Presidencia y Justicia en la Argentina*. Buenos Aires: Temas Grupo Editorial.

Morón, Eduardo, and Cynthia Sanborn. 2006. "The Pitfalls of Policymaking in Peru: Actors, Institutions, and the Rules of the Game." Research Network Working Paper #R-511. Research Department, Inter-American Development Bank, Washington, DC.

Numasawa, Katsumi. 1998. "Health Policy Formulation Practices of the American Medical Association (AMA) and the Japan Medical Association (JMA)," *Research Paper No. 146*, Takemi Program in International Health, Harvard School of Public Health.

Olson, David M. 1994. *Democratic Legislative Institutions*. New York: M.E. Sharpe.

Opello, Walter. 1986. "Portugal's Parliament: An Organizational Analysis of Legislative Performance," *Legislative Studies Quarterly*, Vol. 11, No. 3: 291–319.

Park, Chan Wook. 2002. "Change is Short but Continuity is Long," in Gerhard Loewenberg, Peverill Squire, and D. Roderick Kiewiet (eds.). *Legislatures*. Ann Arbor: University of Michigan Press.

Parodi, Jean Luc. 1972. *Les rapports entre le Legislatif et l'Executif sous la Cinquieme Republique, 1958–1962*. Paris: A. Colin.

Prata, Andrea. 2006. "Government Domination,Consensus or Chaos? A Study of Party Discipline and Agenda Control in National Legislatures," doctoral dissertation, Department of Political Science, University of California San Diego.

Pulzer, Peter. 2003. "The Devil They Know: The German Federal Election of 2002," *West European Politics*, Vol. 26, No. 2: 153–164.

Reid, G. S., and Martyn Forrest. 1989. *Australia's Commonwealth Parliament 1901–1988*. Melbourne: Melbourne University Press.

Remington, Thomas F. 2001. *The Russian Parliament*. New Haven, CT: Yale University Press.

Rose, Richard. 1986. "British MPS: More Bark than Bite?" in Ezra Suleiman (ed.). *Parliaments and Parliamentarians in Democratic Politics*. New York: Holmes & Meier.

Saalfeld, Thomas. 1998. "The German Bundestag: Influence and Accountability in a Complex Environment," in Philip Norton (ed.). *Parliaments and Governments in Western Europe*. London: Frank Cass.

Siavelis, Peter. 2000. *The President and Congress in Postauthoritarian Chile: Institutional Constraints to Democratic Consolidation*. University Park: Pennsylvania State University Press.

Suleiman, Ezra N. 1986. "Toward the Disciplining of Parties and Legislators," in Ezra Suleiman (ed.). *Parliaments and Parliamentarians in Democratic Politics*. New York: Holmes & Meier.

Taylor-Robinson, Michelle. 2001. "Candidate Selection in Costa Rica," paper delivered at the XXIII International Congress of the Latin American Studies Association, Washington, DC, September 6–8, 2001.

Taylor-Robinson, Michelle, and Christopher Diaz. 1999. "Who Gets Legislation Passed in a Marginal Legislature and is the Label Marginal Legislature Still Appropriate? A Study of the Honduran Congress," *Comparative Political Studies*, Vol. 32, No. 5: 590–626.

Woldendorp, Jaap, Hans Keman, and Ian Budge. 1993. "Political Data 1945–1990: Party Government in 20 Democracies," *European Journal of Political Research* Vol. 24, No. 1: 1–120.

Additional Sources

Australia: http://parlinfo.aph.gov.au/parlInfo/search/summary/summary.w3p;adv= yes;order By=priority,title;query=Dataset:billsPrevParl

Brazil: Argelina Cheibub Figueiredo (IUPERJ)

Canada: http://www.parl.gc.ca/LEGISINFO/index.asp?Language=E&Mode=1& Parl=39&Ses=2

Canada: http://www2.parl.gc.ca/HouseBills/billsgovernment.aspx?Parl=39&Ses= 2&Languag e=E&Mode=1

Chile: Eduardo Alemán (University of Houston)

Ecuador: Andrés Mejía-Acosta (University of Sussex)

India: http://164.100.24.219/Bios_Search/search2.aspx

Ireland: http://www.oireachtas.ie/ViewDoc.asp?DocId=-1&CatID=59&m=b

Panamá: Carlos Guevara-Mann (University of Nevada, Las Vegas)

Appendix C

Statistical Analysis (Chapter 8)

Figure 8.2 presents the estimated effects of seat shares on box scores under different ballot access rules in a multivariate context. To generate these results I used the following approach. First, I performed a logit transformation of my dependent variable, the proportion of bills initiated by a chief executive and approved by the legislature of his or her respective country. Next, I regressed these box scores on a series of explanatory variables using ordinary least squares (OLS). The following explanatory variables are considered:

Presidential, Mixed, and **Non-Westminster Parliamentary.** Each of these variables takes the value of 1 if the country has the referred constitutional structure, and 0 otherwise. Constitutional structures were classified according to the criteria developed by Cheibub (2007). The following countries were coded as Westminster-style systems: Canada, Bangladesh, Ireland, Malta, United Kingdom, and New Zealand.

Coalition Government. This is a binary indicator that takes the value of 1 if the government is a multiparty coalition, and 0 otherwise. A government is considered to be a multiparty coalition if two or more political parties represented in the national legislature hold cabinet positions. *Source:* Cheibub et al. (2004) and the author's own calculations.

Government's Seat Share. This variable ranges between 0 and 1 and was constructed by dividing the number of seats held by the party – or parties – included in the government divided by the total number of seats in the lower house of the national legislature. *Source:* Cheibub et al. (2004) and the author's own calculations.

Ballot Access. This is a dummy variable that takes the value of 1 if individual candidates have restricted access to a party label. These situations occur when: (i) parties control access to the ballot, even if they do not control the order in which candidates will receive seats; (ii) parties control access to ballots as well as the order in which individuals will fill the seats that the party wins. The variable takes the value of 0 when candidates face few or no impediments to appear on the ballot. These situations occur under single-member districts if parties allow independent candidates and/or use primaries to select candidates. *Source*: Seddon Wallack, et al. (2003); Johnson and Wallack (2009).

Average District Magnitude. This variable measures the standard magnitude of the average district in the lower house of the national legislature. *Source*: Gaviria, et al. (2003); Johnson and Wallack (2009).

Government's Seat Share*Ballot Access. This variable captures the interaction between the share of government seats and the electoral rules.

Table C1 presents the results of a model in which standard errors are robustly estimated and the disturbance terms for each country are allowed to be correlated.

Figure 8.3 shows the effects of party-centered electoral rules and their interaction with constitutional structure on chief executives' legislative passage rates. The following approach was used to generate these results. As a dependent variable I used the proportion of bills initiated by a chief executive and approved by the legislature of his or her respective country. Then I estimated two separate models, one for the sample of presidential democracies and the other one for non-Westinster parliamentary countries using ordinary least squares (OLS). In addition to **Coalition Government, Ballot Access,** and **Average District Magintude,** the following explanatory variables are considered:

Chief Executive's Seat Share. This variable ranges between 0 and 1 and was constructed by dividing the number of seats held by the chief executive's party divided by the total number of seats in the lower house of the national legislature. *Source*: Cheibub et al. (2004) and the author's own calculations.

Majority Government. This is a binary indicator that takes the value of 1 if the government controls a majority of seats in the lower house of the national legislature, and 0 otherwise. *Source*: Cheibub et al. (2004) and the author's own calculations.

Table C1. *Ballot access and passage rates*

Presidential	−0.213***
	(0.076)
Mixed	−0.204**
	(0.076)
Non-Westminster Parliamentary	−0.085
	(0.068)
Coalition Government	−0.054
	(0.053)
Government's Seat Share	−0.05
	(0.237)
Ballot Access	−1.072***
	(0.186)
Average District Magnitude	0.001**
	(0.0004)
Government's Seat Share*Ballot Access	1.796***
	(0.367)
Intercept	4.524***
	(0.148)
N	415
R^2	0.34

Notes: The omitted category is Westminster-style system (for constitutional structure). Standard errors are in parentheses. * indicates significance at a 10% level; ** indicates significance at a 5% level; *** indicates significance at a 1% level.

Majority Government*Ballot Access. This variable captures the interaction between the government status and the electoral rules.

Table C2 presents the results. In both models, standard errors are robustly estimated and the disturbance terms for each country are allowed to be correlated.

Table C2. *Ballot access and passage rates*

	Parliamentary	Presidential
Coalition Government	1.655	−0.022
	(4.907)	(6.487)
Chief Executive's Seat Share	44.359***	11.731
	(10.868)	(30.011)
Majority Government	−9.508	−3.821
	(7.499)	(4.620)
Ballot Access	−2.928	−27.285***
	(5.563)	(5.145)
Average District Magnitude	0.115**	0.206
	(0.041)	(0.256)
Chief Executive's Seat Share*Ballot Access	9.733	22.065**
	(6.608)	(8.641)
Intercept	64.083***	71.908***
	(5.012)	(13.514)
N	151	180
R^2	0.24	0.36

Notes: Standard errors are in parentheses. * indicates significance at a 10% level; ** indicates significance at a 5% level; *** indicates significance at a 1% level.

Appendix D

Statistical Analysis (Chapter 9)

Sample of Democratic Countries

The sample includes democratic countries with a per capita income below $6,055 (measured in 1985 purchasing power parity dollars). It comprises 292 observations on 32 countries for the 1950–1995 period. The choice of these countries is dictated by data availability.

Country	Observations
Argentina	12
Bangladesh	5
Bolivia	1
Brazil	30
Chile	6
Colombia	6
Costa Rica	23
Denmark	6
Ecuador	17
Finland	2
France	11
Germany	6
Greece	5
Honduras	6
Hungary	4
Iceland	2
India	37
Ireland	3
Israel	13
Italy	14

(cont.)

Country	Observations
Japan	15
Malta	9
Pakistan	2
Panama	2
Paraguay	3
Poland	7
Portugal	12
South Korea	2
Sri Lanka	3
Turkey	13
United Kingdom	4
Uruguay	11
Total	**292**

To generate the results presented in Figure 9.1, I regress data on social upheaval collected by Banks (1996) on my box score measure. The dependent variable, *riots*, measures the number of violent demonstrations or clashes of more than 100 citizens involving the use of physical force. I model the relationship between chief executive's legislative passage rates and social unrest by fitting a second-order polynomial to the data. Hence, my two independent variables are the box score and its squared values.

Table D1 presents the results of OLS, Poisson, and Negative Binomial specifications. In all models, the standard errors are robustly estimated and the disturbance terms for each country are allowed to be correlated.

Table D1. *Riots and passage rates (democracies)*

	OLS	Poisson	Negative Binomial
Box Score	−0.158**	−0.072***	−0.064**
	(0.073)	(0.023)	(0.026)
Box Score^2	0.002**	0.001***	0.001***
	(0.001)	(0.000)	(0.000)
Intercept	4.056**	1.261**	1.133
	(1.525)	(0.628)	(0.805)
N	292	292	292
R^2	0.094		
Log-likelihood		−806.239	−442.28

Notes: Standard errors are in parentheses. * indicates significance at a 10% level; ** indicates significance at a 5% level; *** indicates significance at a 1% level.

Sample of Autocratic Countries

In the analysis presented in Chapter 9 (Figure 9.2), I include all autocracies in my analysis, regardless of their income level. The sample consists of eighty four observations on fourteen countries between 1965 and 1995. As before, the choice of these countries is dictated by data availability:

Country	Observations
Bangladesh	7
Brazil	11
Czechoslovakia	5
Fiji	6
Ivory Coast	6
Jordan	6
Kuwait	6
Malaysia	6
Mexico	14
Paraguay	4
Peru	1
South Africa	6
Spain	3
Sri Lanka	3
Total	84

Table D2 presents the results of OLS, Poisson, and Negative Binomial specifications. In all models, the standard errors are robustly estimated and the disturbance terms for each country are allowed to be correlated.

Table D2. *Riots and passage rates (autocracies)*

	OLS	Poisson	Negative Binomial
Box Score	2.287	4.143**	2.570**
	(1.400)	(1.964)	(1.022)
Box Score^2	−0.013	−0.024**	−0.015**
	(0.008)	(0.011)	(0.006)
Intercept	−95.733	−177.397**	−112.854**
	(58.376)	(84.298)	(44.358)
N	84	84	84
R^2	0.115		
Log-likelihood		−118.288	−74.449

Notes: Standard errors are in parentheses. ∗ indicates significance at a 10% level; ∗∗ indicates significance at a 5% level; ∗∗∗ indicates significance at a 1% level.

Bibliography

Ackerman, Bruce. 2003. "The New Separation of Powers," *Harvard Law Review*, No. 3: 633–729.

Aguayo, Julio Javier. 2004. "The Legislature Strikes Back in Peru: The Role of Congress in the Demise of Fujimori in 2000," Ph.D. dissertation, University of Florida.

Aigner, Erin, Amanda Cox, Farhana Hossain, and Archie Tse. 2008. "The No Votes," *New York Times*, September 30, 2008.

Alcántara, Manuel. 2004. *¿Instituciones o Máquinas Ideológicas? Origen, Programa y Organización de los Partidos Latinoamericanos*. Barcelona: Institut de Ciencies Politiques i Socials.

Alcántara, Manuel (ed.). 2008. *Politicians and Politics in Latin America*. Boulder, CO: Lynne Rienner Publishers.

Aldrich, John H., and Richard McKelvey. 1977. "A Method of Scaling with Applications to the 1968 and 1972 Presidential Elections," *American Political Science Review*, Vol. 71, No. 1: 111–130.

Alemán, Eduardo. 2009. *Legislative Politics in Chile*, unpublished manuscript, Department of Political Science, University of Houston.

Alemán, Eduardo, and Ernesto Calvo. 2006. "Analyzing Legislative Success in Latin America: The Case of Argentina," paper presented at the Conference of Junior Scholars for the Study of Democracy, *Woodrow Wilson Center*, Santiago, Chile, February 9.

Alemán, Eduardo, and George Tsebelis. 2005. "Presidential Conditional Agenda Setting in Latin America," *World Politics*, Vol. 57, No. 3: 396–420.

Alemán, Eduardo, and Sebastian Saiegh. 2007. "Legislative Preferences, Political Parties, and Coalition Unity in Chile," *Comparative Politics*. Vol. 39, No. 3: 253–272.

Alesina, Alberto, and Howard Rosenthal. 1995. *Partisan Politics, Divided Government, and the Economy*. New York: Cambridge University Press.

Ames, Barry. 2001. *The Deadlock of Democracy in Brazil*. Ann Arbor: The University of Michigan Press.

Ames, Barry. 2002. "Party Discipline in the Chamber of Deputies," in Morgenstern, Scott, and Benito Nacif (eds.). *Legislative Politics in Latin America.* Cambridge: Cambridge University Press.

Amorim Neto, Octavio. 2006. "The Presidential Calculus: Executive Policy Making and Cabinet Formation in the Americas," *Comparative Political Studies*, Vol. 39, No. 4: 415–440.

Amorim Neto, Octavio, and Eric Magar. 2000. "Veto Bargaining and Coalition Formation: A Theory of Presidential Policymaking with Application to Venezuela," paper delivered at the XXII International Congress of the *Latin American Studies Association*. Miami, March 16–18, 2000.

Amorim Neto, Octavio, Gary W. Cox, and Mathew McCubbins. 2003. "Agenda Power in Brazil's Câmara Dos Deputados, 1989–98," *World Politics*, Vol. 55: 550–578.

Austen-Smith, David, and Jeffrey Banks. 1988. "Elections, Coalitions, and Legislative Outcomes," *American Political Science Review*, Vol. 82, No. 2: 405–422.

Austen-Smith, David, and Jeffrey Banks. 1996. "Information Aggregation, Rationality, and the Condorcet Jury Theorem," *American Political Science Review*, Vol. 90, No. 1: 34–45.

Banks, Arthur. 1996. "Cross-National Time-Series Data Archive." Binghamton, NY: Center for Social Analysis, State University of New York at Binghamton. http://www2.scc.rutgers.edu/cnts/index.php.

Battaglini, Marco, Rebecca Morton, and Thomas Palfrey. 2007. "Efficiency, Equity, and Timing of Voting Mechanisms," *American Political Science Review*, Vol. 101, No. 3: 409–424.

Bailey, Michael A. 2007. "Comparable Preference Estimates across Time and Institutions for the Court, Congress, and Presidency," *American Journal of Political Science*, Vol. 51, No. 3: 433–448.

Barkan, Joel D., and John J. Okumo. 1974. "Political Linkage in Kenya: Citizens, Local Elites, and Legislators." Occasional Paper No. 1, Comparative Legislative Research Center, Iowa City: Iowa.

Barrett, Andrew W. 2005. "Are All Presidential Legislative Successes Really Victories?: Examining the Substance of Legislation," *White House Studies*, Vol. 5, No. 5: 133–151.

Barry, Brian. 1980. "Is It Better to be Powerful or Lucky? Part 2," *Political Studies*, Vol. 28, No. 3: 338–352.

Bavastro, Roberto. 2001. "The Dynamics of Latin American Presidentialism: Government and Opposition in Argentina, 1983–1995," M.Phil. Thesis, University of Oxford.

Binder, Sarah A. 1999. "The Dynamics of Legislative Gridlock, 1947–96," *American Political Science Review*, Vol. 93, No. 3: 519–533.

Bond, Jon R., and Richard Fleisher. 1990. *The President in the Legislative Arena.* Chicago: University of Chicago Press.

Bond, Jon R., Richard Fleisher, and Glen S. Krutz. 1996. "An Overview of the Empirical Findings on Presidential-Congressional Relations," in James A. Thurber (ed.). *Rivals for Power.* Washington, DC: CQ Press.

Boothroyd, David. 2001. "House of Commons Divisions in Which the Government Was Defeated since 1918," in http://www.election.demon.co.uk/defeats.html

Borges, Jorge Luis. 1962. *Ficciones*. New York: Grove Press.

Bueno de Mesquita, Bruce, Alastair Smith, Randolph M. Siverson, and James D. Morrow. 2003. *The Logic of Political Survival*. Cambridge, MA MIT Press.

Calmes, Jackie. 2008. "A Leadership Breakdown," *New York Times*, September 30, 2008.

Calvo, Ernesto. 2007. "The Responsive Legislature: Public Opinion and Law Making in a Highly Disciplined Legislature," *British Journal of Political Science*, Vol. 37, No. 2: 263–280.

Cameron, Charles M. 2000. *Veto Bargaining*. New York: Cambridge University Press.

Cameron, Charles M., and Jee-Kwang Park. 2007. "A Primer on the President's Legislative Program," in Bert Rockman and Richard Waterman (eds.). *Presidential Leadership: The Vortex of Power*. New York: Oxford University Press.

Campbell, Colin. 1977. *Canadian Political Facts 1945–1976*. New York: Methuen.

Cannon, John. 1984. *Aristocratic Century*. New York: Cambridge University Press.

Capano, Giliberto, and Marco Giuliani. 2001. "Governing Without Surviving? An Italian Paradox: Law-Making in Italy, 1987–2001," *The Journal of Legislative Studies*, Vol. 7, No. 4: 13–36.

Capo Giol, Jordi. 2003. "The Spanish Parliament in a Triangular Relationship, 1982–2000," *Journal of Legislative Studies*, Vol. 9, No. 2: 107–129.

Cárdenas, Mauricio, Roberto Junguito, and Monica Pachón. 2008. "Political Institutions and Policy Outcomes in Colombia: The Effects of the 1991 Constitution," in Ernesto Stein and Mariano Tommasi (eds.). *Policymaking in Latin America: How Politics Shapes Policies*. Washington DC: IDB – Harvard University Press.

Carey, John M. 2002. "Parties, Coalitions and the Chilean Congress in the 1990s," in Morgenstern, Scott and Benito Nacif (eds.). *Legislative Politics in Latin America*. Cambridge: Cambridge University Press.

Carey, John M. 2003. "Transparency Versus Collective Action: Fujimori's Legacy and the Peruvian Congress," *Comparative Political Studies*, Vol. 36, No. 9: 983–1006.

Carey, John. 2007. "Competing Principals, Political Institutions, and Party Unity in Legislative Voting," *American Journal of Political Science*, Vol. 51, No. 1: 92–107.

Carey, John. 2009. *Legislative Voting and Accountability*. New York: Cambridge University Press.

Carey, John M., and Matthew S. Shugart. 1995. "Incentives to Cultivate a Personal Vote: a Rank Ordering of Electoral Formulas," *Electoral Studies*, Vol. 14, No. 4: 417–439.

Carey, John, and Matthew Shugart. 1998. *Executive Decree Authority*. New York: Cambridge University Press.

Casar, Maria Amparo. 2002. "Executive-Legislative Relations: The Case of Mexico (1946–1997)," in Scott Morenstern and Benito Nacif (eds.). *Legislative Politics in Latin America*. Cambridge: Cambridge University Press.

Cheibub, Jose Antonio. 2002. "Minority Governments, Deadlock Situations, and the Survival of Presidential Democracies," *Comparative Political Studies*, Vol. 35, No. 3: 284–312.

Chiebub, Jose Antonio. 2007. *Presidentialism, Parliamentarism, and Democracy*. New York: Cambridge University Press.

Cheibub, Jose Antonio, Adam Przeworski, and Sebastian Saiegh. 2004. "Government Coalitions and Legislative Success Under Presidentialism and Parliamentarism," *British Journal of Political Science*, Vol. 34: 565–587.

Cheibub, Jose Antonio, Jennifer Gandhi, and James Raymond Vreeland. 2010. "Democracy and Dictatorship Revisited," *Public Choice*, Vol. 143, No. 1-2: 67–101.

Cheibub Figueiredo, Argelina. 2000. "Government Performance in Multiparty Presidential Systems: The Experiences of Brazil," paper delivered at the XVIII IPSA World Congress, Quebec.

Chrypinski, Vincent. 1966. "Legislative Committees in Polish Lawmaking," *Slavic Review*, Vol. 25, No. 2: 247–258.

Cohen, Youssef. 1994. *Radicals, Reformers, and Reactionaries: The Prisoner's Dilemma and the Collapse of Democracy in Latin America*. Chicago: University of Chicago Press.

Coleman, John J. 1999. "Unified Government, Divided Government, and Party Responsiveness," *American Political Science Review*, Vol. 93, No. 4: 821–835.

Colley, Linda. 1976. "The Mitchell Election Division, 24 March 1755," *Bulletin of the Institute of Historical Research*, Vol. 49, No. 119: 80–107.

Conaghan, Catherine M. 2005. *Fujimori's Peru*. Pittsburgh, PA: Pittsburgh University Press.

Coppedge, Michael. 1994. "Venezuela: Democratic Despite Presidentialism," in Juan J. Linz and Arturo Valenzuela (eds.). *The Failure of Presidential Democracy*. Baltimore: Johns Hopkins University Press.

Costa, Gabriel B., Michael R. Huber, and John Saccoman. 2008. *Understanding Sabermetrics: An Introduction to the Science of Baseball Statistics*. N. C.: McFarland.

Covington, Cary R. 1988. "Building Presidential Coalitions among Cross-Pressured Members of Congress," *Western Political Quarterly*, Vol. 41, No. 1: 47–62.

Covington, Cary R., J. Mark Wrighton, and Rhonda Kinney. 1995. "A 'Presidency-Augmented' Model of Presidential Success on House Roll Call Votes," *American Journal of Political Science*, Vol. 39: 1001–1024.

Cox, Gary. 1987. *The Efficient Secret*. New York: Cambridge University Press.

Cox, Gary, and Mathew McCubbins. 1993. *Legislative Leviathan: Party Government in the House*. Berkeley: University of California Press.

Cox, Gary, and Matthew Soberg Shugart. 1995. "In the Absence of Vote Pooling: Nomination and Vote Allocation Errors in Colombia," *Electoral Studies*, Vol. 14, No. 4: 441–460.

Cox, Gary, and Mathew McCubbins. 2005. *Setting the Agenda*. New York: Cambridge University Press.

Cox, Gary W., and Scott Morgenstern. 2002. "Epilogue: Latin America's Reactive Assemblies and Proactive Presidents," in Scott Morgenstern and Benito Nacif (eds.). *Legislative Politics in Latin America*. New York: Cambridge University Press.

Crain, William, Randal Holcombe, and Richard Tollison. 1979. "Monopoly Aspects of Political Parties," *Atlantic Economic Journal*, Vol. VII, No. 2: 54–58.

Crisp, Brian F. 2000. *Democratic Institutional Design*. Stanford, CA: Stanford University Press.

Crisp, Brian, and Rachael E. Ingall. 2002. "Institutional Engineering and the Nature of Representation: Mapping the Effects of Electoral Reform in Colombia," *American Journal of Political Science*, Vol. 46 No. 4: 733–748.

Crowe, Edward W. 1980. "Cross-Voting in the British House of Commons: 1945–1974," *Journal of Politics*, Vol. 42, No. 2: 487–510.

Crozier, Michel, Samuel P. Huntington, and Joji Watanuki. 1975. *The Crisis of Democracy*. New York: New York University Press.

Dahrendorf, Ralph. 1980. "Effectiveness and Legitimacy: On the 'Governability of Democracies'," *The Political Quarterly*, Vol. 51, No. 4: 393–410.

Dal Bo, Ernesto. 2007. "Bribing Voters," *American Journal of Political Science*. Vol. 51, No. 4: 789–803.

Dekel, Eddie, and Michele Piccione. 2000. "Sequential Voting Procedures in Symmetric Binary Agendas," *Journal of Political Economy*, Vol. 108, No. 1: 34–55.

Dekel, Eddie, Matthew Jackson, and Asher Wolinsky. 2005. "Vote Buying," unpublished manuscript, *Caltech*.

De Luca, Miguel, Mark P. Jones, and Maria Ines Tula. 2002. "Back Rooms or Ballot Boxes?: Candidate Nomination in Argentina," *Comparative Political Studies*, Vol. 35, No. 4: 413–436.

Denzau, Arthur, William Riker, and Kenneth Shepsle. 1985. "Farquharson and Fenno: Sophisticated Voting and Home Style," *American Political Science Review*, Vol. 79, No. 4: 1117–1134.

Desposato, Scott W. 2003. "Comparing Group and Subgroup Cohesion Scores: A Nonparametric Method with an Application to Brazil," *Political Analysis*, Vol. 11, No. 3: 275–288.

Desposato, Scott W. 2006. "Parties for Rent? Ambition, Ideology, and Party Switching in Brazil's Chamber of Deputies," *American Journal of Political Science*, Vol. 50, No. 1: 62–80.

De Vylder, Stephan. 1976. *Allende's Chile*. Cambridge: Cambridge University Press.

de Winter, Lieven. 1998. "Parliament and Government in Belgium: Prisoners of Partitocracy," in Philip Norton (ed.). *Parliaments and Governments in Western Europe*. London: Frank Cass.

Di Palma, Giuseppe. 1977. *Surviving without Governing*. Berkeley: University of California Press.

Diermeier, Daniel, and Timothy J. Feddersen. 1998. "Cohesion in Legislatures and the Vote of Confidence Procedure," *American Political Science Review*, Vol. 92, No. 3: 611–621.

Diermeier, Daniel, and Razvan, Vlaicu 2007. "Executive Control and Legislative Success." Available at SSRN: http://ssrn.com/abstract=1118163

Dixit, Avinash K., and Barry J. Nalebuff. 1991. *Thinking Strategically*. New York: Norton.

Döring, Herbert (ed.). 1995a. *Parliaments and Majority Rule in Western Europe*. New York: St. Martin's Press.

Döring, Herbert. 1995b. "Time as a Scarce Resource," in Herbert Döring (ed.). *Parliaments and Majority Rule in Western Europe*. New York: St. Martin's Press.

Duch, Jordi, Joshua S. Waitzman, and Luís Nunes Amaral. 2010. "Quantifying the Performance of Individual Players in a Team Activity," PLoS ONE 5(6): e10937. doi:10.1371/ journal.pone.0010937.

Edwards, George C., III. 1980. *Presidential Influence in Congress*. San Francisco: W. H. Freeman.

Edwards, George C. 1989. *At the Margins* New Haven, CT: Yale University Press.

Edwards, George C., III, Andrew Barret, and Jeffrey Peake. 1997. "The Legislative Impact of Divided Government," *American Journal of Political Science*, Vol. 41, No. 2: 545–563.

Edwards, George C., III, and Andrew Barret. 2000. "Presidential Agenda Setting in Congress," in Jon R. Bond and Richard Fleisher (eds.). *Polarized Politics: Congress and the President in a Partisan Era*. Washington DC: CQ Press, pp. 109–133.

Epstein, David and Sharyn O'Halloran. 2008 "Bailout Vote Analysis: Empirics," posted on http://www.reflectivepundit.com/ on September 30, 2008.

Feddersen, Timothy, and Wolfgang Pesendorfer. 1997. "Voting Behavior and Information Aggregation in Elections With Private Information," *Econometrica*, Vol. 65, No. 5: 1029–1058.

Fenno, Richard. 1978. *Home Style: House Members in Their Districts*. Boston: Little Brown.

Figueiredo, Argelina C., and Fernando Limongi. 2000. "Presidential Power, Legislative Organization, and Party Behavior in Brazil," *Comparative Politics*, Vol. 32, No. 2: 151–170.

Fiorina, Morris. 1974. *Representatives, Roll Calls, and Constituencies*. Lexington, MA: Heath.

Fiorina, Morris, and Roger G. Noll. 1978. "Voters, Bureaucrats and Legislators: A Rational Choice Perspective on the Growth of Bureaucracy," *Journal of Public Economics*, Vol. 9, No. 2: 239–254.

Fiorina, Morris. 1996. *Divided Government*. Boston: Allyn Bacon.

Fleisher, Richard, Jon R. Bond, and B. Dan Wood. 2002. "Presidential Success in Congress: Which Presidents Do Better or Worse Than Expected?" paper delivered at the annual meeting of the Southern Political Science Association. Savannah, GA: November 6–9, 2002.

Foord, Archibald S. 1947. "The Waning of 'The Influence of the Crown,'" *The English Historical Review*, Vol. 62, No. 245: 484–507.

Foweraker, Joe. 1998. "Institutional Design, Party Systems and Governability – Differentiating the Presidential Regimes of Latin America," *British Journal of Political Science*, Vol. 28: No. 4: 651–676.

Franzese, Robert J. 2010. "Multiple Policymakers: Veto Actors Bargaining in Common Pools," presented at the Comparative Politics Workshop, Duke University, February 5, 2010.

Friend, Julius W. 1998. *The Long Presidency: France in the Mitterrand Years, 1981–1995*. Boulder, CO: Westview Press.

Gamm, Gerald, and John Huber. 2003. "Legislatures as Political Institutions: Beyond the Contemporary Congress," in Ira Katznelson and Helen Milner (eds.). *Political Science: State of the Discipline*, APSA: W.W. Norton, pp. 313–341.

Gandhi, Jennifer. 2008. *Political Institutions under Dictatorship*. New York: Cambridge University Press.

Gandhi, Jennifer, and Adam Przeworski. 2006. "Cooperation, Cooptation, and Rebellion under Dictatorships," *Economics & Politics*, Vol. 18, No. 1: 1–26.

García, Fátima and Araceli Mateos. 2001. "Élites Parlamentarias en América Latina," *Revista Española de Ciencia Política*, Vol. 5: 173–94.

Gartzke, Erik. 1999. "War Is in the Error Term," *International Organization*, Vol. 53, No. 3: 567–587.

Geddes, Barbara. 2004. "Authoritarian Breakdown," unpublished paper, Department of Political Science, UCLA.

Gertzel, Cherry. 1966. "Parliament in Independent Kenya." *Parliamentary Affairs*, Vol. 19, No. 4: 486–504.

Ginter, Donald E. 1995. *Voting Records of the British House of Commons, 1761–1820*. London: Hambledon Press.

Goldberg, Peter A. 1975. "The Politics of the Allende Overthrow in Chile," *Political Science Quarterly*, Vol. 90, No. 1: 93–115.

Golder, Matt. 2005. "Democratic Electoral Systems around the World," *Electoral Studies*, Vol. 24, No. 1: 103–21.

Green, Matthew, and Kristen Hudak. 2008. "Congress and the Bailout: Explaining The Bailout Votes and Their Electoral Effect," unpublished paper, The Catholic University of America.

Groseclose, Tim, and James M. Snyder. 1996. "Buying Supermajorities," *American Political Science Review*, Vol. 90, No. 2: 303–315.

Groseclose, Tim, and Nolan McCarty. 2001. "The Politics of Blame: Bargaining Before an Audience," *American Journal of Political Science*, Vol. 45, No. 1: 100–119.

Groseclose, Tim, and Jeff Milyo. 2009. "Sophisticated Voying in Congress," unpublished paper, Department of Political Science, UCLA.

Hager, George, and Eric Pianin. 1997. *Mirage: Why Neither Democrats nor Republicans Can Balance the Budget, End the Deficit, and Satisfy the Public*. New York : Times Books/Random House.

Hallerberg, Mark, and Patrik Marier. 2004. "Executive Authority, the Personal Vote, and Budget Discipline in Latin American and Caribbean Countries," in *American Journal of Political Science,* Vol. 48: 571–587.

Hammond, T. H., and J. M. Fraser. 1983. "Baselines for Evaluating Explanations of Coalition Behavior in Congress," *Journal of Politics,* Vol. 45, No. 3: 635–656.

Hammond, T. H., and J. M. Fraser. 1984a. "Judging Presidential Performance on House and Senate Roll Calls," *Polity,* Vol. 16, No. 6: 624–646.

Hammond, T. H., and J. M. Fraser. 1984b. "Studying Presidential Performance in Congress," *Political Methodology,* Vol. 10: 211–244.

Heller, William B. 2001. "Making Policy Stick: Why the Government Gets What It Wants in Multiparty Parliaments," *American Journal of Political Science,* Vol. 45, No. 4: 780–798.

Henisz, Witold J. 2000. "The Institutional Environment for Economic Growth," *Economics & Politics,* Vol. 12, No. 1: 1–31.

Hill, Brian W. 1976. *The Growth of Parliamentary Parties 1689–1742.* London: Allen & Unwin.

Hix, Simon. 2001. "Legislative Behaviour and Party Competition in European Parliament: An Application of Nominate to the EU," *Journal of Common Market Studies,* Vol. 39, No. 4: 663–688.

Holmes, Geoffrey, and Daniel Szechi. 1993. *The Age of Oligarchy.* New York: Longman.

Hoppit, Julian. 1996. "Patterns of Parliamentary Legislation, 1660–1800," *The Historical Journal,* Vol. 39, No. 4: 109–131.

Hoppit, Julian (ed.). 1997. *Failed Legislation, 1660–1800.* London: Hambledon Press.

Hoppit, Julian, Joanna Innes, and John Styles. 1994. "Towards a History of Parliamentary Legislation, 1660–1800," *Parliamentary History,* Vol. 13, No. 3: 312–321.

Hochstetler, Kathryn. 2006. "Rethinking Presidentialism: Challenges and Presidential Falls in South America," *Comparative Politics,* Vol. 38, No. 4: 401–418.

Holmes, Geoffrey. 1986. *Politics, Religion and Society in England 1679–1742.* London: Hambledon Press.

Holmes, Geoffrey, and Daniel Szechi. 1993. *The Age of Oligarchy.* London: Longman.

Horne, Alistair. 1972. *Small Earthquake in Chile.* London: MacMillan.

Howell, William, Scott Adler, Charles Cameron, and Charles Reimann. 2000. "Divided Government and the Legislative Productivity of Congress, 1945–1994," *Legislative Studies Quarterly,* Vol. 25, No. 2: 285–312.

Huang, The-fu. 1997. "Party Systems in Taiwan and South Korea," in Larry Diamond, Marc F. Plattner, Yun-han Chu, and Hung-mao Tien (eds.). *Consolidating the Third Wave Democracies: Themes and Perspectives.* Baltimore: Johns Hopkins University Press.

Huber, John D. 1996. "The Vote of Confidence in Parliamentary Democracies," *American Political Science Review,* Vol. 90, No. 2: 269–282.

Huntington, Samuel P. 1968. *Political Order in Changing Societies*. New Haven, CT: Yale University Press.

Huse, Carl, and David Herszenhorn. 2008. "Leaders Rebuffed in 228-205 Vote – Broad Public Anger Is Cited," *New York Times*, September 30, 2008.

Iaryczower, Matias. 2008. "Strategic Voting in Sequential Committees," unpublished paper, Caltech.

Iaryczower, Matias, Gabriel Katz, and Sebastian Saiegh. 2010. "Voting in the Bicameral Congress: Large Majorities as a Signal of Quality," unpublished paper, Department of Politics, Princeton University.

Ingberman, Daniel E., and Dennis A. Yao. 1991. "Presidential Commitment and the Veto," *American Journal of Political Science*, Vol. 35, No. 2: 357–389.

Inter-Parliamentary Union. 1986. *Parliaments of the World. A Comparative Reference Compendium*. 2nd Edition. Aldershot: Gower House.

Jackson, John E., and John W. Kingdon. 1992. "Ideology, Interest Group Scores, and Legislative Votes," *American Journal of Political Science*, Vol. 36: 805–823.

Johnson, Joel W., and Jessica S. Wallack. 2009. *Electoral Systems and the Personal Vote*, available at: http://dss.ucsd.edu/~jwjohnso/espv.htm

Jones, Charles O. 1994. *The Presidency in a Separated System*. Washington, DC: Brookings.

Jones, Mark. 1995. *Electoral Laws and the Survival of Presidential Democracies*. Notre Dame, IN: University of Notre Dame Press.

Jones, Mark P., Sebastian Saiegh, Pablo Spiller, and Mariano Tommasi. 2002. "Amateur Legislators–Professional Politicians: The Consequences of Party-Centered Electoral Rules in a Federal System," *American Journal of Political Science*, Vol. 46, No. 3: 656–669.

Jones, Mark P., and Wonjae Hwang. 2005. "Party Government in Presidential Democracies: Extending Cartel Theory Beyond the U.S. Congress," *American Journal of Political Science*, Vol. 49, No. 2: 267–282.

Judd, Gerrit P. 1972. *Members of Parliament, 1734–1832*. New Haven, CT: Archon Books.

Kalt, Joseph P., and Mark A. Zupan. 1990. " Apparent Ideological Behavior of Legislators: Testing for Principal-Agent Slack in Political Institutions," *Journal of Law & Economics*, Vol. 33: 103–131.

Kam, Christopher. 2001. "Do Ideological Preferences Explain Parliamentary Behaviour? Evidence from Great Britain and Canada," *Journal of Legislative Studies*, Vol. 7, No. 4: 89–126.

Kam, Christopher. 2009. *Party Discipline and Parliamentary Politics*. New York: Cambridge University Press.

Kane, Paul, and Lori Montgomery. 2008. "How the Numbers Failed the Leaders," *Washington Post*, September 30, 2008.

Kang, Cecilia. 2008. "Rescue Sweetened With Tax Incentives," *Washington Post*, October 4, 2008.

Katz, Richard S., and Bernhard Wessels. 1999. *The European Parliament, National Parliaments and European Integration*. Oxford: Oxford University Press.

Keefer, Philip. 2005. "Database of Political Institutions: Changes and Variable Definitions." Washington, DC: Development Research Group, World Bank.

Kellam, Marisa. 2006. "Shifting Majorities: Multiparty Coalitions and Support for Presidential Agendas within Latin American Legislatures," paper delivered at the annual meeting of the Midwest Political Science Association. Chicago, April 20–23, 2006.

Kennan, John. 1986. "The Economics of Strikes," in Orley Ashenfelter and Richard Layard (eds.). *Handbook of Labor Economics*. Amsterdam: North Holland.

Kernell, Samuel. 1991. "Facing an Opposition Congress," in Gary W. Cox and Samuel Kernell (eds.). *The Politics of Divided Government*. Boulder, CO: Westwiew, pp. 87–112.

King, David C., and Richard Zeckhauser. 2003. "Congressional Vote Options," *Legislative Studies Quarterly*, Vol. 28, No. 3: 387–411.

King, Gary, and Lyn Ragsdale. 1988. *The Elusive Executive*. Washington, DC: CQ Press.

King, Gary, Christopher J. L. Murray, Joshua A. Salomon, and Ajay Tandon. 2004. "Enhancing the Validity and Cross-cultural Comparability of Survey Research," *American Political Science Review*, Vol. 97, No. 4: 567–583.

Kingdom, John. 2003. *Government and Politics in Britain: An Introduction*. Cambridge: Polity Press.

Krehbiel, Keith. 1993. "Where's the Party?" *British Journal of Political Science*, Vol. 23, No. 2: 235–266.

Krehbiel, Keith. 1998. *Pivotal Politics*. Chicago: University of Chicago Press.

Krehbiel, Keith. 2000. "Party Discipline and Measures of Partisanship," *American Journal of Political Science*, Vol. 44, No. 2: 212–227.

Kreppel, Amie. 1997. "Impact of Parties on Legislative Output in Italy," *European Journal of Political Research*, Vol. 31, No. 3: 327–349.

Krugman, Paul. 1994. "The Fall and Rise of Development Economics," published electronically: http://web.mit.edu/krugman/www/dishpan.html

Krutz, Glen S. 2000. "Getting Around Gridlock: The Effect of Omnibus Utilization on Legislative Productivity," *Legislative Studies Quarterly*, Vol. 25, No. 4: 533–549.

Lambert, Paul C, Lucy K. Smith, David R. Jones, and Johannes Botha. 2005. "Additive and Multiplicative Covariate Regression Models for Relative Survival Incorporating Fractional Polynomials for Time-Dependent Effects," *Statistics in Medicine*, Vol. 24: 3871–3885.

Laruelle, Annick, and Federico Valenciano. 2005. "Assessing Success and Decisiveness in Voting Situations," *Social Choice and Welfare*, Vol. 24, No. 1: 171–197.

Laruelle Annick, Ricardo Martinez, and Federico Valenciano. 2006. "Success Versus Decisiveness: Conceptual Discussion and Case Study," *Journal of Theoretical Politics*, Vol. 18, No. 2: 185–205.

Leston-Bandeira, Cristina. 2001. "The Portuguese Parliament During the First Two Decades of Democracy," *West European Politics*, Vol. 24, No. 1: 137–156.

Levin, Jonathan, and Barry Nalebuff. 1995. "An Introduction to Vote-Counting Schemes," *Journal of Economic Perspectives*, Vol. 9, No. 1: 3–26.

Levitt, Steven D. 1996. "How Do Senators Vote? Disentangling the Role of Voter Preferences, Party Affiliation, and Senator Ideology," *American Economic Review*, Vol. 86, No. 3: 425–441.

Levy, Brian, and Pablo T. Spiller. 1994. "The Institutional Foundations of Regulatory Commitment: A Comparative Analysis of Telecommunications Regulation," *Journal of Law, Economics, and Organization*, Vol. 10, No. 2: 201–246.

Lewis, Michael. 2003. *Moneyball: The Art of Winning an Unfair Game*. New York: W. W. Norton & Company.

Lichbach, Mark. 1984. "An Economic Theory of Governability: Choosing Policy and Optimizing Performance," *Public Choice*, Vol. 44, No. 2: 307–337.

Light, Paul C. 1989. "The Focusing Skill and Presidential Influence in Congress," in Christopher J. Deering (ed.). *Congressional Politics*. Chicago: Dorsey Press.

Linz, Juan J. 1978. *The Breakdown of Democratic Regimes: Crisis, Breakdown, and Reequilibration*. Baltimore: Johns Hopkins University Press.

Linz, Juan. 1990. "The Perils of Presidentialism," *Journal of Democracy*, Vol. 1, No. 1: 51–69.

Linz, Juan J. 1994. "Presidential or Parliamentary Democracy: Does It Make a Difference," in Juan J. Linz and Arturo Valenzuela (eds.). *The Failure of Presidential Democracy: The Case of Latin America*. Baltimore: Johns Hopkins University Press.

Linz, Juan J., and Alfred Stepan. 1996. *Problems of Democratic Transition and Consolidation: Southern Europe, South America, and Post-Communist Europe*. Baltimore: Johns Hopkins University Press.

Lipset, Seymour M. 1960. *Political Man; the Social Bases of Politics*. Garden City, NY: Doubleday.

Lockerbie, Brad, Stephen Borrelli, and Scott Hedger. 1998. "An Integrative Approach to Modeling Presidential Success in Congress," *Political Research Quarterly*, Vol. 51: 155–172.

Loewenberg, Gerhard. 1984. "The Division of Political Science into American and Non-American Politics: The Case of Legislatures," *PS*, Summer: 561–563.

Loewenberg, Gerhard, and Samuel C. Patterson. 1979. *Comparing Legislatures*. Lanham, MD: University Press of America.

Londregan, John B. 2000. *Legislative Institutions and Ideology in Chile*. New York: Cambridge University Press.

Londregan, John B. 2002. "Appointment, Reelection, and Autonomy in the Senate of Chile," in Scott Morgenstern and Benito Nacif (eds.). *Legislative Politics in Latin America*. New York: Cambridge University Press.

Lueck, Sarah, Damian Paletta, and Greg Hitt. 2008. "Bailout Plan Rejected, Markets Plunge, Forcing New Scramble to Solve Crisis," *Wall Street Journal*, September 30, 2008.

Lupia, Arthur W., and Kaare Strom. 1995. "Coalition Termination and the Strategic Timing of Parliamentary Elections," *American Political Science Review*, 89: 648–665.

Lust-Okar, Ellen. 2005. *Structuring Conflict in the Arab World: Incumbents, Opponents, and Institutions.* New York: Cambridge University Press.

Lynch, David J. 2008. "It's an 'Extremely Worrisome Situation,'" *USA Today*, September 30, 2008.

Magaloni, Beatriz. 2006 *Voting for Autocracy: Hegemonic Party Survival and Its Demise in Mexico.* New York: Cambridge University Press.

Mainwaring, Scott. 1990. "Presidentialism in Latin America," *Latin American Research Review*, Vol. 25, No. 1: 157–179.

Mainwaring, Scott. 1993. "Presidentialism, Multipartism, and Democracy: The Difficult Combination," *Comparative Political Studies*, Vol. 26, No. 2: 198–228.

Mainwaring, Scott. 1998. "Party Systems in the Third Wave," *Journal of Democracy*, Vol. 9, No. 3: 67–81.

Mainwaring, Scott, and Timothy R. Scully. 1995. "Introduction: Party Systems in Latin America," in Scott Mainwaring and Timothy R. Scully (eds.). *Building Democratic Institutions: Party Systems in Latin America.* Stanford, CA: Stanford University Press.

Mainwaring, Scott, and An'bal Pérez-Liñán. 1997. "Party Discipline in the Brazilian Constitutional Congress," *Legislative Studies Quarterly*, Vol. 22, No. 4: 453–483.

Matthews, Steven. 1989. "Veto Threats: Rhetoric in a Bargaining Game," *Quarterly Journal of Economics*, Vol. 104, No. 2, 347–369.

Mayhew, David. 1990. *Divided We Govern.* New Haven, CT: Yale University Press.

McCarty, Nolan, Keith T. Poole, and Howard Rosenthal. 2006. *Polarized America: The Dance of Ideology and Unequal Riches.* Cambridge, MA: MIT Press.

McCubbins, Mathew, Roger Noll, and Barry Weingast. 2007. "The Political Economy of Law: Decision-Making by Judicial, Legislative, and Executive and Administrative Agencies," in A. Mitchell Polinsky and Steven Shavell (eds.). *Handbook of Law and Economics.* Amsterdam: Elsevier Science.

McMillan, John, and Pablo Zoido. 2004. "How to Subvert Democracy: Montecinos in Peru," *Journal of Economic Perspectives*, Vol. 18, No. 4: 69–92.

Mejía Acosta, Andrés. 2000. "Weak Coalitions and Policy Making in the Ecuadorian Congress (1979–1996)," paper delivered at the Annual Meeting of the Latin American Studies Association, Miami, March 16–18, 2000.

Mejía Acosta, Andrés, Anibal Pérez-Liñán, and Sebastian Saiegh. 2009. "Las bases partidarias de la legislación particularista en Ecuador y Paraguay," in Flavia Freidenberg and Manuel Alcántara (eds.). *Selección de candidatos, política partidista y rendimiento democrático.* México: Universidad Nacional Autónoma de México (UNAM).

Mezey, Michael. 1979. *Comparative Legislatures.* Durham, NC: Duke University Press.

Moe, Terry M., and William Howell. 1999. "The Presidential Power of Unilateral Action," *Journal of Law, Economics, and Organization*, Vol. 15, No. 1: 132–179.

Molinas, Jose, Anibal Perez Linan, and Sebastian Saiegh. 2004. "Political Institutions, Policymaking Processes, and Policy Outcomes in Paraguay, 1954–2003," *Revista de Ciencia Politica* (Chile), Vol. 24: 67–93.

Molinelli, N. Guillermo, M. Valeria Palanza, and Gisela Sin. 1999. *Congreso, Presidencia y Justicia en la Argentina*. Buenos Aires: Temas Grupo Editorial.

Moreno, Erika, and Maria Escobar-Lemmon. 2008. "Mejor Solo Que Mal Acompañado: Political *Entrepreneurs* and List Proliferation in Colombia," in Peter Siavelis and Scott Morgenstern (eds.). *Pathways to Power*. University Park: Pennsylvania State University Press.

Morgenstern, Scott. 2004. *Patterns of Legislative Politics*. New York: Cambridge University Press.

Namier, Lewis B., Sir. 1929. "The Circular Letters: An 18th-Century Whip to Members of Parliament," *English Historical Review*, Vol. 44, No. 176: 588–611.

Namier, Lewis B., Sir. 1957. *The Structure of Politics at the Accession of George III*. New York: St. Martin's Press.

Namier, Lewis B., Sir, and John Brooke. 1964. *The House of Commons, 1754–1790*. New York: Oxford University Press.

Navia, Patricio. 2008. "Legislative Candidate Selection in Chile," in Peter Siavelis and Scott Morgenstern (eds.). *Pathways to Power*. University Park: Pennsylvania State University Press.

Negretto, Gabriel. 2004. "Government Capacities and Policy Making by Decree in Latin America," *Comparative Political Studies*, Vol. 37, No. 5: 531–562.

Negretto, Gabriel. 2006. "Minority Presidents and Democratic Performance in Latin America," *Latin American Politics & Society*, Vol. 48, No. 3: 63–92.

Neher, Clark D. 1971. "Thailand: Toward Fundamental Change," *Asian Survey*, Vol. 11, No. 2: 131–138.

Neumayer, Eric. 2003. "Good Policy Can Lower Violent Crime: Evidence from a Cross-National Panel of Homicide Rates, 1980–97," *Journal of Peace Research*, Vol. 40, No. 6: 619–640.

Nielson, Daniel L. 2003. "Supplying Trade Reform: Political Institutions and Liberalization in Middle-Income Presidential Democracies," *American Journal of Political Science*, Vol. 47, No. 3: 470–491.

Norris, Pippa. 2001. "The British Representation Study," http://www.pippanorris.com

North, Douglass, and Barry Weingast. 1989. "Constitutions and Commitment: Evolution of Institutions Governing Public Choice." *Journal of Economic History*, Vol. XLIX, No. 4: 803–832.

Olson, David M., and Maurice D. Simon. 1982. "The Institutional Development of a Minimal Parliament: The Case of the Polish Sejm," in Daniel Nelson and Stephen White (eds.). *Communist Legislatures in Comparative Perspective*. Albany: State University of New York Press.

Osborne, Martin. 2004. *An Introduction to Game Theory*. New York: Oxford University Press.

Owen, John B. 1975. *The Eighteenth Century, 1714–1815*. Totowa, NJ: Rowman and Littlefield.

Özbudum, Ergun. 1970. *Party Cohesion in Western Democracies: A Causal Analysis*. Beverly Hills, CA: Sage.

Pachón, Mónica. 2002. "El Partido Conservador y sus din‡micas pol'ticas," in Gutiérrez, Francisco (ed.). *Degradación o Cambio: Evolución del Sistema Político Colombiano*. Bogotá: Editorial Norma.

Palfrey, Thomas R., and Keith T. Poole. 1987. "The Relationship between Information, Ideology, and Voting Behavior," *American Journal of Political Science*, Vol. 31: 511–530.

Palmer, R. R. 1959. *The Age of the Democratic Revolution*. Princeton, NJ: Princeton University Press.

Payne, Mark J., Daniel Zovatto G., Fernando Carrillo Flórez, and Andrés Allamand Zavala. 2002. *Democracies in Development: Politics and Reform in Latin America*. Washington, DC: IADB.

Pereira, Carlos, Timothy J. Power, and Lucio Rennó. 2005. "Under What Conditions Do Presidents Resort to Decree Power?" *Journal of Politics*, Vol. 67, No. 1: 178–200.

Pérez-Liñán, Anibal. 2007. *Presidential Impeachment and the New Political Instability in Latin America*. New York: Cambridge University Press.

Peterson, Mark A. 1990. *Legislating Together*. Cambridge, MA: Harvard University Press.

Piketty, Thomas. 2000. "Voting as Communicating," *Review of Economic Studies*, Vol. 67, No. 1: 169–191.

Poole, Isaiah J. 2006. "Presidential Support: Two Steps Up, One Step Down," *CQ Weekly*, January 9, 2006.

Poole, Keith T. 1998. "Recovering a Basic Space From a Set of Issue Scales," *American Journal of Political Science*, Vol. 42, No. 3: 954–993.

Poole, Keith T. 2005. *Spatial Models of Parliamentary Voting*. New York: Cambridge University Press.

Poole, Keith, and Howard Rosenthal. 1987. "Analysis of Congressional Coalition Patters," *Legislative Studies Quarterly*, Vol. 12, No. 1: 55–75.

Poole, Keith T., and Howard Rosenthal. 1997. *Congress: A Political-Economic History of Roll Call Voting*. New York: Oxford University Press.

Power, Timothy, and Mark Gasiorowski. 1997. "Institutional Design and Democratic Consolidation in the Third World," *Comparative Political Studies*, Vol. 30, No. 2: 123–155.

Przeworski, Adam, Susan C. Stokes, and Bernard Manin (eds.). 1999. *Democracy, Accountability, and Representation*. New York: Cambridge University Press.

Przeworski, Adam, Michael Alvarez, Jose Antonio Cheibub, and Fernando Limongi. 2000. *Democracy and Development*. New York: Cambridge University Press.

Przeworski, Adam. 2005. "Democracy as an Equilibrium," *Public Choice*, Vol. 123, No. 3: 253–273.

Przeworski, Adam. 2009. "Representative Institutions, Political Conflicts, and Public Policies," unpublished paper, Department of Politics, New York University.

Purdum, Todd. 2009. "Henry Paulson's Longest Night," in *Vanity Fair*, October 2009, http://www.vanityfair.com/politics/features/2009/10/henry-paulson 200910

Rasmusen, Eric, and J. Mark Ramseyer. 1994. "Cheap Bribes and the Corruption Ban: A Coordination Game among Rational Legislators," *Public Choice*, Vol. 78, No. 3–4: 305–327.

Razin, Ronny. 2003. "Signaling and Election Motivations in a Voting Model with Common Values and Responsive Candidates," *Econometrica*, Vol. 71, No. 4: 1083–1119.

Remington, Thomas F. 2006. "Presidential Support in the Russian State Duma," *Legislative Studies Quarterly*, Vol. 31, No. 1: 5–32.

Remington, Thomas F., Steven S. Smith, and Moshe Haspel. 1998. "Decrees, Laws, and Inter-Branch Relations in the Russian Federation," *Post-Soviet Affairs*, Vol. 14, No. 4: 287–322.

Rivers, Douglas, and Nancy Rose. 1985. "Passing the President's Program," *American Journal of Political Science*, Vol. 29, No. 2: 183–196.

Roberts, Kenneth M. 2006. "Do Parties Matter? Lessons from the Fujimori Experience," in Julio Carrión (ed.). *The Fujimory Legacy*. University Park: Pennsylvania State University Press.

Rosas, Guillermo. 2005. "The Ideological Organization of Latin American Legislative Parties," *Comparative Political Studies*, Vol. 38, No. 7: 824–849.

Rosenthal, Howard, and Erik Voeten. 2004. "Analyzing Roll Calls with Perfect Spatial Voting: France 1946–1958," *American Journal of Political Science*, Vol. 48, No. 3: 620–632.

Royston, Patrick and Douglas Altman. 1994. "Regression Using Fractional Polynomials of Continuous Covariates: Parsimonious Parametric Modelling," *Applied Statistics*, Vol. 43, No. 3: 429–467.

Rudalevige, Andrew. 2002. *Managing the President's Program*. Princeton, NJ: Princeton University Press.

Saalfeld, Thomas. 1995. "On Dogs and Whips: Recorded Votes," in Herbert Döring (ed.). *Parliaments and Majority Rule in Western Europe*. New York: St. Martin's Press.

Saiegh, Sebastian M. 2009a. "Political Prowess or Lady Luck? Evaluating Chief Executives' Legislative Success Rates," *Journal of Politics*, Vol. 71, No.4: 1342–1356.

Saiegh, Sebastian M. 2009b. "Recovering a Basic Space from Elite Surveys: Evidence from Latin America," *Legislative Studies Quarterly*, Vol. XXXIV, No. 1: 117–145.

Scartascini, Carlos, and Mariano Tommasi. 2009. "The Making of Policy: Institutionalized or Not?" unpublished paper, Research Department, Inter-American Development Bank.

Schall, Teddy, and Gary Smith. 2000. "Do Baseball Players Regress Toward the Mean?" *The American Statistician*, Vol. 54: 231–235.

Seddon Wallack, Jessica, Alejandro Gaviria, Ugo Panizza and Ernesto Stein. 2003. "Particularism around the World," *World Bank Economic Review*, Vol. 17, No. 1: 133–143.

Sedgwick, Romney. 1970. *The House of Commons, 1715–1754*. New York: Oxford University Press.

Shepsle, Kenneth A., and Barry R. Weingast. 1987. "The Institutional Foundations of Committee Power," *American Political Science Review*, Vol. 81, No. 1: 85–104.

Shepsle, Kenneth A., and Mark S. Bonchek. 1997. *Analyzing Politics*. New York: Norton.

Scholz, Evi, and Georgios Trantas. 1995. "Legislation on 'Benefits' and on Regulatory Matters: Social Security and Labour Market," in Herbert Döring (ed.). *Parliaments and Majority Rule in Western Europe*. New York: St. Martin's Press.

Shugart, Matthew S. 1998. "The Inverse Relationship Between Party and Executive Strength: A Theory of Politicians' Constitutional Choices," *British Journal of Political Science*, Vol. 28: 1–29.

Shugart, Matthew S., and John Carey. 1992. *Presidents and Assemblies: Constitutional Design and Electoral Dynamics*. Cambridge: Cambridge University Press.

Shugart, Matthew S., Melody E. Valdini, and Kati Suominen. 2005. "Looking for Locals: Voter Information Demands and Personal Vote-Earning Attributes of Legislators Under Proportional Representation," *American Journal of Political Science*, Vol. 49, No. 2: 437–449.

Shull, Steven A. 1983. *Domestic Policy Formation*. Westport, CT: Greenwood Press.

Shull, Steven A. 1997. *Presidential-Congressional Relations*. Ann Arbor: University of Michigan Press.

Siavelis, Peter. 1997. "Continuity and Change in the Chilean Party System," *Comparative Political Studies*, Vol. 30, No. 6: 651–674.

Siavelis, Peter. 2000. *The President and Congress in Postauthoritarian Chile: Institutional Constraints to Democratic Consolidation*. University Park: Pennsylvania State University Press.

Siavelis, Peter, and Scott Morgenstern. 2008. "Political Recruitment and Candidate Selection in Latin America: A Framework for Analysis," in Peter Siavelis and Scott Morgenstern (eds.). *Pathways to Power*. University Park: Pennsylvania State University Press.

Simmons, Bill. 2010. "Finally joining the revolution," ESPN.com, http://sports.espn.go.com/espn/page2/story?page=simmons/100402.

Snyder, James, Michael Ting, and Stephen Ansolabehere. 2005. "Legislative Bargaining under Weighed Voting," *American Economic Review*, Vol 95, No. 4: 981–1001.

Speck, William. 1977. *Stability and Strife*. London: Edward Arnold.

Speck, William. 1981. "Whigs and Tories Dim Their Glories: English Political Parties under the First Two Georges," in John Cannon (ed.). *The Whig Ascendancy: Colloquies on Hanoverian England*. London: Edward Arnold.

Spitzer, Robert J. 1983. *President and Congress*. Philadelphia: Temple University Press.

Stepan, Alfred, and Cindy Skach. 1993. "Constitutional Frameworks and Democratic Consolidation: Parliamentarism Versus Presidentialism," *World Politics*, Vol. 46, No. 1: 1–22.

Stokes, Susan C. 1995. *Cultures in Conflict, Social Movements and the State in Peru.* Berkeley: University of California Press.

Stokes, Susan C. 2001. "Economic Reform and Public Opinion in Fujimori's Peru," in Susan C. Stokes (ed.). *Public Support for Reforms in New Democracies.* New York: Cambridge University Press.

Sundquist, James L. 1992. *Constitutional Reform and Effective Government.* Washington, DC: Brookings.

Svolik, Milan. 2008. "Authoritarian Reversals and Democratic Consolidation," *American Political Science Review*, Vol. 102, No. 2: 153–168.

Taylor-Robinson, Michelle M. 2001. "Candidate Selection in Costa Rica," paper delivered at the XXIII International Congress of the Latin American Studies Association, Washington, DC.

Taylor-Robinson, Michelle M., and Christopher Diaz. 1999. "Who Gets Legislation Passed in a Marginal Legislature and is the Label Marginal Legislature Still Appropriate? A Study of the Honduran Congress," *Comparative Political Studies*, Vol. 32, No. 5: 590–626.

Theakston, Kevin, and Mark Gill. 2006. "Rating 20th-Century British Prime Ministers," in *British Journal of Politics & International Relations*, Vol. 8, No. 2: 193–213.

Theil, Henri. 1971. *Principles of Econometrics.* New York: John Wiley.

Thomas, P. D. G. 1971. *The House of Commons in the Eighteen Century.* Oxford: Clarendon Press.

Toro Maureira, Sergio. 2007. "Conducta legislativa ante las iniciativas del Ejecutivo: unidad de los bloques políticos en Chile," *Revista de Ciencia Política*, Vol. XXVII, No. 1: 23–41.

Tsebelis. George. 1995. "Decision Making in Political Systems," *British Journal of Political Science*, Vol. 25, No. 3: 289–326.

Tsebelis, George. 2002. *Veto Players: How Political Institutions Work.* New York: Princeton University Press and Russell Sage Foundation.

Tsebelis, George, and Jeannette Money. 1997. *Bicameralism.* New York: Cambridge University Press.

Turan, Ilter. 2003. "Volatility in Politics, Stability in Parliament: An Impossible Dream?," *Journal of Legislative Studies*, Vol. 9, No. 2: 151–176.

Valenzuela, Arturo. 1978. *The Breakdown of Democratic Regimes, Chile.* Baltimore: Johns Hopkins University Press.

Valenzuela, Arturo. 1994. "Party Politics and the Crisis of Presidentialism in Chile," in Juan J. Linz and Arturo Valenzuela (eds.). *The Failure of Presidential Democracy: The Case of Latin America.* Baltimore: Johns Hopkins University Press.

Voeten, Erik. 2000. "Clashes in the Assembly," *International Organization*, Vol. 54, No. 2: 185–215.

Vreeland, James Raymond. 2003. *The IMF and Economic Development.* New York: Cambridge University Press.

Vreeland, James Raymond. 2007. *The International Monetary Fund: Politics of Conditional Lending.* New York: Routledge.

Wallack, Jessica Seddon, Alejandro Gaviria, Ugo Panizza, and Ernesto Stein. 2003. "Particularism around the World," *The World Bank Economic Review*, Vol. 17, No. 1: 133–143.

Weisberg, Herbert F. 1978. "Evaluating Theories of Congressional Roll-Call Voting," *American Journal of Political Science*, Vol. 22, No. 3: 554–577.

Wessels, Bernhard. 2004. "Members of Parliament Survey 2003," Study Report, Social Science Research Center, Berlin.

White, R. J. 1968. *The Age of George III*. New York: Walker and Co.

Wright, Joseph. 2008. "Do Authoritarian Institutions Constrain? How Legislatures Affect Economic Growth and Investment," *American Journal of Political Science*, Vol. 52, No. 2: 322–343.

Zoco, Edurne. 2006. "Legislators Positions and Party System Competition in Central America: A Comparative Analysis," *Party Politics*, Vol. 12, No. 2: 257–280.

Index

accountability 10, 94, 116, 157–8, 172, 183
A'court-Ashe, William 123–4
agenda setting 11n, 17, 51–2, 62, 144, 161n, 183
agent(s) 13, 18, 23, 38, 142
Aguayo, Julio Javier 130–1
Aigner, Erin 179
Alcántara, Manuel 135, 143, 143n
Aldrich, John 143n, 144n
Alemán, Eduardo 8n, 66, 68, 143, 150, 168
Alesina, Alberto 21
Alfonsín, Raúl 102
Aliança Renovadora Nacional (ARENA) 79
Alianza Popular Revolucionaria Americana (APRA) 129
Alianza por Chile 146–7, 152n
Allende, Salvador 146, 167–9, 171, 173
Althaus, Dudley 126n
Altman, Douglas 162n
American Revolutionary War 115
Ames, Barry 69, 70n, 134, 143
Amorim Neto, Octavio 8n, 18, 66n, 87
Ansolabehere, Stephen 41n
Argentina 8n, 17, 24n, 31–2, 35, 63, 65, 67–8, 72, 94, 102
Arriaga, Julio 32
Asia 9, 76, 82
Attlee, Clement 101, 101n
Austen-Smith, David 182
Australia 182n
Austria 67
Aylwin, Patricio 152

Bailey, Michael 144, 144n
Bangladesh 77–8, 90n, 202
Banks, Arthur 162, 207

Banks, Jeffrey 182
Barkan, Joel D. 80n
Barret, Andrew W. 8n, 69, 73–4
Barry, Brian 23n, 26n, 34, 105n
baseball 96–7, 97n, 103
Baseball Abstracts 96
Baseball Writers Association of America 96
Battaglini, Marco 182
batting average(s) 61, 69, 92, 103
Bavastro, Roberto 68, 72
Beane, Billy 96
Belgium 62n, 67, 73
Berlin Wall 126
Binder, Sarah 62n, 66, 74
binomial distribution 107
Blainpain, Roger 69n
Blunt, Roy 178
Boehner, John A. 178
Bolivia 67, 169–71
Bolten, Josh 178
Bonchek, Mark S. 21, 21n, 148n
Bond, Jon R. 8n, 61, 70n, 70–2
Boothroyd, David 71n
Borges, Jorge Luis 36n
Borrelli, Stephen 8n, 70, 73
box score(s): and constitutional structures 84–7, 136–7, 140; under democracy 77–8, 136, 163; under dictatorship 79, 82, 164; and electoral systems 138, 138n, 140; expected 105n; and government status 87–89, 136–7, 140; and legislative effectiveness 102, 103; measure 9, 12, 61, 61n, 63, 66–71, 70n, 73, 73n, 75–6, 76n, 77n, 92–4, 98, 101, 103; multivariate analysis of 89–91, 97, 202; and social unrest 11, 162–4, 162nn, 166, 207
Brazil 65, 66n, 73, 78–9, 82, 86

Brerenton-Salusbury, Thomas 124, 124n
Brooke, John 115, 117–20, 119n, 124–5
Brown, Gordon 102n
Brown, Sherrod 65n
Bueno de Mesquita, Bruce 79
Buller, John 124
Bush, George W. 3–5, 22, 43–4, 65, 65n, 177, 178–9

Cáceres Pérez, Róger 129
Cáceres Velásquez, José Luis 129
Cali cartel 167
Callaghan, James 101–2, 102n
Calmes, Jackie 179
Calvo, Ernesto 8n, 68, 68n, 94
Calvo Sotelo, Leopoldo 102
Cambio 90 126
Cameron, Charles M. 8n, 22n, 73, 110
Canada 63, 78, 86, 90n, 182n, 202
Canales Pilaca, Edilberto 129
candidate selection 13, 136, 145; in Chile 142, 145n, 146–7; in Colombia 142, 147n; and legislative behavior 113, 133–4, 150; and party unity 135, 141–2
Cannon, John 115, 118n, 120n
Capano, Giliberto 166
Cárdenas, Mauricio 149, 152
Carey, John 130n, 133–5, 140, 142–3, 150, 159
Carlos Alberto 97
Castañeda Lossio, Luis 129
Chavez Cossio de Ocampo, Martha 129
Cheibub, José 12, 69, 74, 76n, 77n, 89, 92, 140n, 158n, 159, 202–3
Cheney, Dick 178
Chile 13, 65, 133, 142, 145–7, 150, 152–3, 167, 169, 171
Chrypinski, Vincent 80n
Churchill, Winston 101
Clinton, Bill 27–8, 28n
Clive, Robert 121–3
closed-list system(s) 134–6, 135n, 147. *See also* electoral rule(s)
coalition(s): in Bolivia 169–70; bribed 51, 57; in Chile 145–7, 146n, 147n, 152, 152n, 167; in Colombia 153; electoral 145, 147; government 12, 33, 87–89, 90n, 94, 137–8, 158n, 159n, 202–3; least expensive 53; legislative 13, 20, 28, 41, 50–1, 53, 56, 134, 145; majority 87, 89; minimum-winning 8, 31, 46–8, 58, 120, 122, 130, 193; minority 87–8; multiparty 90, 90n, 138, 202; nonflooded 46; oversized 11, 13, 18, 31, 123; policy 133, 153, 173; presidential 8n, 87; social 159; supermajority 8, 58, 130, 131; unbribed 46; winning 7, 11,

13, 18, 30, 31, 46–8, 50–1, 53, 56–7, 115, 123, 130, 179, 193
Cobos, Julio 33–4
Cockburn, Sir James 125n
Cohen, Youssef 146, 168
Cold War 80, 159
Coleman, John J. 62, 74
Colley, Linda 121–3
Colombia 13, 23, 78, 133, 135n, 142, 145, 147, 147n, 149–50, 152–3, 167
Conaghan, Catherine 126–128
Concertación 145, 147, 152, 152n
Congressional Quarterly, also CQ 28, 61n, 65, 73n
constituency 7, 10, 12, 23, 25–8, 80n, 90, 94, 134, 138, 179
Cook Political Report 179
Coppedge, Michael 8n
Costa, Gabriel B. 96
Costa e Silva, Artur da 79
Costa Rica 67, 78, 86
Covington, Cary R. 8n, 23, 73, 110
Cox, Amanda 179
Cox, Gary 38, 62, 66, 66n, 106, 116, 143, 147
Crain, William 62
Crisp, Brian 8n, 135
cross-pressured legislators 5–6, 13, 22, 22n, 29–31, 34–5, 47, 57, 75, 114, 132, 179
Crozier, Michel 157
Cy Young jinx 104
Czechoslovakia 82

D'Acunha Cuervas, Jorge 129
Dahrendorf, Ralph 157, 172–3
Dal Bo, Ernesto 45n, 47
Davenport, Clay 97
Dekel, Eddie 47, 182
de la Rúa, Fernando 17, 102
DeLay, Tom 3
De Luca, Miguel 24n
De Vylder, Stephan 168
de Winter, Lieven 62n
Democrat(s) 3–4, 27, 43–4, 65, 65n, 178–80
Denmark 67, 77–8
Denzau, Arthur 23, 29n, 45n
Desposato, Scott W. 24n, 143
Didi 97
Diermeier, Daniel 22n, 139
differential item functioning (DIF) 143n
Digby, Edward 123
Di Palma, Giuseppe 158, 166
district magnitude 90n, 134–5, 203. *See also* electoral rule(s)
divided government 61, 74

Divided We Govern 74
Dixit, Avinash 19
Döring, Herbert 8, 67n, 67–8, 69n
Dow Jones Industrial Average (Dow) 178
Duch, Jordi 97
Duhalde, Eduardo 17
Dupplin, Lord 121

Ecuador 66, 78, 86
Edwards, George C., III 8n, 61, 74
El Alto 170
electoral rule(s) 89, 89n, 134–6, 140n, 141,
   203–4; in Chile 146; in Colombia 148–9;
   local 7, 12, 90, 94, 138; national 7, 12,
   73, 90, 90n, 94, 134–5, 138;
   party-centered 135–8, 140
Elías Alvaro, José Luis 129
Encyclopedia of Labor Law 69n
Epstein, David 179–80, 179n
equilibrium: Nash 29n, 45n; Strong Nash
   29n; subgame perfect 40
Erdogan, Recep Tayyip 4–5
Escobar-Lemmon, Maria 142, 145, 147n,
   148–9
ESPN 97n
Europe 9, 76, 82
executive-legislative: conflict 8n, 10, 11,
   158–9, 169; relations 6, 12, 61, 65, 70,
   70n, 74, 108, 113, 144
Expreso 131

faction(s) 134; in Britain 115–16; in
   Colombia 150; legislative 41, 43–4, 46,
   53, 56, 110; lists 135, 135n; two-party
   110n
Fane, Thomas 123
Farah Hayn, Eduardo 129
Febres Cordero, León 86
Feddersen, Timothy 140, 182
Fédération Internationale de Football
   Association (FIFA) 95
Fenno, Richard 22
Fernández de Kirchner, Cristina 32–3
Figueiredo, Argelina C. 143
Figueres, José María 86
Finland 67
Fiorina, Morris 22–3
Fleisher, Richard 8n, 61, 110–1
Foley, Tom 27
Foord, Archibald S. 118
Fourth French Republic 159
Foweraker, Joe 159
Fox, Henry 120–1
Fox, John D. 28
France 67
Franzese, Robert 11n, 161n

Fraser, Jane M. 8n, 73, 104n,
   104–6,108,110,110n
Fratto, Tony 178
Free Trade Area of the Americas (FTAA)
   169n
Frei Montalva, Eduardo 168
Frei Ruiz-Tagle, Eduardo 152
Frente Independiente Moralizador (FIM)
   128
Frente Independiente Perú 2000. *See Perú
   2000*
Frente Nacional 149
Friend, Julius W. 112
Fujimori, Alberto 13, 17, 18, 115, 125–32,
   173
Funes the Memorious 36n

game of strategy: lawmaking as 18–9
Gamm, Gerald 8
Gandhi, Jennifer 77n, 79, 79n, 82, 164
García-Diez, Fátima 143n
Garrett, Scott 179
Garrincha 97
Gartzke, Erik 22n
Gasiorowski, Mark 159
Gaviria, Alejandro 203
Geddes, Barbara 79
George I 111
George III 13, 115, 132
German Bundestag 85
Germany 67
Gérson 97
Gertzel, Cherry 80
Gill, Mark 101, 101n
Gillespie, Ed 178
Ginter, Donald E. 124n, 125
Giuliani, Marco 166
Goldberg, Peter A. 169
Golder. Matt 90n
Goldman Sachs, 22
González Inga, Mario 129
governability 10–11, 14, 94, 102, 157–8,
   161, 166–7, 172–3, 181, 183
Greece 67
Green, Matthew 179–80
Grenville, George 119n
Groseclose, Tim 21, 21n, 23, 23n, 40, 45n,
   46
Guatemala 67
Gul, Abdullah 4

Hager, George 27
Hallerberg, Mark 134
Hammond, Thomas H. 8n, 73, 104n,
   104–6, 108, 110, 110n

Hare: formula 147n; method 147;
procedure 135n; quota 149, 149n.
See also electoral rule(s)
Hayes, Robin 3, 43
Heath, Edward 71n
Hedger, Scott 8n, 70, 73
Heller, William B. 21
Henisz, Witold J. 172
Herszenhorn, David 179
Hicks paradox 22n
Hildebrandt, Martha 131
Hill, Brian W. 115
Hix, Simon 143
Hochstetler, Kathryn, 160
Holcombe, Randal 62
Holmes, Geoffrey 115, 118, 118n, 120n,
121
Honduras 63, 67
Hoppit, Julian 111, 118, 124n
Horne, Alistair 168
Hossain, Farhana 179
House of Commons 5, 67, 71, 84, 115–8,
120–2
Houston Chronicle 126, 126n
Howell, William 62, 74
Huamán, María del Milagro 128–9
Huang, The-fu 159
Huber, John 8, 139
Hudak, Kristen 179–80
Huntington, Samuel P. 9, 157
Huse, Carl 179
Hussey, Richard 122–4
Hwang, Wonjae 143

Iaryczower, Matías 182
Iceland 67
ideal point(s) 19–20, 144; of Chilean
legislators 147; of Colombian legislators
150. *See also* ideological position(s)
ideological cohesion 13, 133; in Chile 142,
145.
ideological position(s): of Bolivian
legislators 170n; of Chilean legislators
147, 150; of Chilean parties 147; of
Colombian legislators 150, 152; of
legislators 143, 144n, 150; of Peruvian
parties 126
impuestazo 169–70
India 102, 108
influence 117–8, 118n. *See also* vote
buying.
Ingall, Rachael 135
Ingberman, Daniel E. 21n
International Labor Organization (ILO)
69n
International Monetary Fund (IMF) 5n
Inter-Parliamentary Union 9, 67n

Iraq 4
Ireland 67, 90n, 111, 202
Italy 63, 67, 85, 87n, 108, 159, 166
Ivory Coast 77

Jackson, John E. 143
Jairzinho 97
James, Bill 96
Jeyns, Soame 123
Johnson, Joel 136, 203
Jones, Mark P. 8n, 24n, 143
Jordan 77, 82
Judd, Gerrit P. 115
judicial review 5, 18

Kalt, Joseph P. 23
Kam, Christopher 140n, 142, 144, 182n
Kane, Paul 178–9
Kang, Cecilia 180
Katz, Gabriel 182
Katz, Richard S. 143
Keefer, Philip 89n
Kellam, Marisa 8n, 65
Kennan, John 22n
Kenya African Democratic Union (KADU)
80
Kenyan African National Union (KANU)
80
Kenyatta, Jomo 80
Kernell, Samuel 74
King, David C. 22, 46
King, Gary 71, 143n, 144n
Kingdom, John 102
Kingdon, John W. 143
Kirchner, Néstor 32
Kittikachorn, Thanom 80
Kouri, Alberto 128–30
Krehbiel, Keith 38, 74, 143
Krugman, Paul 36n
Krutz, Glen S. 62, 74
Kuwait 82

Lacalle, Luis 86
Lagos, Ricardo 152–3
Lambert, Paul C. 162n
La Paz 170
Laruelle, Annick 26n
Latin America 9, 76, 82, 145, 159, 166n,
182
Latin America Weekly Report 170n
law of anticipated reactions 22, 106
Lebanon 86, 87n
legal review 5, 18. *See also* judicial review
legislative gridlock 62, 62n, 74, 152, 168
Leston-Bandeira, Cristina 72
Levin, Jonathan 149n

Levitt, Steven D. 23
Lewis, Michael 96
Lib-Lab pact 101
Lichbach, Mark 161
Limongi, Fernando 143
Linz, Juan 76n, 136, 159, 159n, 168
Lipset, Seymour Martin 157, 172
Lockerbie, Brad 8n, 70, 73
Loewenberg, Gerhard 82
Londregan John B. 23, 133, 142–3
Lozada de Gamboa, Carmen 129
Lueck, Sarah 178–9
Luna Gálvez, José León 129
Lupia, Arthur 159
Lust-Okar, Ellen 79
Luttrell, Simon 122–4
Luxembourg 67
Lynch, David J. 178

Mackay, George 123
Macpherson, James 125n
Magaloni, Beatriz 79
Magar, Eric 8n
Mainwaring, Scott 76n, 133–4, 159
Major, John 102n
Major League Baseball 96
majority rule 19–20, 25, 28, 40, 105, 160
Malta 90n, 202
Maradona, Diego Armando 95, 97
Margolies-Mezvinsky, Marjorie 27–8, 28n
Marier, Patrik 134
Martinez, Ricardo 26n
Mateos, Araceli 143n
Matthews, Steven 21n
Mauroy, Pierre 112
Mayhew, David 74
Mayor, John 125n
McCarty, Nolan 21n, 143
McCubbins, Mathew 38, 62, 66, 66n, 106, 143
McKelvey, Richard 143n, 144n
McMillan, John 128, 128n
median legislator: in Bolivian legislature 170; in Chilean legislature 152; in Colombian legislature 152–3; in single dimensional space 19–21
Mejía-Acosta, Andres 134, 135n
Mendoza del Solar, Juan Carlos Miguel 129
Mexico 63, 65, 78
Mezey, Michael 80, 82
Middle East 9, 76
Middleton, Sir William 124, 124n
Milyo, Jeff 23, 40, 45n
Mitchell Election division list 121–3
Mitterand, Francois 112
Molinelli, N. Guillermo 68

Money, Jeannette 73–4
Moneyball 96
Monte Carlo simulation(s) 13, 107
Montesinos Torres, Vladimiro 127–30, 128n, 132
Montgomery, Lori 178–9
Morales, Evo 169, 170n
Moreira Alves, Márcio 79
Moreno, Erika 142, 145, 147n, 148–9
Morgenstern, Scott 116, 133, 135, 142–6, 150
MORI 101
Movimiento al Socialismo 160
Movimiento de la Izquierda Revolucionaria (MIR) 169
Movimiento Democrático Brasileiro (MDB) 79
Movimiento Nacionalista Revolucionario (MNR) 169
multimember district(s) 136. *See also* electoral rule(s)

Nalebuff, Barry 19, 149n
Namier, Lewis 115–21, 119n, 120n, 124–5
Napoli SSC 97
National Association for Stock Car Auto Racing (NASCAR) 180
NATLEX 69n
Navia, Patricio 142, 145–6, 145n, 152
Negretto, Gabriel 160
Neher, Clark D. 80
Netherlands 67, 78
Neudstadt, Richard 70n
Newcastle, Duke of 116, 119–24, 121n, 124n, 132
New York Times 170n
New Zealand 90n, 182n, 202
Nielson, Daniel L. 134
Noll, Roger 23
Norris, Pippa 143
North, Douglass C. 172
North, Frederick (Lord North) 119, 124–5, 125n, 132
North America 9, 76
Norway 67
Nueva Mayoría 126

Oakland Athletics 96
Obey, David 179
O'Halloran, Sharyn 179–80, 179n
Okumo, John J. 80n
Olivera, Fernando 128
Olson, David M. 80
Onslow, Sir Arthur 122
open-list system(s) 134–6, 135n, 145. *See also* electoral rule(s)

Operation Recruitment 127
Osborne, Martin 40
Özbudum, Ergun 142

Pachón, Monica 153
pairing norm 123
Pakistan 77
Palfrey, Thomas 146
Palmer, Pete 97
Palmer, R. R. 115n, 116–8, 120n
Palomo Orefice, Antonio 129
Paniagua, Valentin 131
Paraguay 63, 65, 67, 77
Park, Jee-Kwang 8n, 73, 110
Parliamentary Elites of Latin America
    survey (PELA) 143–4, 143nn, 147, 150,
    152, 170n
parliamentary regime(s) 17, 67, 92, 202–3;
    classification of 84; coalitions under 87;
    legislative passage rates in 12–3, 22n, 84,
    86–90, 93–4, 136–8, 140; parties in 139,
    141, 182n; and political stability 158n,
    159; in South Korea 86, 86n
Partido Conservador (PC) 150, 153
Partido Demócrata Cristiano (DC) 145–6,
    168
Partido Liberal (PLO) 150, 153, 167
Partido Liberal Uribista (PLU) 150, 153
Partido por la Democracia (PPD) 145
Partido Radical Social-Demócrata (PRSD)
    145
Partido Socialista (PS) 145
Partido Solidaridad Nacional (PSN) 129
party-augmented model 105–7, 109
Patterson, Samuel C. 82
Paulson, Henry 22–3, 178
Payne, Mark 66
Peake, Jeffrey 74
Pelé 95, 97
Pelosi, Nancy 178
Pennano Allison, Guido 129
Pérez-Liñan, Aníbal 11, 134, 159–60,
    160n, 166–7, 166n
Peronist party 17, 32–4
personal vote 134–5. *See also* electoral
    rule(s)
Peru 13, 17, 115, 125–6, 128, 128n, 131–2
Perú 2000 17, 127, 131
Perú Posible (PP) 129
Pesendorfer, Wolfgang 182
Peterson, Mark A. 8n, 61, 71, 73n, 110
Pianin, Eric 27
Piccione, Michele 182
Piketty, Thomas 182
Pinochet, Augusto 145–7
Pitt, William (1st Earl of Chatham) 117,
    121n

pivotal offers 47
plurality rule 24, 89n
Polack Merel, Jorge 129
Poland 80
Polish Sejm 80, 83
Poole, Isaiah 65
Poole, Keith 109n, 143–4, 144nn, 146
Portugal 63, 67, 72
Power, Timothy 159
Presidential Power 70n
presidential regime(s) 17, 76, 140, 182,
    203; classification of 84; coalitions under
    87, 158n; legislative passage rates in 12,
    22n, 61n, 66, 69, 86, 88–90, 93–4, 102,
    110, 110n, 136–7, 140, 158n; parties in
    74, 139, 142; and political stability
    158–9, 158n, 159n; in South Korea 86n
principal(s) 23–4, 38–9, 41, 43–8, 50, 53,
    56–7, 75, 188–93. *See also* constituency
prisoners' dilemma 45
proportional representation 89n, 145, 147,
    149. *See also* electoral rule(s)
Przeworski, Adam 12, 77, 77n, 79, 84,
    157, 160–2, 164, 172, 177
public goods 34
Purdum, Todd 22–3

Quintela, Teresita 33

Rached, Julio 33
Ragsdale, Lyn 71
Ramseyer, J. Mark 23, 39n, 41n, 47
Rasmusen, Eric 23, 39n, 41n, 47
Razin, Ronny 182
Reátegui, Rolando 129
Remington, Thomas F. 18
Renovación Nacional (RN) 146–7
Republican(s) 3–4, 43, 65, 65n, 178–80
Richardson, Bill 27
Ríos Salcedo, Waldo Enrique 129
Rivelino, Roberto 97
Rivers, Douglas 8n, 71, 73
Roberts, Kenneth 126–7
Rockingham, Marquess of 119, 124
Rodríguez, Ruby 128, 128n
Rodríguez Saá, Adolfo 17
roll call vote(s) 46, 65–6, 70n, 105, 106n,
    107–8, 108n, 110, 121, 143–4, 144n,
    177, 182
roll rate(s) 66, 66n, 70
Rosas, Guillermo 143
Rose, Nancy 8n, 71, 73
Rosenthal, Howard 21, 109n, 143,
    144n
Rossi, Agustín 32
Rossi, Fabiana 32

Royston, Patrick 162n
Rudalevige, Andrew 8n, 73

Saalfeld, Thomas 62n
sabermetric(s) 96–98, 101–3
Saiegh, Sebastian M. 12, 97–8, 98n, 101, 143, 150, 170n, 182
Salgado, Luz 129
Samper, Ernesto 167
Sánchez de Lozada, Gonzalo 169–71
Sanguinetti, Julio María 103–4
Santos, Nilton 97
Scartascini, Carlos 160
Schall, Teddy 103–4
Scholz, Evi 69
score(s): congruence 65, 70n; success 65; support 65, 70, 70n. *See also* box score(s)
Scully, Timothy 159
Sedgwick, Romney 116, 116n
Selwyn, George Augustus 125n
Servicio de Inteligencia Nacional (SIN) 127
Shadegg, John B. 65n
Shelburne, Earl of 119n
Shepsle, Kenneth 21, 21n, 148n
Shugart, Matthew S. 133–6, 147, 159
Shull Steven A. 8n, 61, 67, 70, 70n, 73
Siavelis, Peter 135, 142, 145–6, 168
Siles, Luis Eduardo 170n
Simmons, Bill 97n
Simon, Maurice D. 80
single-member district(s) 24, 136, 203. *See also* electoral rule(s)
single nontrasferable vote (SNTV) 147, 148n. *See also* electoral rule(s)
Skach, Cindy 159
Smith, Chris 43
Smith, Edward 123
Smith, Gary 103–4
Snyder, James M. 21, 23n, 41n, 46
soccer 95–6
social conflict 160, 160n, 207. *See also* social unrest.
social unrest: in developing countries 11; and governability 11, 160n, 164, 166; passage rates and 11, 14, 161–4, 162n, 207
Society for American Baseball Research (SABR) 96
Solá, Felipe 32
South Korea 86, 86n
Spain 63, 65, 67, 102
Speck, William 115–6, 121n
Spitzer, Robert J. 8n, 73
Sports Illustrated 104
Stepan, Alfred 159
Stephenson, John 121–3

Stokes, Susan 126
Strom. Kaare 159
Suárez, Adolfo 102
Sun Tzu 177
Sundquist, James L. 74
Suominen, Kati 134
Svolik, Milan 79
Sweden 67
Switzerland 67
Szechi, Daniel 115, 118, 120n, 121

Taira, Sobero 129
Tejerazo 102
Thailand 80
Thatcher, Margaret 71n, 101–2, 102n
Theakston, Kevin 101, 101n
Theil, Henry 181n
Third French Republic 159
Thomas, P. D. G. 122–3
Thornton, Ray 27, 29
Ticona Gómez, Gregorio 129
Ting, Michael 41n
Toledo, Alejandro 127–8
Tollison, Richard 62
Tommasi, Mariano 160
topos 127–30
Tories 115, 120
Toro, Sergio 150, 152, 152n
Tostão 97
transfugas 127–8, 130–1
Trantas, Georgios 70
Trilateral Commission 157
Tse, Archie 179
Tsebelis, George 9, 11n, 66, 68, 73–4, 161n
Turkey 4, 9, 63, 85n

UEFA Cup 97
Unión Cívica Radical (UCR) 33
Unión de Centro Democrático (UCD) 103
Unión Democrática Independiente (UDI) 145, 147
United Kingdom, also Britain, England 13, 62n, 67, 77, 84, 90n, 101–2, 102n, 115–6, 125, 131–2, 157, 182n, 202
United States, also U.S. 3–4, 8, 8n, 22–3, 22n, 46, 61n, 62, 65–6, 66n, 69, 70n, 71, 73–4, 76n, 77n, 104n, 110, 143, 144n, 157, 170, 177–8, 180
United Thai People's Party (UTPP) 80
Universidad de Salamanca 143
University College 111
University of Leeds 101
Uribe, Alvaro 153
Uruguay 73, 86, 102–3

Valdini, Melody 134
Valenciano, Federico 26n
Valenzuela, Arturo 76n, 159, 168
Vanity Fair 22
Vara Ochoa, Manuel 129
Vava 97
veto player(s) 11n, 158, 161n
vladivideos 128
Vlaicu, Razvan 22n
Voeten, Erik 143
vote buying 6–8, 26, 26n, 36, 39–40, 114,
    179, 183; with bribes 13, 115, 120;
    budget 37, 50–2; and coalition size 11,
    13, 18, 31, 48, 58, 115, 120, 123,
    129–31; and legislative voting 18;
    strategies 34, 50, 120
Vreeland, James Raymond 5n

Wallack, Jessica 90n, 134, 136, 139, 203
Walpole, Horace 120

Walpole, Robert 115–6, 116n
Wall Street 179
Watanuki, Joji 157
Weingast, Barry 21, 172
Wessels, Bernhard 143
Westminster-style system(s) 89–90, 90n,
    182n, 202
Whigs 115, 120–1
Williams, Pat 27
Wilson, Harold 101
Winter of Discontent 101
World Bank 12
Wright, Joseph 79

Yao Dennis A. 21n

Zeckhauser, Richard 22, 46
Zoco, Edurne 143
Zoido, Pablo 128, 128n
Zupan, Mark A. 23